Migrating from Microsoft Windows NT 4.0 to Microsoft Windows 2000

Migrating from Microsoft Windows NT 4.0 to Microsoft Windows 2000

iUniverse.com, Inc.

San Jose   New York   Lincoln   Shanghai

Migrating from Microsoft Windows NT 4.0 to Microsoft Windows 2000

Published by iUniverse.com, Inc.

For information address:
iUniverse.com, Inc.
5220 S 16th, Ste. 200
Lincoln, NE 68512
www.iuniverse.com

Cover Creation by Shay Jones

Graphic Production by Matt Bromley, Associate Consultant

CD-ROM Duplication by Paragon Media, Seattle, Washington

Domhnall CGN Adams, Corporation Sole—http://www.dcgna.com
5721-10405 Jasper Avenue
Edmonton, Alberta
Canada T5J 3S2
(780) 416-2967
dcgna@yahoo.com

ISBN: 0-595-14822-0

Printed in the United States

Acknowledgments

We are pleased to acknowledge the following people for their important contributions in the creation of this study guide.

Technical Writer—Joe Rawlings

Editors—Nina Gettler and Grace Clark

Indexer—Loral Pritchett

Proofreaders—Kerry Holland and Steve Reed

Cover Creation, Text Conversion and Proofing—Shay Jones, AA, MCSE, MCP

Technical Reviewer—Steve Patrick, MCSE, Cisco, CCNA

Graphic Designer—Matt Bromley

V.P., Publishing and Courseware Development— Candace Sinclair

Course Prerequisites

The Migrating from Microsoft Windows NT 4.0 to Microsoft Windows 2000 study guide targets individuals interested in designing a strategy to migrate from a Microsoft Windows NT Server 4.0 directory services infrastructure to a Microsoft Windows 2000 Active Directory directory service infrastructure.

It is recommended that you meet the following prerequisites before reading this study guide and taking the certification exam:

- Working knowledge of Active Directory planning and design

- Hands-on experience evaluating forest and site designs for strategic upgrades

- Successful completion of: Designing a Microsoft Windows 2000 Directory Services Infrastructure

- Successful completion of: Implementing and Administering Windows 2000 Directory Services

- Successful completion of: Administering Microsoft Windows 2000

- Successful completion of: Installing and Configuring Microsoft Windows 2000

- Successful completion of: Advanced Administration for Microsoft Windows 2000

- In addition, we recommend that you have a working knowledge of the English

- language so that you can understand the technical words and concepts presented in this study guide.

To feel confident about using this study guide, you should have the following knowledge or ability:

- The desire and drive to become a certified MCSE through our instructions, terminology, activities, quizzes, and study guide content

- Basic computer skills, which include using a mouse, keyboard, and viewing a monitor

- Basic networking knowledge including the fundamentals of working with Internet browsers, e-mail functionality, and search engines

- IP, remote connectivity and security

Hardware and Software Requirements

To apply the knowledge presented in this study guide, you will need the following minimum hardware:

- For Windows 2000 Professional, we recommend 64 megabytes of RAM (32 megabytes as a minimum) and a 1-gigabyte (GB) hard disk space.

- For Windows 2000 Server, we recommend a Pentium II or better processor, 128 megabytes of RAM (64 megabytes minimum), and a 2-GB hard drive. If you want to install Remote Installation Server with Windows 2000 Server, you should have at least two additional gigabytes of hard disk space available.

- CD-ROM drive

- Mouse

- VGA monitor and graphics card

- Internet connectivity

To apply the knowledge presented in this study guide, you will need the following minimum software installed on your computer:

- Microsoft Windows 2000 Advanced Server

- Microsoft Internet Explorer or Netscape Communicator

Symbols Used in This Study Guide

To call your attention to various facts within our study guide content, we've included the following three symbols to help you prepare for the Migrating from Microsoft Windows NT 4.0 to Microsoft Windows 2000 exam.

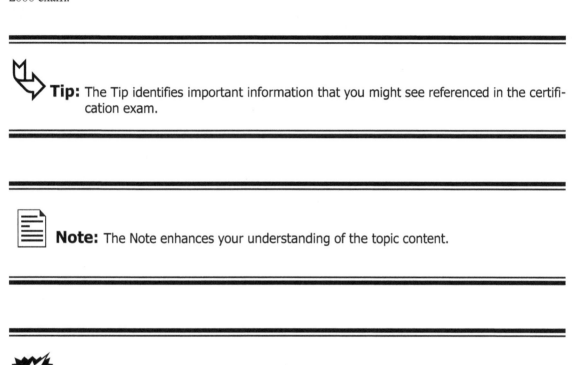

Tip: The Tip identifies important information that you might see referenced in the certification exam.

Note: The Note enhances your understanding of the topic content.

Warning: The Warning describes circumstances that could be harmful to you and your computer system or network.

How to Use This Study Guide

Although you will develop and implement your own personal style of studying and preparing for the MCSE exam, we've taken the strategy of presenting the exam information in an easy-to-follow, ten-lesson format. Each lesson conforms to Microsoft's model for exam content preparation.

At the beginning of each lesson, we summarize the information that will be covered. At the end of each lesson we round out your studying experience by providing the following four ways to test and challenge what you've learned.

Vocabulary—Helps you review all the important terms discussed in the lesson.

In Brief—Reinforces your knowledge by presenting you with a problem and a possible solution.

Activities—Further tests what you have learned in the lesson by presenting ten activities that often require you to do more reading or research to understand the activity. In addition, we have provided the answers to each activity.

Lesson Quiz—To round out the knowledge you will gain after completing each lesson in this study guide, we have included ten sample exam questions and answers. This allows you to test your knowledge, and it gives you the reasons why the "answers" were either correct or incorrect. This, in itself, enhances your power to pass the exam.

You can also refer to the Glossary at the back of the book to review terminology. Furthermore, you can view the Index to find more content for individual terms and concepts.

Introduction to MCSE Certification

The Microsoft Certified Systems Engineer (MCSE) credential is the highest-ranked certification for professionals who analyze business requirements for system architecture, design solutions, deployment, installation, and configuration of architecture components, as well as troubleshooting system problems.

When you receive your MCSE certification, it proves your competence by having earned a nationally-recognized credential as an information technology professional who works in a typically complex computing environment of medium to large organizations. It is recommended that a Windows 2000 MCSE candidate should have at least one year of experience implementing and administering a network operating system environment.

The MCSE exams cover a vast range of vendor-independent hardware and software technologies, as well as basic Internet and Windows 2000 design knowledge, technical skills and best practice scenarios.

To help you bridge the gap between needing the knowledge and knowing the facts, this study guide presents Designing a Microsoft Windows 2000 Migration Strategy knowledge that will help you pass this exam.

 Note: This study guide presents technical content that should enable you to pass the Migrating from Microsoft Windows NT 4.0 to Microsoft Windows 2000 certification exam on the first try.

Study Guide Objectives

Successful completion of this study guide is realized when you can competently understand, explain and identify the tasks involved in migrating a network from Microsoft Windows NT 4.0 to Microsoft Windows 2000.

You must fully comprehend each of the following objectives and their related tasks to prepare for this certification exam:

- Choose a migration path to Windows 2000 Active Directory.

- Develop an upgrade strategy

- Plan for continued productivity during a domain upgrade or a restructure by managing and mitigating risks within a production environment

- Develop a strategy for a domain restructure process

- Thorough understanding of how to plan for a migration deployment

Contents

Figures

Lesson 1: Migration Concepts and Introduction

There are several reasons why an organization might choose to migrate from Microsoft Windows NT 4.0 to Microsoft Windows 2000 Active Directory. The organization might wish to gain a competitive advantage in the marketplace, or it might wish to establish an enterprise architecture that will support anticipated growth. To accomplish such a migration, an understanding of the basic steps is needed.

An enterprise migrating from Microsoft Windows NT 4.0 to Windows 2000 Active Directory Services must consider and include these basic steps when developing an overall migration strategy. This lesson will provide you with the necessary knowledge and foundation to design a migration strategy. You will also learn about the four phases of domain migration planning, and you will learn about the difference between a domain upgrade and a domain restructure.

After completing this lesson, you should have a better understanding of the following topics:

- Migration Planning Concepts

- Business and Migration Goals for an Enterprise

- Domain Upgrade or Restructure Strategy

- Deployment Concepts

Migration Planning Concepts

To successfully migrate from a Microsoft Windows NT 4.0 environment tcrosoft Windows NT 4.0 environment to a Windows 2000 environment, you must perform some in-depth planning based on a very careful analysis of the current corporate and domain infrastructures. Such planning is critical to the success of the operation and must be accomplished. Failure to do so can become a very expensive oversight. You need a migration strategy that takes into consideration the current state and the desired or projected future state of your enterprise.

Planning a Migration Strategy

For your migration efforts to be successful, the migration must be planned. During the planning phase, a project team documents the current network environment of the organization and thoroughly analyzes it. The team can then define future goals and identify the changes that the current environment must undergo to obtain the desired future results. The project team measures the change between the current working environment and the goals for the future environment and defines the steps needed to achieve those results. If a thorough plan is developed, it allows the project team to concentrate on migration essentials, and it provides migration steps that can be implemented effectively.

Tip: Migrating to Windows 2000 impacts the entire organization. The migration project team should include members of diverse business experience to ensure that a complete and thorough plan is developed.

During the planning process, sufficient attention must be paid to the business requirements. Focusing exclusively on the technology during the evaluation and implementation of a new technology is a common error that should be avoided. It is critical to get buy-in from the representatives of various departments of the organization prior to implementing changes in the current architecture. When forming the planning team, you should include members from the following business groups as illustrated in Figure 1.1:

- Account administrators

- Application developers

- Core business representatives

- Desktop engineers

- Domain architects

- LAN or WAN engineers

- Operations personnel

- Security personnel

- Training personnel

- Support personnel

Figure 1.1 Planning Team Members

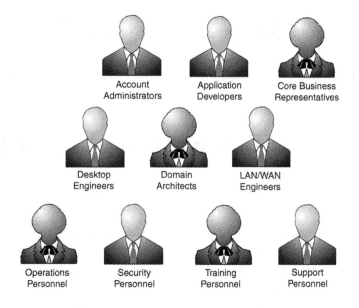

Planning a migration strategy provides an opportunity to align corporate Information Technology (IT) goals with business goals. Planning ahead can provide an opportunity to enhance core business processes, or it can provide an opportunity for a competitive advantage in the marketplace.

An effectively and thoroughly planned migration can secure several other benefits. Planning helps to detect how a change in one area of the enterprise will impact other areas in the enterprise. It allows you to find ways to maximize the changeover while minimizing the negative impact on the overall organization. Planning can identify opportunities to apply technology in an innovative way that will add value to the business side of the organization. Planning provides a mechanism that makes it possible to implement advanced technologies in a proactive, coordinated, and focused manner. Planning can also identify efficient methods that will minimize or eliminate duplication of efforts while maximizing the efficiency of the migration. Planning allows the re-use and leveraging of IT investments and resources. In general, planning reduces the complexity of the migration task and minimizes the risks that change inherently introduces.

 Note: Migrating to the Windows 2000 environment requires a shift in domain and domain administration paradigms because it completely changes how you view domains and their administration.

Migrating from Microsoft Windows NT 4.0 to Windows 2000

Many factors may prompt an organization to migrate to Windows 2000 Active Directory. Windows 2000 Active Directory is a scalable enterprise-class directory service that was built using Internet-standard technologies. It simplifies system administration and provides a wealth of features and capabilities.

Under Active Directory, resources are organized hierarchically in domains. Recall that a Windows 2000 domain is a logical collection or group of network resources, including domain servers, under a single domain name. In a Windows 2000 network, the domain is the basic unit of replication and security, and a Windows 2000 server that is used to manage user access to the network is called a domain controller. User access management includes the following functionalities:

- Logging on
- Authentication
- Access to the directory
- Access to shared resources

Under Active Directory, all domain controllers in the domain are equal. This simplifies administration because you can make changes at any domain controller and the changes are automatically replicated to all other domain controllers in the domain. Active Directory also provides a single point of administration for all objects on the network. An administrator can log on to any computer and administer objects on another computer in the network.

Migrating to Windows 2000 also provides scalability, since Active Directory can store a very large number of objects whose definitions can be modified, augmented, and otherwise customized to the organization and its needs. This is a very powerful feature of Active Directory.

Steps for Developing a Migration Strategy

Developing a migration strategy requires several steps. A complete analysis of the current environment as well as of the desired goals for the environment is necessary. You must design the target environment, decide how you are going to reach that target, develop a strategy to reach it, and then create a plan for deploying the strategy.

Understanding the Four Phases of Domain Migration Planning

A successful migration from Microsoft Windows NT 4.0 to Windows 2000 requires the development of an in-depth plan based on a careful analysis of the current infrastructure. You need to understand the process of planning your strategy before you proceed with the actual migration from a Microsoft Windows NT 4.0 domain structure to Windows 2000 Active Directory. Planning is a four-phase process, each phase containing its own set of plans and action items. The phases that an enterprise must complete to successfully develop a Windows 2000 Active Directory migration strategy consist of the following:

- Design the Active Directory forest

- Choose a migration path

- Develop a domain upgrade or a restructure strategy

- Plan for the deployment of the strategy

Designing the Active Directory Forest

Prior to developing a migration strategy, it is essential to develop the goal of that migration. In this case, depending upon the size and infrastructure of your organization, the goal may be the development of an Active Directory forest. The final design of an Active Directory implementation identifies the ideal domain infrastructure for an organization. This is the end goal of the migration project. This phase involves designing an Active Directory structure that suits your business model and needs. An Active Directory forest is illustrated in Figure 1.2.

Figure 1.2 Active Directory Forest

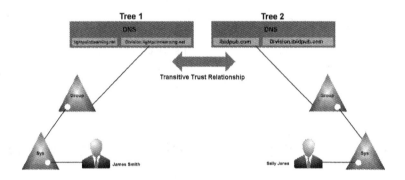

Designing an Active Directory forest is beyond the scope of this book. This course assumes that this first phase has been completed and focuses on the remaining three phases of planning a domain migration.

Choosing a Migration Path to Windows 2000 Active Directory

Selecting the migration path that is right for your organization involves carefully comparing your business needs with the capabilities that a specific migration path will provide to the business. The objective is to select a path that satisfies your business needs, exposes your organization to the least risk, and unfolds as painlessly as possible. You should take great care in determining the migration path because the migration path you choose will affect the remainder of your migration planning.

Part of selecting the migration path is the decision whether to perform an upgrade or a complete restructure. You should note that the two choices are not mutually exclusive. You may choose to upgrade initially and restructure at a later time, or you may choose to restructure from the start.

Developing a Strategy

Once you have carefully selected your migration path, you can begin planning for it. Regardless of whether you are performing an upgrade or a restructure, you need to plan for and define the steps that you will take to achieve the desired Active Directory structure.

Planning for the Deployment of the Strategy

A deployment plan is used to detail the steps required to implement the migration strategy. A deployment plan lists the tasks to be performed and the order in which they must be performed. This plan provides the what, when, and how of the migration effort. It is the final phase of the planning process.

Enterprise Business and Migration Goals

Windows 2000 Active Directory is very powerful and extensible. It allows you to create business elements based in Active Directory technology and to use them in combinations that provide real and practical solutions to pressing business problems. Active Directory allows you to create solutions with which you can leverage opportunities when they present themselves. When you create such solutions, you are using Windows 2000 Active Directory to provide real business value. This is the real key to the success of a Windows 2000 migration.

It is critical that you identify and prioritize your business migration goals. You must also understand the implications of your business migration goals. You must set goals that are achievable and pragmatic.

The goals you set and the priority you assign to them will impact your migration strategy. There are two types of goals that you will want to develop. One set of goals relates to the business, for example, an uninterrupted cash flow. Other goals relate to the migration process itself, for example, no disruption of security. Finally, you will need to develop a map from one type of goal to the other.

Defining Your Business Migration Goals

The decision to migrate to Windows 2000 was made to fulfill the needs of the business, to meet its requirements, or to attain business goals. Windows 2000 provides the technology that can solve business problems and attain business goals. It is important to define how the technological solutions map to the needs and functions of the organization. By doing so, you align the technology with the needs and goals of the business.

Migration Considerations for the Enterprise

During the migration process, a number of business goals might come into play. Common business migration goals include the following:

- Minimizing any disruptions to the business environment
- Minimizing administrative overhead during the migration
- Maximizing value received during the incremental migration
- Maintaining or improving domain security during the migration
- Maintaining or improving security of confidential customer information
- Improving the support of geographically dispersed end users
- Lowering the Total Cost of Ownership (TCO)
- Lowering the cost of administration

Defining Migration Goals

Migration goals are goals that define what you expect to accomplish during the migration and what you expect the migration to accomplish.

Migration goals might be set to consider the potential disruption of network traffic flow. Migration goals can be used as a measuring stick when assessing the success of a completed migration project. For example, if your migration goal is to maintain security without disruption, but a temporary security hole was created during the migration process, the migration might not be considered completely successful.

Migration Considerations

When defining your migration process goals, consider the following possibilities:

- Transparent migration of user accounts

- No new permissions for existing resources

- User access to data, resources, and applications maintained during and after migration

- User's environment maintained during and after the migration

- Earliest possible access to features of the new platform

- Implementation of Group Policy for software distribution and updates

- No impact on security policy other than improvement

Mapping Business Goals to Migration Goals

Business goals should map to migration goals. This ensures the alignment of process and technological goals with business objectives. If conflicts arise during the migration project, the mapping of business goals to migration goals helps to remind the project team of the driving business interests that initially precipitated the migration. For example, the business goal of minimizing administrative overhead during the migration might map to the following migration goals:

- Transparent migration of user accounts

- No new permissions for existing resources

- User access to data, resources, and applications maintained during and after migration

- User's environment maintained during and after the migration

Domain Upgrade or Restructure Strategy

The process of migration involves moving from an existing Microsoft Windows NT 4.0 environment to Windows 2000 Active Directory. In order to plan your migration strategy, you must first decide when, or even if you are going to restructure your existing network infrastructure. You may choose to restructure from the start, upgrade first and restructure later, or you may choose not to restructure at all.

Upgrading Versus Restructuring

To achieve migration from a Microsoft Windows NT 4.0 environment to the desired Active Directory infrastructure, you can perform a domain upgrade or a restructure or both.

Because the process of performing a Windows 2000 upgrade is very flexible, organizations have the choice to only upgrade, upgrade first and then restructure, or restructure from the start. When deciding between an upgrade versus a restructure, consider whether you wish to maintain as much of the current environment as possible or to restructure and obtain a better model of your corporate infrastructure.

Domain Upgrade

A domain upgrade is the process of upgrading a Microsoft Windows NT 4.0 domain to Windows 2000 Active Directory. In an upgrade, the Primary Domain Controller (PDC) and all Backup Domain Controllers (BDCs) are upgraded from Microsoft Windows NT 4.0 to Windows 2000. The process of a domain upgrade is designed to maintain as much of your current environment as possible. Because a domain upgrade retains most of your system settings, preferences, and network service configurations, it may represent the easiest migration route with the lowest associated risk. A domain upgrade, illustrated in Figure 1.3, is sometimes referred to as an in-place upgrade or simply an upgrade.

A domain upgrade accomplishes the following objectives:

- Maintains the current domain model

- Retains most system settings, preferences and applications

Figure 1.3 Domain Upgrade

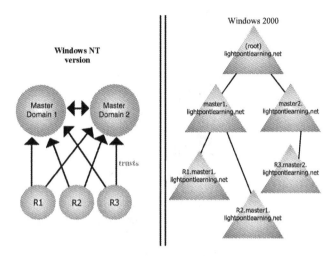

Domain Restructure

A domain restructure is a process in which you redesign the structure of the domain based on the needs of your organization. Because a domain restructure creates a model of a unique entity, your organization, the end result could be any number of different outcomes. However, the process typically reorganizes your current domain structure into a structure of fewer but larger domains. The concept of a domain restructure is illustrated in Figure 1.4.

Figure 1.4 Domain Restructure

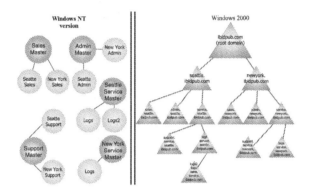

When you restructure, you are redesigning your network infrastructure. Security principals, such as Administrators, Authenticated Users and Server Operators, are reorganized and moved between domains. An organization can first design it's ideal Active Directory forest and then, during implementation, populate it with users, groups, and computers. The organization can also simplify administration and improve manageability in the process by reducing the number of domains and trusts that require administrative overhead.

- A domain restructure can result in the following aspects:

- Fewer but larger domains

- Reduced administrative overhead

Deployment Concepts

Upgrading from a Microsoft Windows NT domain to Windows 2000 Active Directory is not a trivial process. Considerable planning is necessary. Domain controllers, the PDC and all BDCs, must be upgraded in a specific order. The PDC must be upgraded first. Member servers, standalone servers, and client computers can be upgraded at any time before or after the actual domain is upgraded.

Before upgrading your existing Microsoft Windows NT domain, it is important to assess the current network and to plan the upgrade approach you want to take. You need to do the following:

- Document the existing trust relationships

- Document the number and location of domain controllers

- Document account and resource domains

- Document the Domain Name System (DNS) namespaces

- Inventory the application servers

- Plan to upgrade or decommission existing Microsoft Windows NT 3.51 servers

- Create a recovery plan

- Plan the first Active Directory tree

- Plan the site topology

- Devise a general upgrade strategy

Planning to Deploy a Migration Strategy

After you have documented the existing network infrastructure, made a recovery plan, designed the Active Directory trees, planned the site topology, and devised your upgrade strategy, you can create the actual upgrade plan. This plan will specify how you are going to deploy the migration strategy.

Enterprise-Wide Considerations

Thorough migration planning presents the following business opportunities:

- Aligning IT goals with business goals

- Enhancing core business processes

- Providing a competitive advantage in the marketplace

- Analyzing how change in one area impacts another area

- Identifying ways to add value to the organization's business with innovative technologies

- Implementing technology based on business strategy

- Leveraging IT investments and resources

- Eliminating duplication of effort

- Reducing complexity

- Reducing risk

- Simplifying migration

The following are some general guidelines that apply to any domain upgrade:

- Make sure the PDC has enough compute power and storage space

- Create a new root domain before upgrading the PDC

- Upgrade the PDC first

- Immediately upgrade the BDCs

- Independently upgrade clients and member servers

- Schedule the domain upgrade

Vocabulary

Review the following terms in preparation for the certification exam.

Term	Description
BDC	A Backup Domain Controller is a computer running Microsoft Windows NT 4.0 Server that receives a copy of the domain's directory database in a Microsoft Windows NT 4.0 Server domain.
domain controller	A Windows 2000 server that is used to manage user access to the network.
DNS	The Domain Name System is a static, hierarchical name service for Transmission Control Protocol/Internet Protocol (TCP/IP) hosts.
PDC	A Primary Domain Controller is a computer running Microsoft Windows NT 4.0 Server that authenticates domain logons and maintains the directory database for a domain in a Windows NT 4.0 Server domain.
TCO	The Total Cost of Ownership includes the total amount of money and time associated with purchasing, configuring, and maintaining hardware and software. This includes updates, maintenance, administration, and technical support.
TCP/IP	Transmission Control Protocol/Internet Protocol is a set of networking protocols that is used on the Internet. It provides communication across interconnected networks that are made up of diverse computers and operating systems.

In Brief

If you want to...	Then do this...
Migrate to Windows 2000 Active Directory	Carefully plan the migration. You should design your forest, choose a migration path, develop a migration strategy, and then plan for the deployment of that strategy.
Produce an effective migration strategy that best serves the needs of the business	Involve members of various groups and functions of the enterprise that will be influenced by the migration. Doing so will ensure that the decisions made for one part of the organization will not adversely impact another part of the organization.

Lesson 1 Activities

Complete the following activities to prepare for the certification exam.

1. Discuss the phases that an enterprise must complete to successfully develop a migration strategy.

2. List at least four possible business migration goals.

3. List at least four possible migration goals.

4. List four business opportunities presented by a migration to Windows 2000.

5. Discuss the necessary steps that should be accomplished prior to developing an upgrade plan.

6. Discuss the possible results of a domain restructure.

7. Discuss why a domain upgrade might be preferred over a restructure.

8. Discuss why business goals should be mapped to migration goals.

9. List the items concerning your current network environment that you should document when planning an upgrade.

10. Discuss some of the benefits of a restructure.

Answers to Lesson 1 Activities

1. The four phases of migrating to Windows 2000 are the following:

    *   Design the Active Directory forest

    *   Choose a migration path

    *   Develop a migration strategy

    *   Develop a deployment plan

2. Common business migration goals include the following:

    *   Minimizing any disruptions to the business environment

    *   Minimizing administrative overhead during the migration

    *   Maximizing value received during the incremental migration

    *   Maintaining or improving domain security during the migration

    *   Maintaining or improving security of confidential customer information

    *   Improving the support of geographically dispersed end users

    *   Lowering the Total Cost of Ownership (TCO)

    *   Lowering the cost of administration

3. The following are possible migration process goals:

    *   Transparent migration of user accounts

    *   No new permissions for existing resources

    *   User access to data, resources and applications maintained during and after migration

    *   User's environment maintained during and after the migration

    *   Earliest possible access to features of the new platform

    *   Implementation of Group Policy for software distribution and updates

    *   No impact on security policy other than improvement

4. Migrating to Windows 2000 presents the following business opportunities:

    - Aligning IT goals with business goals

    - Enhancing core business processes

    - Providing a competitive advantage in the marketplace

    - Identifying ways to add value to the organizations business with innovative technology

    - Implementing technology based on business strategy

    - Leveraging IT investments and resources

    - Eliminating duplication of effort

    - Reducing complexity

    - Reducing risk

    - Simplifying migration

5. Prior to developing an upgrade plan, you should have accomplished the following steps:

    - Documented the existing network infrastructure

    - Made a recovery plan

    - Designed the Active Directory trees

    - Planned the site topology

    - Devised your upgrade strategy

    - Upgrade or decommission existing Microsoft Windows NT 3.51 servers

6. A domain restructure can yield the following benefits:

    - Fewer domains

    - Larger domains

    - Reduced administrative overhead

7. A domain upgrade might be preferred because it minimizes the changes to the current infrastructure. A domain upgrade maintains the current domain model while retaining most configuration settings, preferences and applications.

8. The mapping of business goals to migration goals ensures the alignment of migration goals and technological goals with business objectives. If conflicts arise during the migration project, the mapping of business goals to migration process goals helps to remind the project team of the driving business interests that initially precipitated the migration.

9. When planning an upgrade from a Microsoft Windows NT 4.0 environment, you should document the following elements:

   - The existing trust relationships

   - The number and location of domain controllers

   - Account and resource domains

   - Domain Name System (DNS) namespaces

   - Inventory the application servers

   - Plan to upgrade or decommission existing Microsoft Windows NT 3.51 servers

   - Create a recovery plan

   - Plan the first Active Directory tree

   - Plan the site topology

   - Devise a general upgrade strategy

10. A restructure can benefit the organization by simplifying administration and improving manageability by reducing the number of domains and trusts that require administrative overhead.

Lesson 1 Quiz

These questions test your knowledge of features, vocabulary, procedures, and syntax.

1. Before you proceed with a migration to Windows 2000, which task do you need to accomplish first?
   A. Choose the migration path
   B. Develop a migration strategy
   C. Plan deployment of the migration strategy
   D. Design the Active Directory forest

2. Part of developing a migration strategy is deciding when you will restructure your current domain architecture. At which point in the process can you restructure?
   A. From the start of the migration process
   B. Later, after the upgrade has been performed
   C. Only if an upgrade has been performed
   D. Only from an in-place domain upgrade

3. Which of the following statements are true regarding upgrading from a Microsoft Windows NT 4.0 domain to Windows 2000 Active Directory?
   A. Domain controllers, the PDC and all BDCs, must be upgraded in a specific order.
   B. The PDC must be upgraded first.
   C. Domain controllers can be upgraded in any order.
   D. Member servers, standalone servers, and client computers can be upgraded at any time.

4. If your domain contains Microsoft Windows NT 3.51 servers, what should be done with these servers?
   A. They should be upgraded or decommissioned.
   B. They can be used as security providers and authentication servers.
   C. They must first be upgraded to Microsoft Windows NT 4.0.
   D. They can be used without modification in the Active Directory forest.

5. What is the final phase in migration planning?
    A. Deciding whether or not to restructure from the start
    B. Developing a migration strategy
    C. Developing a deployment plan
    D. Developing an upgrade strategy

6. In an existing Microsoft Windows NT 4.0 domain with multiple domain controllers, what is upgraded first?
    A. The BDCs
    B. It does not matter
    C. The PDC
    D. All domain controllers must be upgraded simultaneously

7. To ensure that changes to the existing infrastructure have a minimized impact on the business, what should you do?
    A. Perform a complete restructure of your domain infrastructure
    B. Upgrade all member servers and clients to Windows 2000 before you perform a complete restructure
    C. Upgrade all BDCs before you upgrade the clients
    D. Create a project team with members from various departments within the organization

8. What are the typical results of a reconstructure?
    A. Smaller domains
    B. Fewer domains
    C. Larger domains
    D. Reduced administrative overhead

9. In general, what does planning for a migration require or achieve?
    A. Requires that some parts of the organization benefit when other parts of the organization realize no benefit and possibly a reduction in service
    B. Should be accomplished by relatively few people to reduce confusion
    C. Reduces the complexity of the migration task
    D. Minimizes the risks that change inherently introduces

10. What does a domain upgrade do?
    A. Maintains the current domain model
    B. Retains most configuration settings and preferences
    C. Retains most applications
    D. Introduces the greatest risk

Answers to Lesson 1 Quiz

1. Answer D is correct. The first thing that needs to be done when moving into a Windows 2000 environment is to design the forest.

    Answers A, B, and C are incorrect. These operations cannot be performed until after the Active Directory forest is designed.

2. Answers A and B are correct. You may restructure at any time. You can restructure from the start of the migration or you can perform an in-place upgrade and restructure at a later time.

    Answers C and D are incorrect. You need not restructure immediately and restructuring does not require an in-place upgrade be accomplished beforehand or simultaneously.

3. Answers A and B are correct. The PDC must be upgraded before the BDCs.

    Answer D is correct. Member servers and clients can be upgraded at any time.

    Answer C is incorrect. There is a specific order for domain server upgrades.

4. Answer A is correct. Microsoft Windows NT 3.51 servers should be either upgraded or decommissioned.

    Answer B in incorrect. Microsoft Windows NT 3.51 servers cannot support the security capabilities of the Windows 2000 environment

    Answer C is incorrect. A Microsoft Windows NT 3.51 server does not need to be upgraded to Microsoft Windows NT 4.0 before being upgraded to Windows 2000.

    Answer D is incorrect. A Microsoft Windows NT 3.51 server should be upgraded or decommissioned.

5. Answer C is correct. The final phase in planning for a migration is the development of the deployment plan.

    Answer A is incorrect. Deciding whether or not to restructure from the start is accomplished prior to developing the migration strategy.

    Answer B is incorrect. Developing a migration strategy is accomplished before developing a plan to deploy the strategy.

Answer D is incorrect. You develop the upgrade strategy if you plan to upgrade rather than restructure. This is accomplished prior to developing the migration strategy.

6. Answer C is correct. The PDC is upgraded first.

    Answer A is incorrect. The BDCs are upgraded after the PDC.

    Answer B is incorrect. The domain controllers must be upgraded in a specific order.

    Answer D is incorrect. The PDC is upgraded before the BDCs.

7. Answer D is correct. You should create a project team with members from various departments within the organization.

    Answer A is incorrect. When you perform a complete restructure of your domain infrastructure, you introduce the greatest change and the greatest chance for negative impact. A complete restructure must be accomplished only with the highest level of planning.

    Answer B is incorrect. You can upgrade member servers and clients to Windows 2000 at any time.

    Answer C is incorrect. You can upgrade clients at any time.

8. Answers B, C and D are correct. The end result will most likely be that you have fewer but larger domains whose administrative overhead has been reduced.

    Answer A is incorrect. Most likely, you will not find that you end up with smaller domains.

9. Answers C and D are correct. Planning reduces the complexity of the migration task and minimizes the risks that change inherently introduces.

    Answer A is incorrect. One of the goals of planning is that all parts of the organization benefit and no parts of the organization realize a reduction in service.

    Answer B is incorrect. The planning should involve all aspects of the business to minimize negative impacts caused by change.

10. Answers A, B, and C are correct. A domain upgrade maintains the current domain model and retains most configuration settings, preferences and applications.

    Answer D is incorrect. A domain upgrade presents the least risk of change in a migration strategy.

Lesson 2: Migration Path to Windows 2000 Active Directory

The migration to Microsoft Windows 2000 Active Directory should be well planned. When developing your migration strategy, the first step is to select an appropriate migration path. The selection of the appropriate migration path can be a complex decision; fortunately, there is no one right or wrong solution. The perfect strategy for one organization's migration may be completely inappropriate for another's. The business needs and the tolerance for risk to production and business environments can differ from one organization to the next. Microsoft has provided methodologies to upgrade in a variety of ways so that you can better meet the needs of your organization.

When selecting a migration path that meets your organizational or business needs, you should carefully compare your migration and business goals to the capabilities of each migration path. The migration path that you choose will affect the remainder of migration planning.

After completing this lesson, you should have a better understanding of the following topics:

- Migration Path Introduction
- Existing Domain Environment Identification
- Information Gathering for Current Network Environment
- Migration Goals
- Active Directory Design Analysis
- Migration Path Choices

Migration Path Introduction

When selecting a migration path to Windows 2000 Active Directory, an enterprise must consider it's current network environment and it's target network environment. This section will provide the student with an overview of the steps that an organization should follow to achieve their migration goals.

Choosing a Migration Path

Selecting the correct migration path for a specific organization requires that the organization perform the following tasks:

- Identify and document the existing domain environment

- Gather information about and document the current network environment

- Define the business and migration goals for the migration

- Examine the organization's Active Directory design

- Determine the organization's possible migration paths

- Evaluate the issues that may result in a decision to upgrade

- Evaluate the issues that may result in a decision to restructure

Identify and Document the Existing Domain Environment

The process of identifying and documenting the existing Microsoft Windows NT 4.0 domain environment defines the starting point of the migration. This process also allows an organization to evaluate the effectiveness of it's current domain model in meeting the present business needs.

Gather Information about and Document the Current Network Environment

An informed and precise view of the information and technologies that an organization currently uses and needs to fulfill business requirements is required to analyze the impact a migration will have on an organization's production environment. To this end, the current network environment should be thoroughly investigated and documented.

Define the Business and Migration Goals for the Migration

You will need to identify and prioritize your business and migration goals. Your migration goals will relate to the business and to the migration itself.

Examine the Organization's Active Directory Design

The migration project's end goal is the ideal domain infrastructure for the organization. This is identified by the Active Directory design. An initial review of the Active Directory design must be conducted because the domain hierarchy it proposes will influence, if not dictate, the migration path you choose. Once you select to perform either a domain upgrade or a restructure, a more thorough examination of the Active Directory design will help to direct the remaining migration planning. It will also ensure that the business goals of the two designs are aligned.

Determine the Organization's Possible Migration Paths

To determine the organization's possible migration paths, you need to identify the different ways in which you can accomplish migration to Windows 2000. You then carefully compare your migration goals to the capabilities and features provided by each of the migration paths in order to select the path that best meets your organization's needs.

Evaluate the Issues that May Result in a Decision to Upgrade

You will need to examine the issues and decision points associated with selecting an upgrade as the migration path. You also need to understand the reasons for selecting upgrade over a restructure.

Evaluate the Issues that May Result in a Decision to Restructure

You must also examine the issues and decision points associated with selecting a restructure as the migration path. Understand the reasons for choosing to restructure instead of upgrade.

Identifying the Existing Microsoft Windows NT 4.0 Components

The Microsoft Windows NT 4.0 components currently incorporated in your network have to be identified and documented. In addition to identifying the Microsoft Windows NT 4.0 components, they must also be prepared for the migration. These Windows NT 4.0 components consist of the following:

- Servers

- Domains

- Network services

Servers

Servers are the foundation of a Microsoft Windows NT 4.0 network. To facilitate the upgrade of existing Microsoft Windows NT 4.0 servers you may want to consider evaluating the current state of the servers. Will the existing hardware support Windows 2000 or will a memory upgrade and possibly a processor upgrade be desirable or required? You may wish to consider moving resources, such as file and print services, off existing domain controllers so that your domain controllers are dedicated to authentication of users only.

You should ensure that all Microsoft Windows NT 4.0 servers have been upgraded to at least Service Pack 4. You may wish to remove Domain Naming Service (DNS), Windows Internet Name Service (WINS), and Dynamic Host Configuration Protocol (DHCP) services from the domain controllers that are intended for Windows 2000 so that you do not have to worry about keeping the various service databases intact during the upgrade. You will also want to standardize all your Microsoft Windows NT 4.0 servers and ensure that the latest Service Pack is installed so that you can minimize the number of variables encountered during the migration.

Domains

To simplify the migration, you should investigate and organize your user accounts, groups, naming conventions, and network shares. Clean up unused and disabled accounts and examine special accounts. Redundant or extinct global and local groups should be removed. Evaluate naming conventions, ensure that they are standardized across the organization, and clean up extinct personal and group shares.

During your assessment of the current Microsoft Windows NT 4.0 components that are incorporated into your network, trim and pare the use of Microsoft Windows NT 4.0 resources. You will need to identify ownership of these resources including the following:

Personal shares—Determine which resources are named and shared with a user's account.

Group shares—Identify the owner of the share and its description.

Servers—Ensure that the description field is updated including hardware, ownership, and location.

Workstations—Ensure that the owner name truly reflects ownership.

Customer groups—You will need to know the owner and backup owner as well as a description of the group's purpose.

Printers and print queues—You will need to identify the printer type, location, and other special characteristics.

Network Services

WINS and DHCP services under Windows 2000 and under Microsoft Windows NT 4.0 are very similar. However, DNS has changed considerably. You will need to understand your company's DNS namespace thoroughly to effectively plan the integration of the Windows 2000 namespace into the existing DNS namespace.

You will also need to ensure that your Network Basic Input/Output System (NetBIOS) names fit standard DNS naming conventions. Request for Comments (RFC) standard DNS servers do not support underscores in resource names. However, to support legacy NetBIOS naming rules, Microsoft DNS will support underscores.

It is also necessary to prepare DHCP and WINS services for Windows 2000. At least one of the DHCP services should be moved to a DNS server to facilitate DHCP and DNS integration under Windows 2000. For further information on service preparation for Windows 2000 migration, refer to the Microsoft web site at www.microsoft.com.

Existing Domain Environment Identification

The first step in selecting a migration path is identifying the existing domain environment. The current domain components should be well documented prior to attempting the migration to Windows 2000. Further, identifying the domain model is an important step that must be taken prior to beginning an upgrade to Active Directory.

 Tip: The Microsoft Windows NT 4.0 Resource Kit provides utilities that can assist in documenting your current domain's account details. Third-party tools are also available.

Identifying the Existing Domain Environment

While this is the first step toward selecting a migration path, for larger organizations, it can be a sizeable undertaking. Since this step is key in determining an effective migration strategy, the project plan should allow the project team adequate time to accomplish this step.

You should consider the following factors when you examine your existing Microsoft Windows NT 4.0 directory services and domain structure:

- Domain model

- Existing trust relationships

- Quantity and location of domain controllers

- Accounts and administration

Domain Model

A typical Microsoft Windows NT 4.0 domain model may include several account domains and many resource domains. Your existing domain structure will influence the Windows 2000 migration path you ultimately choose when migrating or upgrading existing domains. Examining the existing domain structure can pinpoint unnecessary complexities or inefficient domains, such as those that were created reactively for a now obsolete purpose or function.

 Note: An organization with a single domain model has no need to restructure when planning an upgrade to Windows 2000. A single domain model only permits a single domain.

Some common Microsoft Windows NT domain model types include the single, single master domain model, a multiple-master domain model, and a complete trust domain model. The single master domain model, as shown in Figure 2.1, consists of a master user domain and a resource domain model. The master user domain is used to maintain user accounts. The resource domain is used to manage resources. The single master domain model forms an administrative hierarchy.

Figure 2.1 Single Master Domain Model

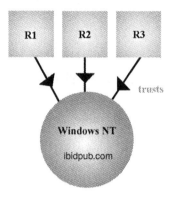

A multiple-master domain model is illustrated in Figure 2.2. The multiple-master domain model forms an administrative hierarchy, exactly like the single master domain model. The difference between a single master domain model and a multiple-master domain model is that the multiple-master domain model uses multiple-master user domains.

Figure 2.2 Multiple-Master Domain Model

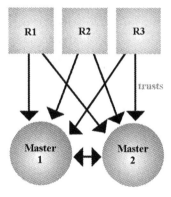

Both single and multiple-master domain models form administrative hierarchies wherein the greatest level of administrative control is at the top of the hierarchy. The complete trust domain model, illustrated in Figure 2.3, does not form a hierarchy. This model is difficult to manage because it forms an interconnected web of trust relationships.

Figure 2.3 Complete Trust Domain Model

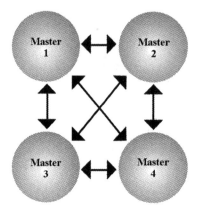

Existing Trust Relationships

You need to document all existing one-way and two-way trust relationships in your current network environment. In addition, you should identify any domains and trust relationships you do not want to move into your Windows 2000 forest. Microsoft Windows NT 4.0 domains that are upgraded to Windows 2000 domains and are members of the same forest will use transitive trust relationships to connect to other Windows 2000 domains as illustrated in Figure 2.4.

Figure 2.4 Windows 2000 Domains

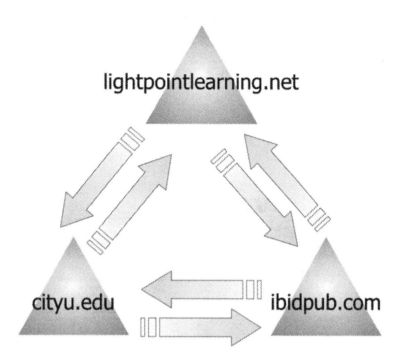

It is necessary to create explicit trust relationships between Windows 2000 domains and down-level domains that are not moved into the new forest.

Quantity and Location of Domain Controllers

When planning your migration, you will need to determine the number and location of all existing domain controllers on your network. You should construct physical and logical network diagrams to show this information. A physical network diagram is illustrated in Figure 2.5. Identify your Primary Domain Controllers (PDCs) and Backup Domain Controllers (BDCs) on both types of network diagrams, noting their geographical locations and configuration details.

Figure 2.5 Physical Network Diagram

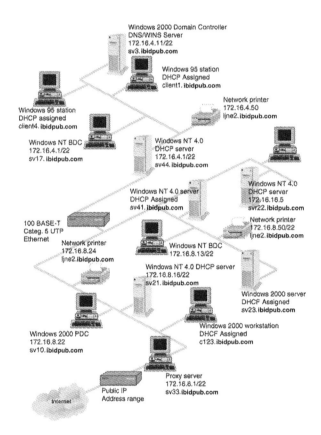

A logical network diagram is illustrated in Figure 2.6.

Figure 2.6 Logical Network Diagram

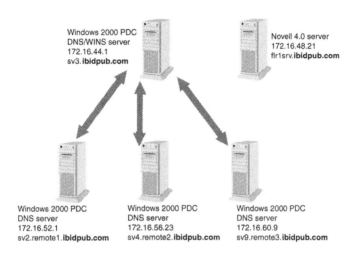

Windows 2000 PDC
DNS/WINS server
172.16.44.1
sv3.**ibidpub.com**

Novell 4.0 server
172.16.48.21
flr1srv.**ibidpub.com**

Windows 2000 PDC
DNS server
172.16.52.1
sv2.remote1.**ibidpub.com**

Windows 2000 PDC
DNS server
172.16.56.23
sv4.remote2.**ibidpub.com**

Windows 2000 PDC
DNS server
172.16.60.9
sv9.remote3.**ibidpub.com**

Accounts and Administration

The number and distribution of user, group, and computer accounts may affect the migration path you choose. The domain location of user, group, and computer accounts must be documented. You should also record key account properties, such as group account membership, permissions to shares, and any special rights assignments. This information is used during the pilot trial migrations to validate the deployment plan. The information can also be used to determine whether any accounts in the enterprise are obsolete or inaccurate. This will prevent data that is no longer used from migrating into the Active Directory service.

Some Information Technology (IT) organizations centralize security assignment but allow for decentralized day-to-day user administration. Other IT organizations may strictly control all administrative functions. Examining and documenting an organization's domain administration will reveal the type of existing administrative traditions. The examination should also reveal the reasons for those traditions. Investigation and documentation of existing administrative policy may also expose security gaps, outdated policies, or unneeded redundancies.

Current Network Environment Information

The second step in developing your migration plan is gathering information about the current network environment. Two important parts in planning your   Windows 2000 Active Directory migration are the documenting of your existing network's physical and logical topology and compiling a complete and accurate inventory of the organization's information, applications, and technologies.

 Note: You should identify locations external to the Microsoft Windows NT Security Accounts Manager (SAM) database in which user account information is stored. An example of this would be Microsoft Exchange.

Gathering Information about the Current Network Environment

An understanding of the current network environment is necessary before network architects can plan for and move to a better network environment. When evaluating whether progress is necessary, the current environment is an important reference point. You will need to document some areas of your current network environment as illustrated in Figure 2.7 and listed in the following:

● Information store inventory

● Hardware and software inventory

● Network infrastructure

● DNS infrastructure

● File, Print and Web Servers, PDCs, and BDCs

● Business applications

Figure 2.7 Typical Network Environments

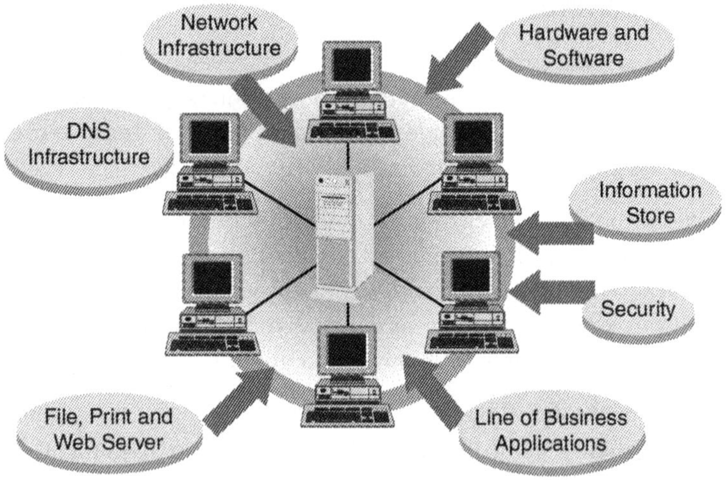

Information Store Inventory

What the organization needs to know to run its business and operations is detailed in an information store inventory. This inventory specifies where and how information is stored throughout the organization. It also specifies how data is moved and shared throughout the organization. The information store inventory identifies the following:

- Data-management policies

- Information origination

- Data ownership

- Patterns of information consumption

- Patterns of information production

Your inventory should also address any statutory or legal restrictions that affect your data and information needs, such as encryption.

Hardware and Software Inventory

You should create hardware and software inventories of all server and client computers in use on your network. Also, include hardware, such as routers, hubs, printers, scanners, modems, and any other hardware in use on the network, for example a Redundant Array of Inexpensive Disks (RAID) data store or a Remote Access Service (RAS) server.

Your software inventory should be extensive. All application programs found on any server should be listed in the software inventory. The inventory should also include the version numbers of any Dynamic-Link Libraries (DLLs) associated with any of the applications on your system. You will need to document all hardware drivers and their versions, as well as any service packs that you may have applied to either your operating system or to any server applications.

Ensure that the latest version of the Basic Input/Output System (BIOS) is installed on all machines, that the BIOS is Windows 2000 compatible, and that both facts are documented. Document the network configurations for all your servers and client computers. For example, you will want to document the Internet Protocol (IP) and gateway addresses and the DNS server name.

Network Infrastructure

To document your network infrastructure, you will need to obtain hardware and software data. The hardware data is used to document your infrastructure's physical structure. The software data is used to document the existence and configuration of the protocols in use on your network. You will also need to document the logical organization of your network including name and address resolution methods, the existence and configuration of services used, such as the Windows Internet Name Service (WINS) topology, and Dynamic Host Configuration Protocol (DHCP) reservations. You should also document option configurations to ensure that these services function appropriately after the migration is complete.

To assist you in making the appropriate installation decisions regarding replication, document the geographic locations, physical connectivity, and available bandwidth between the service providers. Also, document all statically assigned IP address assignments and the presence of any other network operating systems in the network infrastructure.

In addition, all DHCP servers on the network must be documented. Document any IP addresses that have been assigned to servers or clients. You should document DHCP settings such as the default gateway and the number of subnets and hosts on the network, their IP addresses, as well as any subnet masks employed. If you lease IP addresses to clients, you should record the lease duration and expiration.

If you have users who are remote or mobile, then you will need to detail the remote access and dial-up configurations. For Virtual Private Network (VPN) connections, you will need the current VPN connection configuration.

 Note: When you evaluate your current VPN connections, you should do so with the goal of migrating to a Windows 2000 VPN.

Finally, you should document your connectivity. Measure and document the speed of all network links between network segments and between physical geographical locations at low, normal, and high traffic conditions.

DNS Infrastructure

It is important to record any DNS namespaces in use in your organization. Since an Active Directory forest requires a unique DNS namespace, you will need to identify all zones and the configuration of zone transfers. You will also want to document all DNS and WINS servers. In addition to hardware details, note the configuration and version information of software running on the server. If you have a DNS server on the network that is running a Network Operating System (NOS) other than Microsoft Windows NT 4.0, you will need to determine whether that operating system can support dynamic registration and Service (SRV) resource records. If not, you will need to find out if an upgrade to this capability is available from the DNS software manufacturer.

If you have other hosts on the network running non-Windows operating systems, you should document the services and versions that they use and provide. You should document Service Advertising Protocol (SAP) and Routing Information Protocol (RIP) service providers. Detailing the versions of all services that are in use is important so that you can determine if you need to upgrade a particular service. For example, UNIX Berkeley Internet Name Domain (BIND) versions prior to version 4.9.4 are not compatible with Windows 2000.

File, Print and Web Servers, PDCs and BDCs

The configuration details of all file, print, and web servers also need to be recorded. Besides, you will need to document your PDCs and BDCs. Note any unique configurations, for example, a server hosting a bank of modems or multiple network adapters. Identify any of these servers or services that rely on special protocols or drivers. You ought to determine if any service requires a specific environment to run. For example, if a product needs to run on a BDC, it may no longer function when the BDC is upgraded to Windows 2000. Verify that any and all hardware and associated drivers are Windows 2000 compatible; use the Windows 2000 Hardware Compatibility List (HCL) to do so.

Business Application Requirements

Your enterprise uses software applications to perform its core mission. Such applications might be a financial package, a database, or an email system. You will need to verify that the applications are compatible with Windows 2000 Active Directory and, if not, determine if an upgrade is available or planned.

Establishing Security Requirements

A review of the organization's security standards is important when you are making any modifications to your network infrastructure. Review your security standards, as well as their current implementation, in light of your target security environment under Windows 2000. You should document and review the standards and procedures for the following elements:

- Mobile and desktop users

- Internal and external networks

- Dial-up and remote access accounts

You must also document how administrative tasks are performed and by whom. Identify if administrative tasks are performed by a centralized group or by several groups. Review the membership lists of these groups and the specific rights and privileges of these groups. Administrative groups perform the following tasks:

- Creating users, groups, and file shares

- Changing passwords

- Configuring device and object attributes

You will need to document the types of relationships that currently exist between physical and logical units in your organization. Such units can be identified as follows:

- Office locations

- Business units

- Divisions

Record any existing user and enterprise security policies. You will need to identify the types of information that is made available to various groups as well as the groups themselves. You should make a note of any significant restrictions that are needed or required for certain specific types of information, such as accounting or other confidential data.

If your organization has guidelines for network usage or Web access, you should document these as well. Keep track of which staff members can access the Web, the reasons and purpose of the Web access, and what is considered prohibited or inappropriate access.

Your organization's relationships with outside entities, and how these relationships affect security measures should be taken into consideration in your migration strategy. You will want to consider the following entities:

- Vendors

- Customers

- Joint-venture partners

- Business partners

Determine if you have any service-level commitments with your business partners. Also, document if you permit business partners access to your network as recognized users. Examine and document your company's policies regarding your business partners' access to your network data and resources. Find out if they can view data on a read-only basis, or if they can modify or augment data already existing on your network, and document your findings. Determine and document how you restrict access to applications. Document your password standards, for example, longevity and content including the minimum length and character types.

You will also need to document the security and encryption standards that are currently employed in your organization, as well as those that are planned for the future. You should document user and user group security permissions. Also, examine and detail your existing domains and the trust relationships as they currently exist between domain controllers. You should record the security protocols that are currently in use on your network, and how you authenticate external users from sources such as the following:

- Internet

- Dial-up

- Wide Area Network (WAN)

A user may have multiple accounts. If this is the case, then document the types of these various accounts. For example, the user may have a Windows NT 4.0 account and a UNIX account. You must record the permissions, all user and group memberships, and any other account-related detail for each user.

Determine if you are going to implement additional security protocols, policies, or procedures such as distributed security. Identification of any related issues during the planning stage will help you identify the types of security risks you might face during your migration and how to meet them.

While in the process of documenting your existing and future security configuration, you should also review and document your backup policies and procedures. An examination of your disaster recovery plan and insurance that it is up-to-date should be accomplished and documented. Determine if your disaster recovery and backup schemes are appropriate for your current network size and demands as well as their applicability to your anticipated future growth.

Identifying Areas that Require Documentation

Each organization differs in some way from every other organization. This difference makes a listing of documentation requirements nearly impossible to generate on a generalized basis. This lesson has provided you with a generalized overview of your documentation needs. You will need to examine your network in detail to determine if these generalized needs are sufficient for your specific requirements. You may find areas of importance not covered in this lesson. This does not mean that those areas are of any less consequence to your organization, but rather that you should include them in your documentation.

In general, any setting, configuration, resource, protocol, policy, procedure, method, or piece of hardware that is connected to or interacts with your network should be documented. The more that you can document and save, the easier it is to plan your migration and anticipate and minimize any migration problems.

Migration Goals

There are fundamentally two types of migration goals. The first type, the business migration goal, defines how the technology employed will be used to satisfy the needs and functions of an organization. The second type relates to the migration itself and is called simply a migration goal. For your migration to be successful, it is critical to identify and prioritize your migration goals.

Defining Business Goals for Migration

Business migration goals will vary from one organization to the next depending upon the type of organization, its structure, and its business needs. The goals for a small industrial manufacturer will differ from those of a large multinational one. Typically, it is business needs that drive the decision of the business to migrate to the Windows 2000 Active Directory environment.

The key to success is determining the business goals for the migration and then defining how the technology can be employed to meet those goals. Business goals may include or be derived from the following elements:

- Scalability
- Security
- Manageability
- Availability
- Business needs
- Business requirements

Prioritizing Migration Goals

Like business goals, migration goals will differ from one organization to the next. In general, migration goals will tend toward some commonalities regardless of the organization's infrastructure. Such goals might include the following:

- A minimum uptime of 85%

- Users maintain their current passwords

- Users maintain their current environment

- No new permissions are required for existing resources

- Security will not be interrupted or adversely impacted

Mapping Business Goals to Migration Goals

To ensure the alignment of business goals with technological objectives, you should create a map that relates your business goals with migration goals. Each business goal should be cross-referenced with similar migration goals. Creating this map gives you a baseline for the migration project. If any conflicts arise, you will be able to show how the migration goal is related to the business objectives that drove the migration in the first place.

Active Directory Design Analysis

When you have completed defining your business and migration goals, compare them to the goals defined during the Active Directory design. You may find some conflicts when doing so. You can also find conflicts when you attempt to validate the proposed Active Directory design in the current network environment. These conflicts may present a significant risk to a successful migration. Conflicts must be resolved before you begin the upgrade. You should define a process that will enable you to discover and then resolve any design-related conflicts. The definition of such a process can be critical to the success of the migration.

Examining the Active Directory Design of Your Organization

Before you begin the migration process, you will need to carefully and diligently compare the goals defined for the Active Directory design with the goals you defined for your migration. As stated earlier, you need to identify conflicts between the two sets of goals. In addition to conflicts, you need to look for inconsistencies between the goals and designs. Like conflicts, inconsistencies may appear when you validate the proposed Active Directory design against the current network environment. Examine the goal sets carefully. Identifying conflicts and inconsistencies and resolving them during the planning stage is much more efficient and cost-effective than dealing with them during the migration implementation.

Identifying Goal Conflicts

After you have defined your migration goals, you will need to identify the goals created during the design of the proposed Active Directory infrastructure. You should verify that the migration goals reflect the Active Directory design goals. The Active Directory design goals should both support and complement the migration goals and vice-versa.

When Active Directory and migration goals are in conflict, a successful migration is at a high risk. For example, an organization's business migration goal is to reduce the Total Cost of Ownership (TCO). However, an Active Directory design goal is to divide the organization into multiple forests. These two goals are in conflict because the Active Directory design goal will cause the TCO to increase rather than decrease. This conflict is illustrated in Figure 2.8.

Figure 2.8 Goals in Conflict

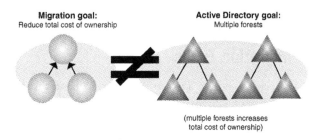

Identifying Design Conflicts

In addition to comparing the Active Directory design goals to the migration goals, you should also compare the Active Directory design components to the current network environment. Any conflicts found can create barriers to the upgrade. Conflicts always present significant risk to the migration success. For example, assume you have a site with a single domain controller and the Wide Area Network (WAN) connection is unreliable. Further, assume one of your Active Directory design goals is for all sites to be independently fault-tolerant. There would be a conflict between the environment and the goal.

Resolving Conflicts

You must mitigate all conflicts with the Active Directory design before your migration begins. Conflicts with the migration goals, as well as conflicts with the current network environment, can usually be resolved. The first step in resolving these conflicts is to identify the business need that has driven the proposed design or strategy that presents a conflict. You must then ensure that the business need is accurately reflected in your migration goals. Finally, you must verify the alignment of the Active Directory design goals with your migration goals. If you still cannot resolve the conflict, then you will need to change something. Either the proposed Active Directory design will require rethinking or your migration goals will need to be reconsidered.

Migration Path Choices

Migrating a domain from Microsoft Windows NT 4.0 to Windows 2000 is a very flexible process with many possible implementation permutations. An organization can choose to upgrade but not restructure, to restructure from the start, or to upgrade and restructure at a later time. In addition, an organization may choose to restructure the entire infrastructure or limit the restructure to a collection of infrastructure components.

Choosing Possible Migration Paths

The migration is driven by business needs. The direction or path of the migration to the Windows 2000 Active Directory environment and infrastructure will also be driven by business needs and requirements. Choosing the correct migration path for your organization can be a complex decision.

There are pros and cons associated with the various migration paths that you need to be aware of before you can effectively make the decision regarding which path your organization should take.

Reasons to Restructure

A domain restructure may be appropriate if your current domain structure does not meet your current business objectives and a re-alignment of technology to business needs can rectify that situation. You may find that an upgrade alone will affect your production environment negatively and decide to restructure. Other reasons to restructure include the desire to lower administrative costs, as well as long-term hardware costs, or the need to repair ineffective or remove obsolete domain structures. Finally, you may choose to restructure if you do not plan to re-use any of the existing infrastructure.

Reasons Not to Restructure

You may choose not to restructure if you find that your current domain infrastructure meets your current business goals, or there is a potential increase in short-term hardware costs. Another reason may be that your organization's needs determine that the network must stay in mixed mode. You may also choose not to restructure if the roles and responsibilities the new infrastructure would impose are not yet defined.

Reasons for Upgrading

You may choose to upgrade without restructuring if you have found that your current infrastructure meets your business goals, you have limited short-term resources, or you need to be able to recover your original environment. You may also choose to upgrade if you decide that an infrastructure change would require significant or excessive changes to the organization or to current business processes. You may also decide to upgrade if you have an application running that presents incompatibilities with a restructure. A final reason to upgrade rather than restructure could be that you need to migrate quickly to the Windows 2000 Active Directory infrastructure.

Reasons for Not Upgrading

You may choose not to upgrade if your current domain infrastructure is ineffective or outdated. You may also choose not to upgrade if you find that there is little or no reduction of administrative or hardware costs associated with upgrading instead of restructuring. Finally, you may decide not to upgrade because there is no savings in server costs as the number of servers needed is not significantly different from one environment to the other.

Reasons for Upgrading First and Restructuring Later

An upgrade followed by a restructure of your domain may be appropriate if your current domain structure is meeting your business objectives, and you can initially upgrade to Windows 2000 and then perform the restructure to fix any problems encountered during the upgrade. You may also choose to upgrade first and restructure later if you need to slowly evolve various corporate Local Area Networks (LANs) into a more centralized infrastructure. Finally, you may choose this route if you need to lower the initial short-term administrative and hardware costs.

Reasons for Not Upgrading First and Restructuring Later

There are some very good reasons for not upgrading first and restructuring later. A two-phased migration takes much longer to plan and much longer to deploy. An additional factor is that the extra details and steps needed increase the chance of error. A two-step process has a much higher risk factor.

Migrating to the Active Directory Infrastructure

An organization may choose to migrate to the Active Directory infrastructure in a number of different ways. Following are some possible migration paths:

- Domain upgrade

- Domain upgrade followed by restructure

- Domain restructure

Upgrading Domains

An organization that is satisfied with its current domain infrastructure may choose to migrate to Windows 2000 Active Directory by performing a domain upgrade. Likewise, an organization that cannot make major changes to its current domain model may choose to upgrade.

An organization that has an effective domain structure but desires to modify some parts of the model could upgrade initially. These organizations can later restructure the domain components that no longer effectively serve the needs of the organization.

Restructuring Domains

An organization that desires to redefine its current domain structures in part or as a whole may choose to perform a domain restructure. The methodology of the restructure that you employ will depend upon your existing domain model, your Active Directory design goals, and your migration goals.

Once an organization has determined that its current domain structures are obsolete or ineffective, but that it cannot afford to put the stability of their current production environments in jeopardy during migration, it may decide to build an isolated Windows 2000 environment. An ideal Active Directory infrastructure can be designed and implemented. After the organization constructs the new Active Directory forest, it can slowly migrate users, groups, and resources into the new infrastructure. This process minimizes the risks associated with a mass migration.

Post Upgrade Phase

You can perform a domain restructure after the domain upgrade is completed. The restructure occurs as the second phase of the migration to Windows 2000 Active Directory. In this case, the restructure is geared to reworking and integrating components of the existing domain structure in such a way as to reduce the complexity of the tasks. In addition, you can securely bring resource domains with administrators that are not trusted into the forest.

Vocabuary

Review the following terms in preparation for the certification exam.

Term	Description
BDC	A Backup Domain Controller is a computer running Microsoft Windows NT 4.0 Server that receives a copy of the domain's directory database in a Microsoft Windows NT 4.0 Server domain.
BIND	Berkeley Internet Name Domain is a name resolution service that runs under UNIX.
BIOS	The Basic Input/Output System is the low level machine code used by the computer to communicate with system hardware components.
complete trust domain model	This is a domain model with few benefits. It is used to support organizations that require completely decentralized administration. This model is difficult to manage because it forms an interconnected web of trust relationships.
DHCP	Dynamic Host Configuration Protocol is a networking protocol that offers dynamic configuration of IP addresses and ensures that address conflicts do not occur.
DLL	Dynamic Link Library is a file containing a set of functions to which applications can be dynamically linked at run time.
DNS	The Domain Name System is a static, hierarchical name service for Transmission Control Protocol/Internet Protocol (TCP/IP) hosts.

Term	Description
HCL	The Microsoft Hardware Compatibility List is a catalog of hardware that has been certified by Microsoft as compatible with Microsoft Windows 2000.
IP	Internet Protocol is one of the major protocols used in networking.
IT	Information Technology refers to a group or organization whose product or mission is the analysis of information.
multiple-master domain model	This is a domain model in which there are multiple-master user domains and an administrative hierarchy.
NetBIOS	The Network Basic Input/Output System is an application programming interface that provides a set of commands for requesting lower level network services.
NOS	A Network Operating System is an operating system that is network-aware. Examples of a NOS are Windows 95, Windows for Workgroups v3.11, Microsoft Windows NT 4.0 and Microsoft Windows 2000.
PDC	A Primary Domain Controller is a computer running Microsoft Windows NT 4.0 server that authenticates domain logons and maintains the directory database for a domain in a Microsoft Windows NT 4.0 Server domain.
RAID	A Redundant Array of Inexpensive Disks is used to store data securely by distributing it over several disk drives in such a way that the loss of one disk will not cause corruption of the data. In some RAID configurations, a failed disk may be replaced and the new disk will be automatically populated with the data from the failed disk.
RAS	The Remote Access Service is a Microsoft Windows NT 4.0 service that provides remote access to networks.

Term	Description
RFC	A Request For Comment is a document that represents the working version of a proposed standard.
RIP	The Routing Information Protocol is used to propagate routing information.
SAM	The Security Accounts Manager is a Microsoft service used to maintain user account information.
SAP	A Service Advertising Protocol is a protocol that advertises the services of the server upon which it resides.
SRV	A Service Resource Record is a resource record that is used in a zone to register and locate TCP/IP services.
TCP/IP	Transmission Control Protocol/Internet Protocol is a set of networking protocols that is used on the Internet. It provides communications across interconnected networks that are made up of diverse computers and operating systems.
TCO	The Total Cost of Ownership includes the total amount of money and time associated with purchasing, configuring and maintaining hardware and software. This includes updates, maintenance, administration and technical support.
VPN	A Virtual Private Network is a connection that can provide secure remote access to networks over the Internet.
WAN	A Wide Area Network is a network that extends beyond a single location, which utilizes leased lines to connect geographically separate computers or other network devices.
WINS	The Windows Internet Naming Service is a service that dynamically maps IP addresses to computer NetBIOS names.

In Brief

If you want to...	Then do this...
Obtain the network settings of an computer running Microsoft Windows NT 4.0	1. Choose **Start**, select **Settings**, **Control Panel**. 2. Double-click **Network**. 3. Document the information on the Identification, Services, Protocols, Adapters and Bindings tabs.
Resolve a conflict between an Active Directory design goal and a migration goal or between an Active Directory design goal and the current network infrastructure	The process for resolving these conflicts is: • Identify the business need that drives the proposed design or strategy that presents a conflict • Ensure that the business need is accurately reflected in your migration goals • Verify the alignment of the Active Directory design goal with your migration goals

Lesson 2 Activities

Complete the following activities to better prepare you for the certification exam.

1. Discuss the possible migration permutations.

2. List the seven steps to determine a migration path.

3. Specify the end goal of the migration project.

4. Discuss the reasons an organization might cite for not selecting a migration path in which it upgrades first and restructures later.

5. Discuss why an organization may decide to construct an isolated   Windows 2000 environment and then gradually migrate to it.

6. Discuss why an organization might select to upgrade rather than restructure it's domain.

7. Discuss the importance of discovering conflicts and inconsistencies early in the planning process.

8. Describe the two types of migration goals.

9. Discuss the value of identifying and documenting the existing Microsoft Windows NT 4.0 domain environment.

10. Describe why you should map business goals to migration goals.

Answers to Lesson 2 Activities

1. The possible migration permutations include the following:

   - Upgrade only

   - Upgrade and restructure later

   - Restructure from the start

2. Selecting the correct migration path for a specific organization requires that the organization perform the following seven steps:

   - Identify and document of the existing domain environment

   - Gather information about and document the current network environment

   - Define the business and migration goals for the migration

   - Examine the organization's Active Directory design

   - Determine the organization's possible migration paths

   - Evaluate the issues that may result in a decision to upgrade

   - Evaluate the issues that may result in a decision to restructure

3. The migration project's end goal is the ideal domain infrastructure for the organization.

4. There are some very good reasons for not upgrading first and restructuring later. A two-phased migration takes much longer to plan and much longer to deploy. An additional factor is that the more details and steps, the greater the chance of error. A two-step process has a much higher risk factor.

5. An organization that has determined that its current domain structures are obsolete or ineffective but cannot afford to put the stability of their current production environments in jeopardy during migration may decide to build an isolated Windows 2000 environment.

6. An organization may choose to upgrade without restructuring if one of the following is true:

   - The current infrastructure meets your business goals

   - Short-term resources are limited

- A need exists to be able to recover the original environment

- An infrastructure change would require significant or excessive changes to the organization or to current business processes

- An application presents incompatibilities with a restructure

- There is a need to migrate quickly to the Windows 2000 Active Directory infrastructure

7. Identifying conflicts and inconsistencies and resolving them during the planning stage is much more efficient and cost-effective than dealing with them during the migration implementation.

8. There are two types of migration goals. The first type is the business migration goal, which defines how the technology employed will be used to satisfy the needs and functions of an organization. The second relates to the migration itself and is simply called a migration goal. For your migration to be successful, it is critical to identify and prioritize your migration goals.

9. The process of identifying and documenting the existing Microsoft Windows NT 4.0 domain environment defines the starting point of the migration. The process also allows an organization to evaluate the effectiveness of the current domain model in meeting the present business needs.

10. Creating this map will give you a baseline for the migration project. It will allow you to ensure the alignment of business goals with technological objectives. If any conflicts arise, you will be able to show how the migration goal is related to the business objectives that initially drove the migration.

Lesson 2 Quiz

These questions test your knowledge of features, vocabulary, procedures, and syntax.

1. When you are planning your migration what type of goal can conflict with the Active Directory design goals?
    A. The current network environment
    B. Migration goals
    C. The design goals of the Active Directory forest
    D. Business migration goals

2. Which of the following would be a reason to restructure rather than upgrade?
    A. You have limited short-term resources.
    B. You need to be able to recover to the original environment.
    C. Your current domain structure does not meet your current business objectives.
    D. You need a fast migration solution.

3. What type of items should you include in your hardware inventory?
    A. Routers
    B. Printers
    C. Connections
    D. RAS Servers

4. Before you migrate to Windows 2000, what is the minimum service pack to which you should upgrade Microsoft Windows NT 4.0?
    A. Service Pack 2
    B. Service Pack 4
    C. Service Pack 5
    D. Service Pack 6

5. Why is it important to document any DNS namespaces in use?
    A. DNS by itself will not map into the Active Directory forest.
    B. DNS is not supported by default.
    C. The version of DNS you are currently using is probably incompatible with Active Directory.
    D. An Active Directory forest requires a unique DNS namespace.

6. Which of the following are possible migration paths?

    A. Restructure of the domain from the beginning

    B. An upgrade followed by restructure

    C. A restructure followed by an upgrade

    D. An upgrade alone

7. What drives the need for an organization to migrate to Windows 2000?

    A. Technological advances

    B. E-commerce

    C. Business needs, requirements, and goals

    D. Windows 2000 provides higher connection speeds

8. What type of trusts do Windows 2000 domains in the same forest use?

    A. Explicit trusts

    B. Transitive trusts

    C. One-way trusts

    D. Two-way trusts

9. What is the preferred method for determining if your hardware is   Windows 2000 compatible?

    A. Use the Microsoft Hardware Compatibility List.

    B. Check compatibility with the latest version of Microsoft Windows NT 4.0.

    C. Install Windows 2000 and then resolve incompatibilities.

    D. Check with vendors of the equipment.

10. Why is mapping business goals to migration goals important?

    A. It identifies conflicts with the Active Directory design goals.

    B. It ensures the alignment of business and technological objectives.

    C. It allows you to identify hardware incompatibilities.

    D. It serves as a reminder of the business goals that drove the migration.

Answers to Lesson 2 Quiz

1. Answers A, B and D are correct. You must identify and rectify any goal conflicts since they represent a significant risk to the migration.

    Answer C is incorrect. Your Active Directory forest design goals should be in alignment with your Active Directory design goals by default.

2. Answer C is correct. If your current domain structure does not meet your current business objectives, you should restructure your domain rather than upgrade it.

    Answers A, B and D are incorrect. If you have limited short-term resources, need to be able to recover the original environment, or need a faster migration path, you should choose to upgrade.

3. Answers A, B, C and D are correct. You should include any hardware connected to the network in your hardware inventory.

4. Answer B is correct. Your NT 4.0 servers should be upgraded to at least Service Pack 4 prior to the migration.

    Answers A, C and D are incorrect. Service Pack 2 is insufficient to the needs of Windows 2000. You do not need to upgrade to either Service Pack 5 or Service Pack 6.

5. Answer D is correct. An Active Directory forest requires a unique DNS namespace.

    Answers A, B, and C are incorrect. Active Directory supports DNS and, in fact, relies upon it.

6. Answers A, B and D are correct. You may select to upgrade only, upgrade and then restructure, or upgrade from the start.

    Answer C is incorrect. You cannot upgrade after a restructure as you will already be using Active Directory after the restructure. This option makes no sense.

7. Answer C is correct. The need to migrate to Windows 2000 is driven by business needs, requirements, and goals.

    Answers A, B and D are incorrect. Technology should not drive business decisions because the technology was created to solve business problems not make them. Also, Windows 2000 does not of itself promote the use of higher connection speeds nor is the need to migrate driven just by E-commerce since Microsoft Windows NT 4.0 has satisfied those needs.

8. Answer B is correct. A Windows 2000 domain uses transitive trust relationships to connect to other Windows 2000 domains in the same forest.

    Answers A, C and D are incorrect. Windows 2000 can support explicit one-way and two-way trusts but does not employ them when connecting Windows 2000 domain controllers in the same forest.

9. Answer A is correct. You should check the Microsoft Hardware Compatibility List (HCL) to verify that your hardware is compatible with Windows 2000.

    Answers B, C and D are incorrect. Windows 2000 differs significantly from Microsoft Windows NT 4.0 so that compatibility with NT 4.0 does not mean compatibility with Windows 2000. You should verify compatibility before you install to ensure that your computer will operate correctly after the install. Hardware vendors are not always aware of compatibility issues. You would be better off checking with the manufacturer than the vendor.

10. Answers B and D are correct. You ensure the alignment of business and migration goals and produce a record of the business objectives that are driving the migration when you map business goals to migration goals.

    Answers A and C are incorrect. Although you should verify the Active Directory design goals against the migration goals, the Active Directory design goals are a separate entity with a different purpose. Mapping goals will not identify hardware incompatibilities.

Lesson 3: Domain Upgrade Strategy Development

The Microsoft Windows 2000 environment provides several new features, such as improved security, improved administration and easier management. An upgrade of a Microsoft Windows NT version 4.0 domain infrastructure gives an organization an opportunity to take advantage of these new features. The upgrade strategy that you employ will depend upon your current network environment, your migration goals and your Active Directory design goals. This lesson shows you how to analyze your Active Directory design goals. It will also provide you with a methodology for creating an upgrade strategy.

- After completing this lesson, you should have a better understanding of the following topics:

- Domain Upgrade Strategy Risks

- Active Directory Design Analysis

- Site Design

- Domain Upgrade Risks

- Domain Upgrade Management

Domain Upgrade Strategy

Changes to business process or infrastructure are always accompanied by risk. This is especially true if the change is brought to bear on something as fundamental as an operating system or network infrastructure. When planning to deploy such a significant change, you must plan for the unexpected.

One key tool in your arsenal for planning is risk assessment. You can identify possible risks and potential problems before they manifest and have a method for a rapid response to those that surprise you. If you have a well thought-out, proactive risk management plan, it should help you with the following areas:

- Reducing the likelihood that a problem will occur

- Reducing the impact and loss if a problem occurs

- Altering the response to and consequences of a problem

- Mitigating risk and potential problems during the deployment

Perhaps the biggest risk to a successful migration is an ill-conceived schedule. You must have the time to analyze the impact of change on the organization as well as the risk that change presents to the organization. You can produce a schedule that minimizes risks and potential problems by basing the schedule on task-level time estimates with major and minor milestones. This concept is illustrated in Figure 3.1.

Figure 3.1 Task-Level Based Schedules

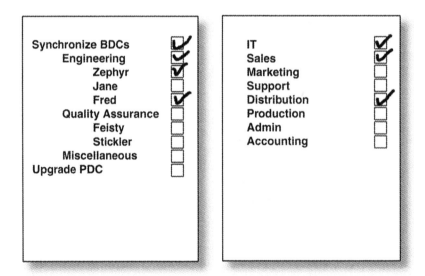

A method that allows you to reduce the overall risk in the upgrade is to schedule higher risk tasks early in the migration. This not only prevents you from being blindsided near the end of the migration, it also helps diminish overall risk because the consequences of high-risk changes have been addressed.

Analyzing the Impact of a Production Environment Upgrade

Before you deploy changes to your network in a production environment, you must be confident that the changes will have as little negative impact as possible. The way to obtain that confidence is to know exactly the consequences of the change.

You must test your proposed design and its implementation schedule in a separate environment that emulates your production environment. The only way to ensure that your changes will have minimal impact is to set up and use a comprehensive test environment. You must implement your changes in the test lab before you do so in the production environment.

Your well-designed test lab gives you a controlled environment where all proposed changes can be tested and verified. It also provides an environment in which you can experiment with the technology, contrast different implementation methods or solutions, and refine the rollout process.

You should also verify your planned rollout schedule by replicating it in the test lab. Be sure to test the implementation process as well as the implementation.

Another consideration that you must analyze is the impact of the upgrade on functioning applications. Testing applications is a significant component of design verification. Before you accomplish the upgrade in the production environment, you must know if server applications will remain fully functional. Some applications may not work and will require a Microsoft Windows NT 4.0 environment as the underlying operating system. Your upgrade plan should include application verification to ensure that applications are compatible with Windows 2000.

You will need to test server applications for functionality and interoperability in the new environment. If the application fails to run under Windows 2000, you must determine if an application Service Pack or newer version of the application is available that is Windows 2000-compatible. If no such update is available you must determine if the application is required to implement or satisfy business needs and then if the application can be run from a Microsoft Windows NT 4.0 member server. This process is illustrated in Figure 3.2.

Figure 3.2 Application Testing Flow Chart

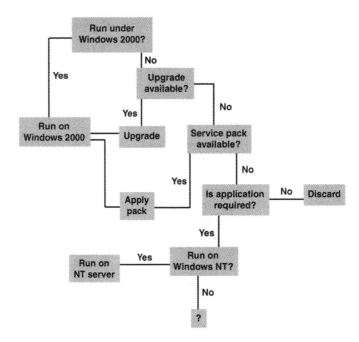

The first step in preparing to test applications is to inventory client and server applications and their requirements. You should include all applications, no matter how trivial. You then need to determine if the application is active and if so, how many users it has. After you complete gathering the data, you can begin to prioritize the applications. You must decide if each application will function correctly and address any issues prior to the upgrade to avoid impacting users and their workflow.

As you compile your application information, you should consider including the following information for each application:

- Name and version

- Vendor

- Current status

- Number of users and their business function
- Importance to the company
- Platform requirements
- Security and installation requirements
- Support contact names and phone numbers
- Web site addresses used by the application

While you are constructing your inventory and analyzing the applications, you have an opportunity to simplify your application environment and make it more manageable and cost-effective. Simplification also reduces the potential risks to the upgrade, makes it easier to test for compatibility and to transition to Windows 2000, and makes the resulting environment easier to manage.

 Note: If an application that requires Microsoft Windows NT 4.0 is currently running on a Backup Domain Controller (BDC), then you will not be able to upgrade the BDC to Windows 2000. This means that you will not be able to switch to native mode later. If possible, you should move such an application to a member server running Microsoft Windows NT 4.0. Doing so will allow you to both upgrade the BDC and to later switch the Windows 2000 domain to native mode.

When you have completed the initial testing, you should conduct a pilot program. A pilot is the last major step you will have to take before you begin the full-scale deployment. During the pilot run, you validate your design using a controlled environment modeled after your real-world environment as illustrated in Figure 3.3. Users will perform their normal business tasks on the pilot using the new features of Windows 2000. The pilot program will help you to find problems and obstacles that were undiscovered during the design and testing processes.

Figure 3.3 Pilot Models the Real-World

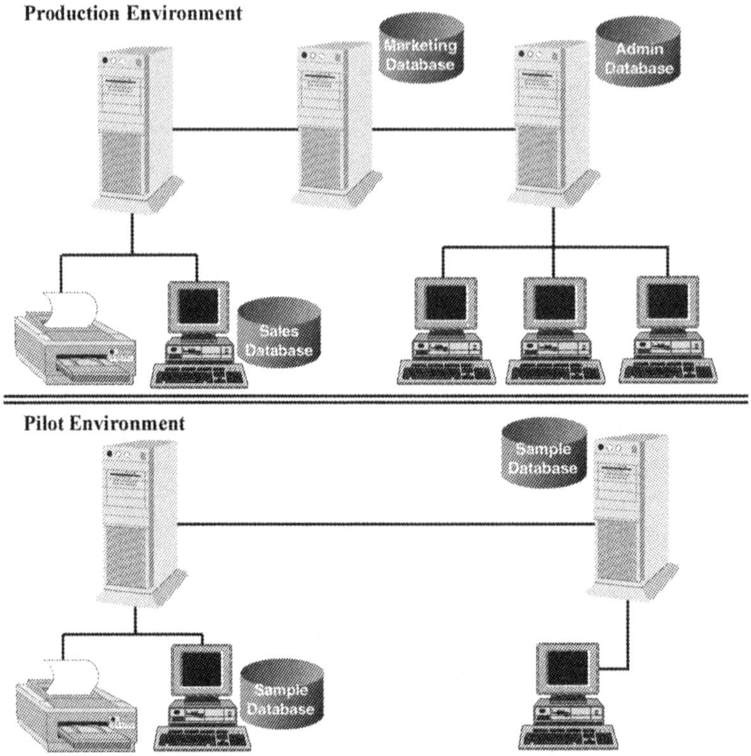

Active Directory Design Analysis

To conduct a thorough assessment of your Windows 2000 Active Directory design, you will need to examine your forest design, the site design, and your plans for administration and security. This concept is illustrated in Figure 3.4. Since an Active Directory deployment is the goal of an upgrade, you must re-examine its design continually to ensure that your business and migration goals are in alignment.

Figure 3.4 Active Directory Design

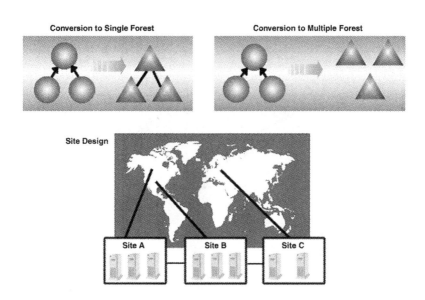

Analyzing the Active Directory Design for an Organization

You should have already identified and documented your business and migration goals. If during the process of doing so, you determined that the preferred migration strategy was to upgrade your current Microsoft Windows NT 4.0 domain model, you will need to examine the proposed infrastructure of your Active Directory design to ensure that your business and migration plans are not compromised during the upgrade.

The examination of your proposed Active Directory structure is important as it provides a mechanism through which you can determine and address migration issues. You will need to know if your Active Directory design proposes a single-forest or a multiple-forest environment. Further, you will also need to establish if the Active Directory design will address or solve immediate and long-term administrative issues. This concept is illustrated in Figure 3.5

Figure 3.5 Proposed Environment and Goals

You will need to examine the proposed site design to identify any barriers it might present to upgrading your domain model. You also have to determine if your site design plan will impact your ability to meet your migration goals and mitigate any differences.

You will need to examine the administrative plans, as well as the plans for security to help determine if and when to make new features available. You should ensure that your administrative and security changes are scheduled so that the introduction of new features does not disrupt the upgrade process. To do this, you need to determine the order in which the new features will be deployed and how the implementation of the new features can be validated in your test environment.

Note: It is vital that you ensure the successful deployment of your Active Directory design while you protect your business and migration goals.

Comparing Single versus Multiple Forests

One of the first tasks that should be accomplished during an analysis of your Active Directory design is deciding whether you can upgrade to a single forest or if you will need multiple forests.

Upgrading to a Single-Forest Environment

In an upgrade migration, the simplest environment to create and maintain is the single-forest environment as illustrated in Figure 3.6. In such an environment, the first domain you upgrade becomes your Active Directory forest root. No additional trust configuration is required as you upgrade additional domains into the forest. In this case, users do not need to be aware of the Active Directory hierarchy because a Global Catalog is used to present them with a unified view.

Figure 3.6 Single-Forest Environment Upgrade

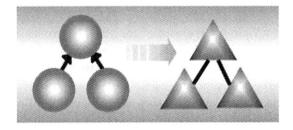

Upgrading to a Multiple-Forest Environment

Upgrading to a multiple-forest environment is considerably more complex than the single-forest upgrade as shown in Figure 3.7. All forests have shared elements. All administrators must agree on the content and administration of shared elements, such as schemas.

Figure 3.7 Multiple-Forest Environment Upgrade

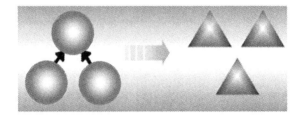

There are several reasons that might cause an organization to decide that it needs to upgrade to multiple forests. For example, an organization may wish to prevent cross-divisional administration so that they can decentralize their administrative model, allowing separate administration of various organizational divisions.

If administrators cannot agree on how to manage forest-wide components, such as schemas or forest-wide group memberships, then a multiple-forest solution is indicated. Multiple forests may be defined to incorporate and accommodate the differences in the ways the administrators manage their forest-wide Active Directory components.

Another reason to select a multiple-forest environment would be that it allows administrators of a forest to restrict access to resources within the forest. A forest uses transitive trusts between its trees and domains. Using transitive trusts allows users from any domain in the forest to be permitted access to resources in any other domain in the forest. In a multiple-forest environment, administrators are, by default, prevented from assigning resource permissions to security principals outside their own forest. This is illustrated in Figure 3.8.

Figure 3.8 External Accesses to Forest Resources Denied

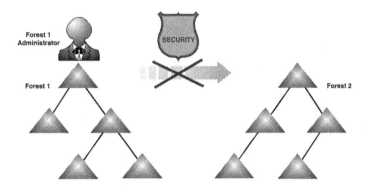

Between forests, an explicit trust relationship must be created and maintained to allow users in one forest to gain access to resources in the other forest. The resources in the supplying domain are imported into the user's domain and are stored in the domain's Global Catalog. The user queries the Global Catalog to find the resource and then access it. This process is illustrated in Figure 3.9.

Figure 3.9 Inter-Forest Resources Access

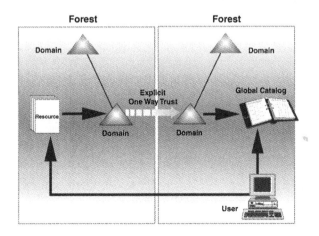

A multiple-forest environment upgrade is more complex than the single-forest upgrade. Planning is also more complex because there is the need to define child domain and multiple-forest root hierarchies. There is also more to consider in planning for a multiple-forest upgrade.

Your Active Directory design was created to support the needs of your organization, as were your business and migration goals. Your Information Technology (IT) organization will have some immediate concerns and needs, all of which should be addressed in your Active Directory design, migration goals, and strategy. However important, these needs should not be allowed to override or obscure the real business needs that drove the migration in the first place.

Warning: Before deploying a multiple-forest upgrade you should carefully consider the long-term impact of the upgrade. The only way to move domains or domain objects between forests is through a restructure. This can have serious consequences if you find in the future that you need to merge forests.

In an upgrade to a multiple-forest environment, the user stands to lose the most. The user will not have a single or consistent view of the Active Directory hierarchy. Additionally, the access to inter-forest resources must be manually configured and a process put in place to automatically update the imported data of any changes in the source domain. These and other issues introduce risk to the upgrade and the possibility of unexpected and unpredictable results when measuring the migration's success.

Site Design

When analyzing your Active Directory design, it is important to examine your site design carefully. You must try to determine if any aspects of your site design might present a barrier to obtaining your migration goals. Any issues you discover that can have a serious impact on your ability to upgrade your domain model should be addressed immediately.

Another factor to consider is the sequence in which sites are implemented and domains are upgraded, as illustrated in Figure 3.10. The sequence of these events can have a serious and significant impact on logon and replication traffic during the upgrade process.

Figure 3.10 Site and Domain Sequence

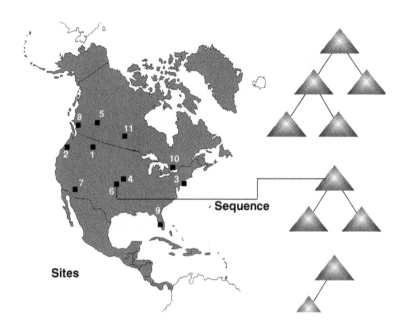

Analyzing the Current Site Environment

You will need to analyze the current site environment to determine any site upgrade needs. You should compare the site's current environment to your proposed site design to identify any issues that may present barriers to a successful upgrade. Any issues you discover must be addressed prior to beginning the upgrade. Failure to do so may result in unexpected setbacks and delays to the upgrade process.

One potential problem you should be aware of is the increased Wide Area Network (WAN) traffic due to domain-upgrade replication. You should analyze how this increased traffic will affect key business operations during peak usage times.

You should determine the current and planned use of site-aware applications and plan accordingly. A site-aware application is an application such as the Distributed File System (DFS) or Microsoft Exchange Server.

You will need to evaluate your fault tolerance requirements and determine if you have a sufficient number of domain controllers at key sites. You may need to augment the number of domain controllers to ensure fault tolerance during the upgrade.

Validating the Site Design against Migration Goals

To validate your site design against your migration goals, you will have to compare the proposed site design with the migration goals. You must ensure that the site design does not adversely impact your ability to meet your migration goals. If you discover any inconsistencies, you must resolve them prior to the upgrade. The migration goals of one organization are not necessarily reflected in another organization; however, some potential commonalties can be addressed.

If your site design calls for a single domain controller at a site, but you have a migration goal of ensuring high availability to Active Directory data during and after the migration, you will have a site design conflict. You should address your site design and modify it to reflect your migration goal.

If you have a site upgrade plan that requires the installation of new equipment and that installation will take a year to negotiate, license, and complete, your site design may conflict with a business goal of completing the migration in less than six months. In this case, the business goal is unrealistic and should be re-examined.

Examine your site network traffic if you have critical data stored at the site. If one of your business goals is to provide worldwide availability to data stored on site and your scheduled replication coincides with your peak usage times, you will need to address the issue prior to upgrading to prevent a possible interruption in data flow.

The above are a few examples of how a business or migration goal can conflict with your site design. You will need to be complete and thorough in your analysis of your site design when comparing it to your goals. The importance of this analysis cannot be overstated.

Preventing Site Design Conflicts

Conflict represents risks. If you have any conflicts between your proposed site design and any migration goal, you have considerable risk to the success of the migration effort. All such conflicts must be resolved prior to beginning an upgrade.

You can minimize conflicts if you ensure that elements of the proposed site design reflect business needs. When you create your site design with your business needs in mind first, you reduce the chance of a conflict. When performing this analysis, it is recommended that you re-verify that your Active Directory design goals align with your migration goals, and that your migration goals reflect the needs of the business as shown in Figure 3.11.

Figure 3.11 Align Goals with Business Needs

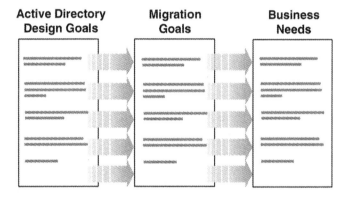

Domain Upgrade Risks

The primary upgrade risks are those that present a potential interruption or cessation of services or cause a breakdown in security. Taking the following precautions can mitigate most of these risks:

- Careful planning

- Design verification in the test lab

- Experimental deployment in a pilot project

An upgrade affects the entire network, including access to network services such as Domain Name Service (DNS) and Dynamic Host Configuration Protocol (DHCP). Other services at risk might include support for Local Area Network (LAN) Manager replication and the File Replication Service (FRS).

Security must be maintained during the complete upgrade process. You will need to be aware of how changes in trusts affect administrative access. Since the trust relationships have changed, you will need to consider security administration and implementation when identifying risks to the upgrade process.

You will also need to identify and analyze the impact of the upgrade on mission-critical applications. It is essential that you determine the impact of the upgrade on these applications in terms of compatibility, required bandwidth, and availability.

An upgrade to a multiple-forest environment is even more susceptible to risk. You must verify that your Active Directory implementation does not cause an interruption to access of services across different forests during the upgrade process.

Along with an interruption in service, another risk is an interruption of performance. You must validate the site design against the current and future needs of each site to ensure that there is no risk of an interruption of network performance during the upgrade.

Maintaining Upgrade Reliability

One of the most important factors in maintaining network reliability during an upgrade is the sequence in which network components are upgraded. This includes the implementation of domains and sites.

When you upgrade a domain, you should first synchronize all Backup Domain Controllers (BDCs) to ensure that they are completely upgraded with all changes that have been made at the domain's Primary Domain Controller (PDC). This concept is illustrated in Figure 3.12. Once this has been accomplished, the PDC is upgraded and becomes the domain's PDC emulator.

Figure 3.12 BDC Synchronization

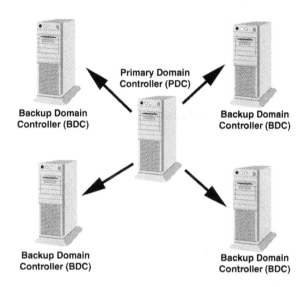

In deciding on the order in which your domains will be upgraded, you should consider upgrading account domains before resource domains. Selecting an account domain with fewer users and the easiest access to domain controllers allows you to minimize disruption and risk and, at the same time, verify the results of the test lab and pilot projects.

While your test lab and pilot project will identify the vast majority of risks and possible disruptions to your network, there will always be some issue that are not discovered until the upgrade is performed in the production environment. Part of your migration planning and risk assessment must include contingency planning for just such an event.

Domain Upgrade Management

You must carefully manage the transition to an Active Directory environment. You have to ensure that you have defined a proper forest namespace so that you do not have to restructure the forest to correct namespace problems. You must also choose the root domain of each forest carefully. Once the root domain has been created, you cannot change it.

Carefully manage the creation of child domains. If a child domain is joined to the wrong part of a forest, a restructure is the only way to repair the problem. Such a restructure is something you want to avoid, since it will be beyond your contingency error response plans. This concept is shown in Figure 3.13.

Figure 3.13 Planning to Avoid Restructure

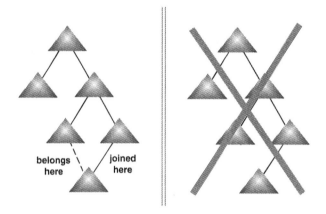

Maintaining Upgrade Availability

During the upgrade to Windows 2000 Active Directory, it is important to maintain availability to network resources. It is necessary to ensure that server applications and resources are available without interruption during the upgrade. You also need to maintain security during the upgrade so that users do not have to wait for available network resources.

Note: You must ensure that your plan causes the user the least problems possible.

An upgrade is a complicated and sophisticated process, and some interruptions to service will almost certainly be experienced. Your job is to minimize these interruptions.

The first step in maintaining availability during the upgrade is to identify any possible points of failure. A point of failure could be a printer or other hardware device, or it could be a software application. Another one could be an external dependency, such as your Internet connectivity. Figure 3.14 illustrates this concept. You should minimize as much as possible the number of points of failure in the environment you are currently upgrading.

Figure 3.14 Identify Points of Failure

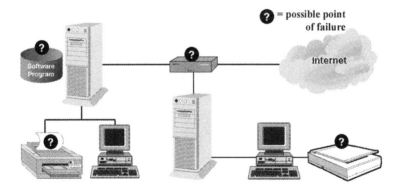

You should provide some mechanism to maintain these services when and if a failure does occur. For example, you might have replacement disks and controllers available. You might also have spare components on hand that exactly match the currently used components, especially when it comes to network components, such as Network Interface Cards (NICs) or Small Computer System Interface (SCSI) adapters. You should provide Uninterruptible Power Supply (UPS) protection for servers, clients, and network components such as routers, hubs, etc.

Vocabulary

Review the following terms in preparation for the certification exam.

Term	Description
BDC	A Backup Domain Controller is a computer running Microsoft Windows NT 4.0 Server that receives a copy of the domain's directory database in a Windows NT 4.0 Server domain.
DFS	The Distributed File System is a Windows 2000 service that transparently links shared folders into a single namespace for improved load sharing and availability.
DHCP	Dynamic Host Configuration Protocol is a networking protocol that offers dynamic configuration of IP addresses and ensures that address conflicts do not occur.
DNS	The Domain Name System is a static, hierarchical name service for Transmission Control Protocol /Internet Protocol (TCP/IP) hosts.
domain	An administrative and security boundary. Active Directory data is replicated between domain controllers within a domain.
forest	A group of Active Directory domain trees that share a common schema, but do not have a contiguous namespace.
FRS	The File Replication Service is a service used by the Distributed File System to replicate topological and Global Catalog information across domain controllers.

Term	Description
LAN	A Local Area Network is made up of computers and other devices connected by a communications link that allows one device to interact with any other in a limited area.
NIC	A Network Interface Card is an adapter board that provides connectivity between a computer and the network.
PDC	A Primary Domain Controller is a computer running Microsoft Windows NT 4.0 Server that authenticates domain logons and maintains the directory database for a domain in a Microsoft Windows NT 4.0 Server domain.
SCSI	The Small Computer System Interface specification is a standard for a high-speed parallel interface between a small computer system and various peripheral devices.
site	Sites are a collection of IP subnets. A site object represents a site in Active Directory. Sites are not tied in any way to the Active Directory domain namespace. The name of a directory object does not reflect the site or sites in which the object is stored. A site may contain Domain Controllers (DCs) from several domains, and DCs from a domain may be present in several sites.
TCP/IP	Transmission Control Protocol/Internet Protocol is a set of software networking protocols used on the Internet. It provides communication across interconnected networks of computers with diverse hardware architectures and operating systems. TCP/IP includes standards for how computers communicate and conventions for connecting networks and routing traffic.

Term	Description
tree	A group of Active Directory domains that share a common schema and a contiguous namespace.
UPS	An Uninterruptible Power Supply provides power to a computer system or other device in the advent of a power failure. Many such devices can notify a computer system of such a failure so that the computer can initiate shutdown procedures.
WAN	A Wide Area Network is a network that extends beyond a single location, connecting geographically separated computers or other network devices.

In Brief

If you want to...	Then do this...
Determine the upgrade needs of a site	Compare the site design to the current environment of the site. Decide if the site has sufficient hardware to meet your site design goals. You should also compare your site design to your migration goals. Doing so will also identify the need for equipment upgrades, replacements, and additions.
Minimize the impact of failures	You should first identify all potential points of failure. Then you should provide a mechanism by which the impact of a failure can be minimized. You may want to have backup disk controllers, hubs, routers, printers, internet connections, or NICs.
Maintain network reliability during the upgrade	Carefully plan the sequence in which network components are upgraded. This includes the implementation of domains and sites.
Analyze the impact of application changes to the environment	First, inventory all applications used by all users, no matter how trivial. Then test these applications for compatibility, bandwidth, and functionality in your test lab. Verify your findings with a pilot project, before you deploy them in the production environment.

Lesson 3 Activities

Complete the following activities to better prepare you for the certification exam.

1. Discuss how you can minimize conflicts between your site design and your migration goals.

2. Discuss how you can minimize impacts on availability during the upgrade.

3. Describe the importance of a pilot program.

4. List some of the reasons that an organization might decide to implement a multiple-forest | environment.

5. Discuss the importance of managing the creation of child domains.

6. Describe why you must choose the root domain of each forest carefully.

7. What are some of the additional benefits of a test lab?

8. Discuss the most important factor in maintaining network reliability during an upgrade.

9. Discuss why a single-forest implementation is the easiest to create and maintain.

10. Describe some of the attributes of an application that you might inventory.

Answers to Lesson 3 Activities

1. You can minimize conflicts between your site design and your migration goals by ensuring that, since your migration goals are driven by business needs, your site design be driven by business needs as well. If both are driven by the same needs, then the potential for conflict is minimized.

2. You can minimize impact on availability by identifying all potential points of failure and providing either backups or alternatives to those areas in case of a failure.

3. A pilot program is essential to ensuring a smooth transition to Windows 2000 because it provides a simulation of the production environment. It allows you to access the viability of your target environment and to verify your deployment and support plans.

4. An organization might decide to implement a multiple-forest environment if domain administrators do not trust each other's administration, cannot agree on change policies, or want to limit the scope of trust relationships between domains or to limit access to domain resources.

5. If a child domain is joined to the wrong part of a forest, a restructure is the only way to repair the problem. Such a restructure is something you want to avoid, since that will be an eventuality for which you have not planned.

6. You must choose the root domain of each forest carefully. Once the root domain has been created, it cannot be changed.

7. A test lab can provide an environment in which you can experiment with the technologies. It allows you to contrast different implementation methods or solutions and refine the rollout process.

8. One of the most important factors in maintaining network reliability during an upgrade is the sequence in which network components are upgraded. This includes the implementation of domains and sites.

9. In a single-forest environment, the first domain you upgrade becomes your Active Directory forest root. No additional trust configuration is required as you upgrade additional domains into the forest. In the single-forest environment users do not need to be aware of the Active Directory hierarchy because a Global Catalog is used to present them with a unified view.

10. As you compile your application information, you should consider including the following information for each application:

   - Name and version

   - Vendor

   - Current status

   - Number of users and their business function

   - Importance to the company

   - Platform requirements

   - Security and installation requirements

   - Support contact names and phone numbers

   - Web site addresses used by the application

Lesson 3 Quiz

These questions test your knowledge of features, vocabulary, procedures, and syntax.

1. How does a user gain access to resources found in a different forest?
    A. A user cannot gain access to inter-forest resources.
    B. A user automatically gains access, when the upgrade to Windows 2000 is performed.
    C. The user must have a logon in the other forest.
    D. Access is gained by manually configuring the access.

2. What is the biggest risk to a successful upgrade?
    A. Lack of financial resources
    B. Lack of proper equipment
    C. A poorly conceived schedule
    D. Mapping business goals to migration goals

3. What should you do to determine the upgrade needs of a site?
    A. Compare the site design to the current site environment.
    B. Compare the site design to your migration goals.
    C. Compare the site design to your business goals.
    D. Compare your migration goals with the Active Directory Design.

4. Why synchronize your BDCs before upgrading your PDC?
    A. It ensures that the time stamps for all modifications are consistent.
    B. It guarantees that your upgrade will proceed smoothly.
    C. It ensures that your BDCs have been upgraded with all changes to the PDC.
    D. It provides a mechanism by which all domains in the forest can share resources.

5. If you have a required application that requires Microsoft Windows NT 4.0 running on a BDC, and you want to upgrade the BDC to Windows 2000, what should you do?

   A. Replace the application with one that will run under Windows 2000.

   B. Adjust your migration plans to include a Microsoft Windows NT 4.0 BDC.

   C. Construct a Microsoft Windows NT 4.0 subnet.

   D. Determine if the application can run on a member server and, if so, move it there.

6. What are the goals of the test lab and pilot program?

   A. Build confidence in the migration plan

   B. Verify connectivity

   C. Reduce risk

   D. Reduce or eliminate any interruption to network reliability or availability

7. What type of network design presents the most change to the user?

   A. Single forest

   B. Multiple-tree forest

   C. Multiple forest

   D. Multiple-site forest

8. Can you move domain objects between forests and if so, how?

   A. Yes, it is a simple administrative task

   B. No, you cannot move domain objects between forests

   C. Yes, but only through a restructure

   D. Yes, but you will need to redefine the forest schema to do so

9. What is the first thing you should do to maintain availability during an upgrade?

   A. Provide hardware backups of all critical components

   B. Determine the need for access to resources

   C. Identify all potential points of failure

   D. Upgrade the BDCs first

10. What do you do if you inadvertently join a child domain to the wrong part of the forest?

A. Move the child domain to the correct part of the forest

B. Duplicate the domain in the correct part of the forest, delete the error

C. Re-load the server and start all over again

D. The only way to fix the problem is to restructure

Answers to Lesson 3 Quiz

1. Answer D is correct. Access to inter-forest resources must be manually configured.

    Answers A, B, and C are incorrect. The user can gain access to resources from another forest without having a logon in the other forest, but such access is not provided automatically.

2. Answer C is correct. The biggest risk to a successful upgrade is a poorly conceived schedule. The success of the upgrade depends upon determining the correct upgrade order and allowing the time to perform the various tasks correctly.

    Answers A, B, and D are incorrect. Any lack in finances or hardware should have been identified prior to the initiation of the upgrade and planned for accordingly. Mapping business goals to migration goals helps to reduce risk rather than present it.

3. Answer A is correct. You need to compare your site design with the current site environment to determine the upgrade needs of the site.

    Answers B, C, and D are incorrect. While you need to accomplish these tasks to ensure a successful upgrade, they will not help you determine site needs.

4. Answer C is correct. Synchronizing your BDCs prior to upgrading your PDC ensures that all changes to the PDC are up to date and stored on the BDCs.

    Answers A, B, and D are incorrect. The synchronization of BDCs does not address time/date stamp issues, nor will it ensure a smooth transition to Windows 2000 Active Directory. Synchronization does not provide access to intra-forest resources.

5. Answer D is correct. You should determine, if the application will run on a Microsoft Windows NT 4.0 member server and, if so, move the application to the member server.

    Answers A, B, and C are incorrect. While replacing your application is a potential solution, it may be one that is time-consuming, expensive, and has a very large impact upon the applications users. You cannot have a BDC in a Windows 2000 network, as all domain controllers are equal. For the same reason, you cannot create a Microsoft Windows NT 4.0 subnet.

6. Answers A, C, and D are correct. Using a test lab and pilot program verifies your migration plans, minimizes risk to the network, and reduces the chances of interruptions to network operations.

    Answer B is incorrect. Both the test lab and the pilot program are separate entities from your network and do not verify network connectivity.

7. Answer C is correct. The user will not have a single consistent view of the Active Directory hierarchy in a multiple-forest environment.

    Answers A, B, and D are incorrect. Each of these implementations presents a single-forest environment, which minimizes the impact on the user.

8. Answer C is correct. The only way to move domains or domain objects between forests is through a restructure.

    Answers A, B, and D are incorrect. Moving domain objects between forests is not a simple administrative task. It can be done, but only through a restructure; modifying the Active Directory schema will not accomplish the task.

9. Answer C is correct. The first thing to do in maintaining availability is to identify all potential points of failure.

    Answers A, B, and D are incorrect. While you should provide backup for critical components, and you should determine the access needs of those components, doing so is not the first step in maintaining availability. You must first identify those components. You do not upgrade BDCs first.

10. Answer D is correct. The only way to repair the problem of adding a child domain to the wrong part of a forest is to restructure.

    Answers A, B, and C are incorrect. You cannot move the child domain once it has been added, nor can you duplicate it and then delete it. Reloading the server will not help, since the structure was replicated to other domain controllers when you added the child domain.

Lesson 4: Domain Upgrade Path Planning

When planning an upgrade from Microsoft Windows NT 4.0 to Windows 2000 Active Directory, you prepare for and plan for a new network environment. You must ensure that the new environment functions correctly and that it meets the business needs of your organization. To make certain that your chosen structure satisfies your business requirements, you must carefully consider your current and future environments and produce an appropriate upgrade plan.

After completing this lesson, you should have a better understanding of the following topics:

- Domain Upgrade Path Planning

- Security Plans and Administration

- Recovery Plan Development

- Domain Upgrade Sequence

- Domain Controller Upgrade Strategy

- Native Mode

- Post-Upgrade Tasks

Domain Upgrade Path Planning

The importance of a complete and thorough upgrade plan cannot be over-emphasized. You must carefully plan your domain upgrade to ensure that it is successful. This will require some careful thought and consideration.

Before you implement any changes to your network, you should ensure that your current environment is as stable as you can make it. You will need to identify and repair any problems. The following list provides some examples of potential network issues that should be addressed prior to the upgrade:

- Network transmission bottlenecks

- Poorly functioning hardware

- Unstable configurations

- Problematic configurations

Failure to address these and other similar issues prior to the upgrade will allow unnecessary risk into the upgrade process and make it hard to attain your migration goals. You should also insure that your hardware maintenance schedule is up to date before you begin the upgrade. If any network components need to be replaced, you must ensure that you replace them with Windows 2000 compatible devices. You can verify the components compatibility with Windows 2000 by using the Microsoft Hardware Compatibility List (HCL).

You will also need to perform a review of your network protocols. If your organization employs an Ethernet network, then you may find that you use a variety of protocols in combination. For example, your network may employ Transmission Control Protocol/Internet Protocol (TCP/IP), Network Basic Input/Output System (NetBIOS) Enhanced User Interface (NetBEUI), Internetwork Packet Exchange/ Sequenced Packet Exchange (IPX/SPX), or other protocols. The protocols in use will depend upon your organization's networking, authentication and security needs, as well as the capabilities of the operating systems in use. When you perform this review, you should consider eliminating or replacing protocols that may not be required after all clients are upgraded. For example, when your upgrade clients that use IPX/SPX protocol to Windows 98 or Windows 2000 Professional, consider replacing the IPX/SPX protocol. Doing so may free up some bandwidth.

You should also consider using only TCP/IP suite protocols to simplify your network and reduce network traffic. Microsoft has implemented more functionality in the Windows 2000 version of TCP/IP than can be found in any previous version of Windows. For example, the Windows 2000 TCP/IP suite now supports large window and selective acknowledgement functionality. To take advantage of some of the advanced features in Windows 2000 and to gain Active Directory support, you will need to use the Microsoft Windows 2000 TCP/IP protocol suite.

The Windows 2000 TCP/IP suite offers advanced features including improved communication link security. Previous versions of Microsoft Windows NT 4.0 use the Point-to-Point Protocol (PPP) to support communication security. The Windows 2000 TCP/IP suite provides PPTP support as well as Layer 2 Tunneling Protocol (L2TP), which improves functionality and communication link security as illustrated in Figure 4.1.

Figure 4.1 Improved Communication Security

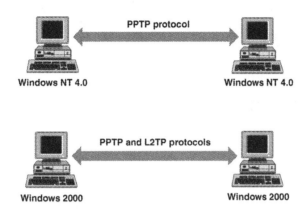

Planning a Domain Upgrade

You must carefully consider all aspects of a domain upgrade prior to implementation. With adequate planning, an upgrade can be a relatively painless procedure. Failure to plan, however, can have some serious consequences. In planning for your domain upgrade, you should perform the following:

- Develop a recovery plan
- Determine the upgrade path
- Determine the upgrade order
- Develop a strategy for upgrading domain controllers
- Determine when to switch to native mode
- Identify post-upgrade tasks

Creating an Upgrade Recovery Plan

You will need to have an upgrade recovery plan in place before you change anything in the current environment. A plan to recover any data accidentally lost during the upgrade will ensure that you can return to the original configuration if necessary. Data is the lifeblood of your organization and must not be put at risk.

Identifying Network Performance Issues

You must evaluate the capabilities or your existing network infrastructure, including the quality and bandwidth of network components. Will your current components support your planned environment? Do the cabling, hubs, and other devices provide the quality of signal as well as the bandwidth to support your plans? You should identify any applications that may be affected by changes in connectivity and ensure that the required bandwidth will be available. You should also plan for replication traffic and ensure that the required links can support the required speeds.

You will need to verify that your hardware is compatible with Windows 2000, including the following:

- Network Interface Cards (NICs)

- Modems

- Certain kinds of hubs

Windows 2000 provides Local Area Network (LAN) Emulation (LANE) services that provide a migration pathway from shared-media networks to Asynchronous Transfer Mode (ATM). Internet Protocol (IP) over ATM is supported as well. If you currently use ATM under Microsoft Windows NT 4.0, then you will need to ensure that your ATM vendor can provide you with updated drives for Windows 2000. If you are currently using Microsoft Windows NT ATM or plan to use Windows 2000 ATM, it is very important to ensure that your ATM adapters are listed in the HCL.

If you plan to deploy a Virtual Private Network (VPN), as illustrated in Figure 4.2, you will need to consider configurations that will provide a secure connection. For example, how do you plan to integrate proxy servers with the VPN server? You will need to examine your existing network infrastructure if you plan to deploy a VPN. Does your network currently support secure Wide Area Network (WAN) connectivity?

Figure 4.2 VPN Connection

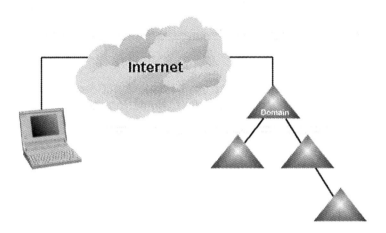

Creating an Upgrade Path

You must determine whether the current operating system running on a client or server can be upgraded directly to Windows 2000. You should accomplish this step very early in the planning process, as it will determine the upgrade path you take for each computer.

To determine the upgrade path for a computer, you will need to decide the version of Windows 2000 that you will be upgrading, too. Some operating systems can be upgraded to Windows 2000 Server that cannot be upgraded to Windows 2000 Advanced Server. Some can be upgraded to Windows 2000 Advanced Server but cannot be upgraded to Windows 2000 Server.

You cannot upgrade to any version of Windows 2000 Server if you are currently running any of the following operating systems:

- Microsoft Windows NT 3.1

- Microsoft Windows NT Advanced Server 3.1

- Microsoft Windows NT Workstation 4.0

To upgrade a computer running an operating system whose upgrade is not supported, you must first perform an interim upgrade to a supported operating system. When documenting your migration path, you must include any intermediate upgrades to ensure that they are accomplished.

 Note: If you are running either Microsoft Windows NT Server 3.51 or 4.0, you should apply the latest service packs before you perform the upgrade.

You can upgrade to Windows 2000 Server if the computer is currently running one of the following operating systems:

- Windows 95

- Windows 98

- Microsoft Windows NT Workstation 3.51

- Microsoft Windows NT Server 4.0

 Note: You cannot upgrade to Windows 2000 Server if you are currently running Microsoft Windows NT Server Enterprise 4.0. You can only upgrade such a computer to Windows 2000 Advanced Server.

In addition to the listed operating systems from which you cannot upgrade to any version of Windows 2000 Server, you cannot upgrade to Windows 2000 Advanced Server from the following operating systems:

- Windows 95

- Windows 98

- Microsoft Windows NT Workstation 3.51

You can upgrade to Windows 2000 Advanced Server from the following operating systems:

- Microsoft Windows NT Server 3.51

- Microsoft Windows NT Server 4.0

- Microsoft Windows NT Server Enterprise Edition 4.0

You will also need to determine the function and current operating system of the computer you plan to upgrade. Is the computer a domain controller, a member server, or a client? Is the computer running Microsoft Windows NT v3.51 or later? Has the computer been upgraded with the latest service pack?

A Primary Domain Controller (PDC) or a Backup Domain Controller (BDC) computer running Microsoft Windows NT v3.51 or 4.0 can become a Windows 2000 domain controller, as illustrated in Figure 4.3.

Figure 4.3 Domain Controller Upgrade

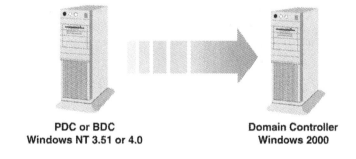

PDC or BDC
Windows NT 3.51 or 4.0

Domain Controller
Windows 2000

Tip: You can upgrade a Microsoft Windows NT 4.0 BDC as a member server under Windows 2000.

When upgrading member servers running Microsoft Windows NT 3.51 or 4.0, you can continue the current functionality as a member server or you can optionally upgrade the member server to a domain controller as shown in Figure 4.4.

Figure 4.4 Member Server Upgrade

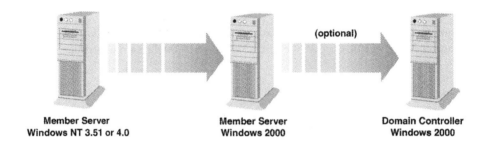

Member Server
Windows NT 3.51 or 4.0

Member Server
Windows 2000

(optional)

Domain Controller
Windows 2000

You cannot directly upgrade computers running versions of Microsoft Windows NT prior to 3.51. These computers must be upgraded to a later version of NT, such as 3.51 or 4.0 prior to the upgrade to Windows 2000, as illustrated in Figure 4.5. When you do so, remember you will need to apply all available service packs.

Figure 4.5 Upgrading Older Versions of Microsoft Windows NT

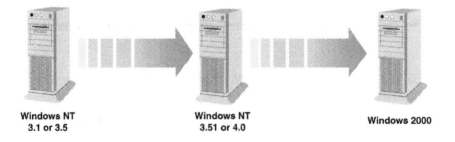

Windows NT
3.1 or 3.5

Windows NT
3.51 or 4.0

Windows 2000

Security Plans and Administration

Windows 2000 provides many new security and administrative features. Most likely, your migration goals will require that several of these features be implemented. You need to examine your existing administrative and security strategies and develop a plan that provides a scheduled implementation of the new features. Your plan should consider the following aspects:

- What new features to adopt
- When to make them available
- What order to deploy them
- Your test lab validation needs

When making your plans for security and administration, you need to ensure that your Active Directory design goals and migration goals are met.

Planning for Domain Upgrade Security

If your Active Directory design implements new security features, you will need to verify that your upgrade plan defines which of the features to implement during the upgrade process and when to implement them. You will also need to define a process for implementing the new features. The implementation process must maintain acceptable levels of security during the upgrade without adding unnecessary delays to the migration.

When planning your migration, you need to verify your security plan by comparing your existing security infrastructure with the features of the proposed Active Directory design so that you can discover and address problems such as the examples in the following list:

- Security gaps
- Outdated policies
- Redundancies

You will need to resolve any such issues in a manner that does not disrupt the upgrade process.

Defining Administrative Functions

Windows 2000 Active Directory provides several new administrative features that you may choose to adopt. The implementation of these new features may cause an Information Technology (IT) group to assess its current culture and perhaps reorganize so that the needs of the business are better served. Reorganizing an IT group requires serious planning. Such planning should be accomplished prior to implementation of any changes in the current system. The reorganization plan should also be constructed in a manner that keeps the IT department focused on the upgrade and minimizes disruptions to the upgrade process.

If you plan to implement new administrative functions made available by Windows 2000, then you should ensure that the features that will be adopted and the sequence, in which they will be adopted, are reflected in your upgrade plans. You will need to define a process that transitions the current administrative model into the new model. You will also need to identify upgrade responsibilities during the transition.

Before you perform an upgrade, you must validate the proposed administrative plan in your test lab. Examine the Active Directory design to determine the following:

- Organization Unit (OU) hierarchy

- Delegation of administration

- Group policy deployment

You must ensure that the implementation of these features complement and support each other and meet your migration goals as well.

Recovery Plan Development

To prevent the accidental loss of data during an upgrade, you must develop a recovery plan. You need to have a rollback strategy in place to ensure recovery from any upgrade problems. Your plan must detail how you will back up domain controllers, application software, databases, and other data sources, as illustrated in Figure 4.6. Your plan should also detail how you will keep such data available and secure during the upgrade.

Figure 4.6 Backup Plans

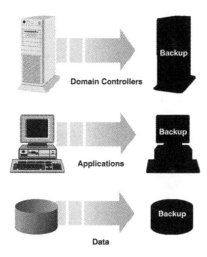

Creating a Recovery Plan

Your recovery plan should ensure that the domain could be returned to its pre-upgrade state. While the needs and architecture of any given domain differ, there is a minimum set of issues that you must consider in your recovery plans.

If you have a Microsoft Windows NT domain with a single domain controller, you should add a BDC to the domain as illustrated in Figure 4.7. If the PDC fails during the upgrade, your domain will not become orphaned if you have a BDC.

Figure 4.7 BDC Recovery Plan

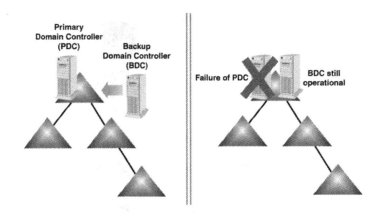

You will need to document the configuration of all PDC and BDC services and applications. For example, Dynamic Host Configuration Protocol (DHCP), Domain Name System (DNS), or file and print services should be documented.

After you have accomplished a complete backup of all services and applications, you should test the backup by performing a complete restoration. Do this in your test lab instead of in a production environment.

Fully synchronize all BDCs with the PDC using the Microsoft Windows NT Server Manager. This will ensure that the Security Accounts Manager (SAM) database is fully up to date on all BDCs. This concept is illustrated in Figure 4.8.

Figure 4.8 BDC Synchronization

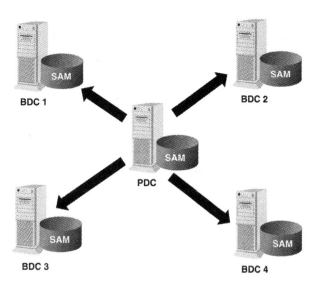

If you have more than one BDC, then after you fully synchronize the BDCs, take one of them off-line before you begin the upgrade, as shown in Figure 4.9. Doing so will ensure that you have preserved all security principals residing in the SAM database of your current Microsoft Windows NT 4.0 domain.

Figure 4.9 Synchronized BDC Offline

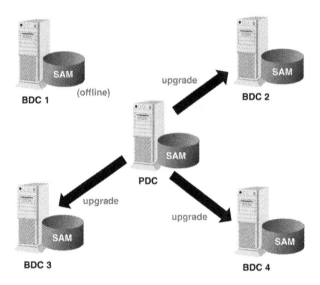

When you have completed the upgrade process, bring the isolated BDC back online and make it available to the network. If any problems arise, you can take all computers running Windows 2000 offline, removing them from the production environment, and then promote the isolated BDC to a PDC. This will cause the newly promoted PDC to replicate itself to any remaining BDCs and return the domain to its previous state.

Tip: During the upgrade process, while still in mixed mode, periodically add the isolated BDC to the network so that its directory information is updated. If you fail to do so, then all changes made to the SAM while the BDC was offline will be lost.

Domain Upgrade Sequence

Once you have completed your recovery plans and determined your strategy for upgrading your domain controllers, you need to determine which domain to upgrade first and the order in which to upgrade subsequent domains. If you have an existing domain that you wish to become the forest root, you must upgrade that domain first. If no existing domain is suitable as the forest root, you will need to create a dedicated domain. If you plan to restructure some of your domains, there is little to be gained in upgrading these domains prior to upgrading others.

Defining the Forest Root

The forest root is the starting point or root of the Active Directory. The first domain that you create in Active Directory becomes the forest root. All additional domains are derivatives of the root domain. You will need to examine your Active Directory design to determine whether you can use an existing domain as the forest root.

If your Active Directory design calls for a dedicated forest root, then you must plan accordingly. Your upgrade plan must provide for the creation of the new dedicated domain whose sole purpose is to serve as the forest root. This concept is illustrated in Figure 4.10. This domain must be created before any domains are upgraded.

Figure 4.10 Dedicated Domain as a Forest Root

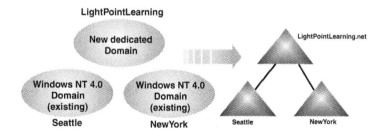

If your Active Directory design does not require a dedicated domain to serve as the root domain, and an existing domain is suitable to the purpose, then you can upgrade an existing Microsoft Windows NT 4.0 domain as the forest root as shown in Figure 4.11.

Figure 4.11 Existing Domain as a Forest Root

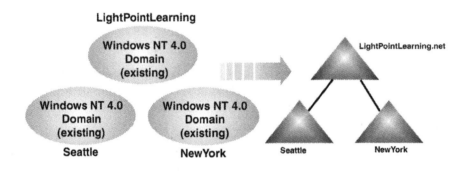

Upgrading Account Domains

A network usually has more user accounts than it does resource accounts. You will realize the most benefit from upgrading your account domains first to take advantage of benefits offered by Windows 2000 including:

- Improved scalability

- Delegated user administration

Windows 2000 Active Directory provides improved scalability. Organizations that are pushing the upper limits of the SAM database will realize an immediate benefit when their account domains are upgraded. The limit on the number of user and group accounts in the Microsoft Windows NT SAM database is not encountered under Windows 2000 Active Directory.

Windows 2000 Active Directory provides for the delegation of administrative authority. It provides a fine granularity of delegation control without granting absolute power to local administrators.

If your network infrastructure contains more than one account domain, you will need to determine the order in which they are upgraded.

To help you to decide upon the upgrade sequence, consider the following factors:

- Physical access

- Risks and disruptions

- Confidence in the process

- Account domains that require restructure

It is far easier to upgrade a domain to which you have physical access. However, you need to know where in the forest that domain will reside. You must ensure that the domain is added to the correct part of the forest. Once a domain is added to the forest, it cannot be moved without a complete restructure.

You will need to mitigate risks and minimize disruptions. Testing your upgrade strategy in a test lab will aid in identifying risks. Further evaluation of your plans in a pilot program will help to minimize disruptions. However, employing both techniques will not eliminate all risks nor will it provide all the data you need to ensure that no disruptions occur. To reduce risk, you should first upgrade the account domain that provides the easiest access. Selecting a domain with fewer users minimizes the potential disruption of services to the largest number of users.

Once you have successfully upgraded a domain, you should have gained the experience to give you confidence in your planned upgrade process. You will have reduced the risk factor and can now move on to upgrading larger account domains.

If you are planning to restructure your domains during the migration, you should create or upgrade the domains you have targeted for restructure. You can than consolidate other domains into the target domain. You will need to identify all account domains that are to be restructured.

 Note: You cannot consolidate domains into a target domain that does not yet exist. You must create a target domain before you begin your consolidation.

Upgrading Resource Domains

If your network infrastructure has more than one resource domain, you should consider the following factors when planning the upgrade sequence:

- Domains with applications that require Windows 2000 features

- Domains with a large number of workstations

- Resource domains that are to be restructured

If you are deploying an application that requires the Windows 2000 infrastructure or requires features provided by Windows 2000 in a resource domain, that domain should be upgraded first. An example of such an application is Microsoft Exchange 2000, which requires Windows 2000 Active Directory.

You should next upgrade any resource domain that contains a large number of workstations. This provides you with the ability to take advantage of Windows 2000 infrastructure components, for example, Microsoft IntelliMirror.

Finally, if you are planning to restructure your resource domains, you should upgrade the domains that will contain objects from restructured domains. You should do this early in the upgrade process because, like account domains, you cannot consolidate domains into a target domain that does not yet exist.

Domain Controller Upgrade Strategy

The first domain controller to be updated to Windows 2000 Server is the PDC. When you upgrade the PDC you establish the forest root domain. In general, BDCs can be upgraded in any order after the PDC is upgraded.

 Note: Existing security principals are maintained during the upgrade. The properties of these principals are also maintained.

Upgrading the PDC

When you upgrade your PDC, you create a new Windows 2000 domain. After you perform the operating system upgrade of the PDC, the Active Directory Installation Wizard will automatically start. The installation wizard will require you to choose to do one of the following:

- Join an existing domain, tree or forest
- Create a new domain, tree or forest

You will also be required to provide the DNS name for the domain. Your Active Directory design will define the DNS namespace for your Windows 2000 domains.

 Warning: You must not choose a random DNS name for your new domain.

When you run the Active Directory Installation Wizard, it will automatically install all components that are required on the domain controller. This includes the Kerberos 5 protocol that is used for authentication as well as the directory data store. By copying the existing SAM security principals from the registry into the new Active Directory data store, upgrading preserves the following features:

- Existing user accounts
- Existing group accounts
- Existing computer accounts

 Note: The process of preserving security principal data can be time-consuming for large account domains.

In Windows 2000, a container is an object that can contain other objects. For example, a folder is a container object. During the upgrade, existing Microsoft Windows NT 4.0 built-in groups are placed in the built-in container. Built-in groups are common groups that are pre-defined for you, for example the Administrators group. In Windows 2000, the built-in container holds all the built-in groups. Created global and local groups are placed in the Users container.

 Note: During the Active Directory installation on a PDC of a child domain, transitive trusts are automatically created between a child domain and the parent domain.

You establish the forest root domain when you upgrade the first PDC. By default, this computer will assume the roles of domain-naming master and schema operations master for the entire forest. Each PDC that is upgraded will become a PDC emulator. In addition, any PDC that is upgraded will also become the Relative Identifier (RID) master as well as the infrastructure master of the domain in which it resides.

After the PDC has been upgraded to a Windows 2000 domain controller, it can synchronize changes to security principals to any remaining Microsoft Windows NT 4.0 BDCs. It uses the Active Directory data store to do so. The Active Directory data store is compatible with Microsoft Windows NT 4.0 BDCs.

 Tip: If your existing PDC should not be upgraded first, you can demote the PDC by promoting a more suitable BDC to PDC.

Upgrading BDCs

After you have completed upgrading the network PDC, it is time to upgrade the Microsoft Windows NT 4.0 BDCs to Windows 2000 Active Directory. In general, you can upgrade your BDCs in any order. However, it is important to verify that applications running on BDCs are compatible with

Windows 2000. If you have an application that is not compatible, you can either move the application to a member server running Microsoft Windows NT 4.0 or you can choose not to upgrade the BDC.

When you determine your BDC upgrade sequence, you should consider any network services running on BDCs and ensure that these services go uninterrupted.

 Note: You should upgrade your BDCs to minimize the impact of having Microsoft Windows NT 4.0 BDCs that do not support Windows 2000 features.

Native Mode

Windows 2000 Server runs in one of two modes, mixed mode and native mode. A domain whose Microsoft Windows NT 4.0 PDC has not been upgraded to Windows 2000 is considered to be a Microsoft Windows NT 4.0 domain. When you install or upgrade to Windows 2000 Server, the default mode is mixed mode. Running in mixed mode allows your Windows 2000 domain controller to interact with Microsoft Windows NT 4.0 domain controllers. You can continue to run in mixed mode indefinitely.

You may want to consider switching to native mode once you have upgraded all your domain controllers. Since this is a serious step in your migration process, you must manually set a switch to convert to native mode. You set this switch using the Active Directory Domains and Trusts Microsoft Management Console (MMC) snap-in as illustrated in Figure 4.12.

Figure 4.12 Active Directory Domains and Trusts

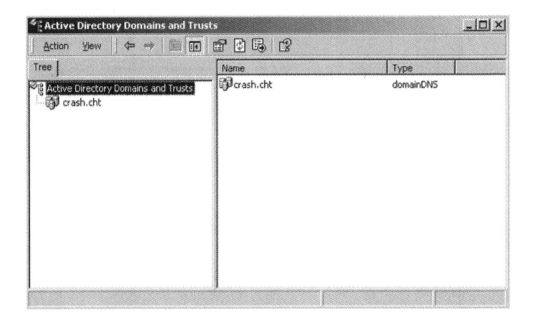

The path from a Windows NT 4.0 domain to Windows 2000 running in native mode is shown in Figure 4.13. You should be certain you will not be adding any Microsoft Windows NT 4.0 domain controllers to the domain in the future.

Figure 4.13 Domain Types

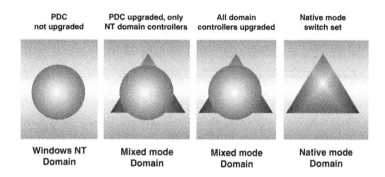

PDC not upgraded	PDC upgraded, only NT domain controllers	All domain controllers upgraded	Native mode switch set
Windows NT Domain	Mixed mode Domain	Mixed mode Domain	Native mode Domain

Switching to Native Mode

Native mode is the preferred mode of operation. There are many benefits derived from native mode. Under native mode, your overall network functionality is enhanced, new group types specific to native mode become available, and you can use universal groups, as well as new group nesting features.

When you upgrade your PDC, there is no immediate effect on groups. Your local and global groups under Microsoft Windows NT 4.0 become your local and global groups under Windows 2000. When you convert to native mode, your local groups on the PDC become domain local groups. Domain local groups are another new feature of Windows 2000. However, domain local groups are available only when your network is running in native mode.

Domain local groups can contain members from the following sectors:

● Anywhere in the forest

● Anywhere is a trusted forest

● Anywhere in a trusted pre-Windows 2000 domain

Native mode does not provide support for pre-Windows 2000 replication. You cannot have any domain controllers in your domain that are running anything other than Windows 2000.

Note: Once you switch to native mode, you will no longer be able to add a Microsoft Windows NT 4.0 domain controller to the domain.

Some features provided by Windows 2000 in native mode have limited availability in a mixed mode domain. Clients running Windows 2000 Professional or Server will be able to access more functions and features than will clients or servers running a different operating system.

Windows 2000 features that are available in mixed mode include the following:

- Microsoft Windows Installer

- Microsoft Management Console (MMC)

- Security configuration and analysis

Services that will only be available to client computers running either Windows 2000 Professional or Server include:

- Kerberos v5 authentication

- IntelliMirror

- Group Policy

 Note: Non-Microsoft clients that support Kerberos 5 authentication are supported in mixed mode.

Mixed mode also supports the use of Active Directory Organizational Units (OUs), but they will not be able to be administered from servers running Microsoft Windows NT 4.0. If all BDCs have been upgraded to Windows 2000 and are running Active Directory, then the scalability of Active Directory is enabled. Active Directory multiple-master replication is available between the PDC and any BDC that has been upgraded to a Windows 2000 domain controller.

You will need to evaluate your migration goals to determine if remaining in mixed mode will present an obstacle to attaining those goals. You may find that the trade-offs you make to remain in mixed mode are acceptable.

Tip: Switching to native mode is a one-way path. Once in native mode, you cannot switch back to mixed mode.

Remaining in Mixed Mode

A domain in which the PDC has been upgraded is considered to be in mixed mode, whether or not the BDCs have all been upgraded. Until you set the native mode switch, the domain will remain in mixed mode.

You may decide to remain in mixed mode if you find that you have applications running on BDCs that require Microsoft Windows NT 4.0 and are not Windows 2000-compatible. You could decide to remain in mixed mode in order to be able to return to a Microsoft Windows NT 4.0 environment.

When deciding to switch to native mode, another factor to consider is the physical security of your BDCs. Since Microsoft Windows NT 4.0 used a single master for directory updates, the security of BDCs was sometimes relaxed. When a BDC is upgraded to a Windows 2000 domain controller, multiple-master replication becomes a factor. Multiple-master replication means that updates can be made from any domain controller.

If you cannot provide appropriate security to your BDCs, you may consider demoting them to member servers during the upgrade. Replacing the BDC with a Windows 2000 domain controller in a different location could also solve your security problems. If the security problem is significant enough, you may have to reconsider your proposed domain structure.

Post-Upgrade Tasks

A very important component of your migration plan is validating the basic configuration of domain controllers after the upgrade. Your plan should specify how you intend to perform the verification. At a minimum, your plan should include the following elements:

- Verifying TCP/IP configuration

- Reviewing services in Computer Management

- Checking the Event Viewer

- Optimizing memory settings

Verifying TCP/IP Configurations

You will need to verify your TCP/IP configurations. You should check the following items:

- IP address settings

- DNS settings

- Windows Internet Name Service (WINS) settings

- Default gateway configurations

You can check these items by using the **IPCONFIG /ALL** command at the command prompt as shown in Figure 4.14.

Figure 4.14 **IPCONFIG /ALL** Command Results

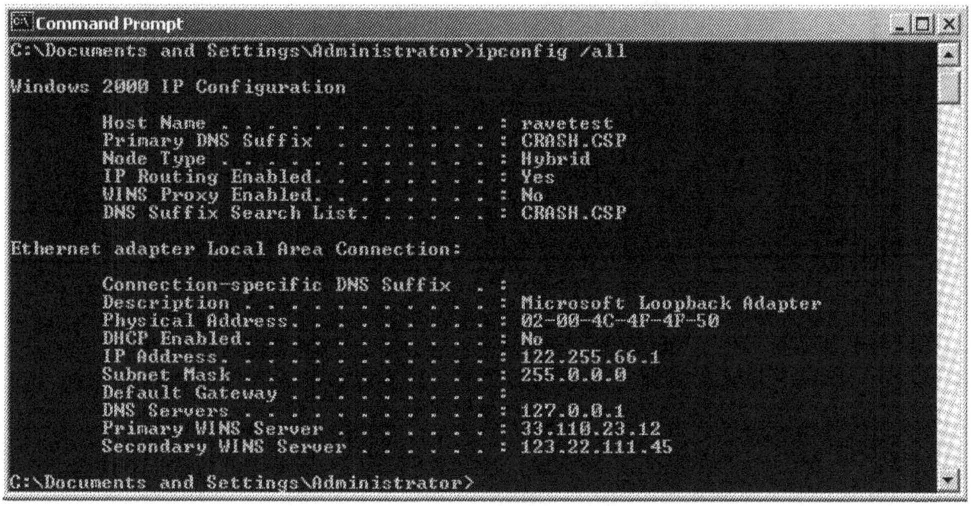

```
Command Prompt                                                    _ □ ×
C:\Documents and Settings\Administrator>ipconfig /all

Windows 2000 IP Configuration

        Host Name . . . . . . . . . . . . : ravetest
        Primary DNS Suffix  . . . . . . . : CRASH.CSP
        Node Type . . . . . . . . . . . . : Hybrid
        IP Routing Enabled. . . . . . . . : Yes
        WINS Proxy Enabled. . . . . . . . : No
        DNS Suffix Search List. . . . . . : CRASH.CSP

Ethernet adapter Local Area Connection:

        Connection-specific DNS Suffix  . :
        Description . . . . . . . . . . . : Microsoft Loopback Adapter
        Physical Address. . . . . . . . . : 02-00-4C-4F-4F-50
        DHCP Enabled. . . . . . . . . . . : No
        IP Address. . . . . . . . . . . . : 122.255.66.1
        Subnet Mask . . . . . . . . . . . : 255.0.0.0
        Default Gateway . . . . . . . . . :
        DNS Servers . . . . . . . . . . . : 127.0.0.1
        Primary WINS Server . . . . . . . : 33.110.23.12
        Secondary WINS Server . . . . . . : 123.22.111.45

C:\Documents and Settings\Administrator>
```

After you have verified the TCP/IP configuration, you will need to verify network connectivity. You can use the Packet Internet Groper (PING) command to accomplish this test as shown in Figure 4.15. You will need to verify that TCP/IP is installed correctly, the local host was added correctly, the default gateway is functioning correctly, and that you can communicate through a router. To accomplish this, PING the following addresses:

- 127.0.0.1 (Loop back address)

- The IP address of your local host

- The IP address of the default gateway

- The IP address of a remote host

Figure 4.15 PING Command Use

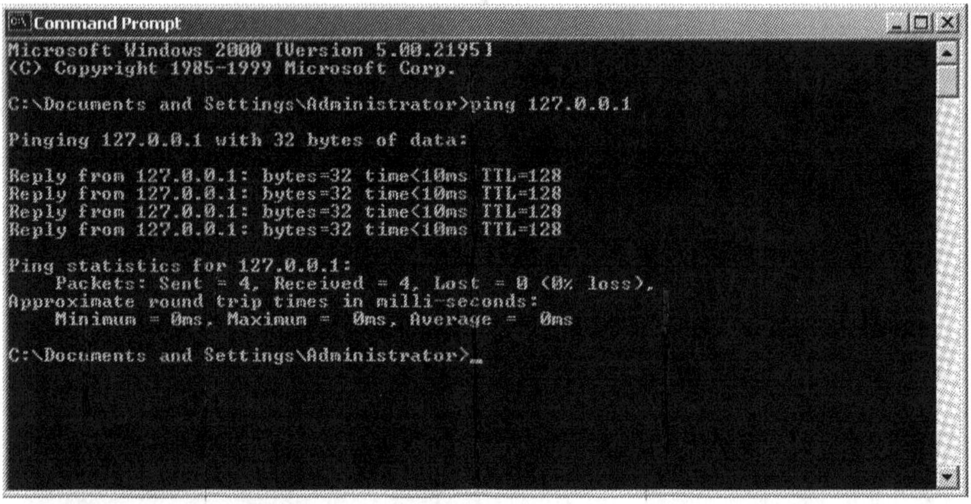

Reviewing Services in Computer Management

You should use the Computer Management administrative tool to ensure that all services that are supposed to start automatically did so. You should also verify that the services started without user intervention or multiple retries. The Computer Management tool is illustrated in Figure 4.16.

Figure 4.16 Computer Management Tool

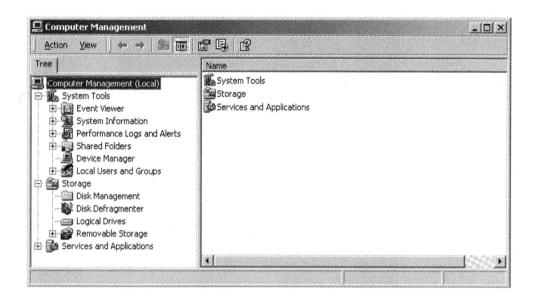

Checking the Event Viewer

Check the Event Viewer, illustrated in Figure 4.17, for any messages that can be associated with the upgrade or with the startup process. Look for any logs generated because of performance problems. You should also check to ensure that your Event Log size and log wrappings are defined to match your business and security requirements.

Figure 4.17 Event Viewer

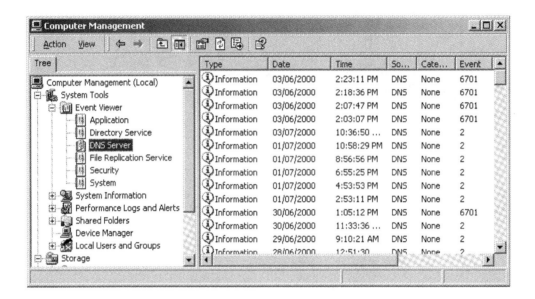

Optimizing Memory Settings

Optimization settings needs vary, depending upon the role of the computer in the domain. Use Network and Dial-up Connections in Control Panel to view or modify these settings. Network and Dial-up Connections is illustrated in Figure 4.18.

Figure 4.18 Network and Dial-up Connections

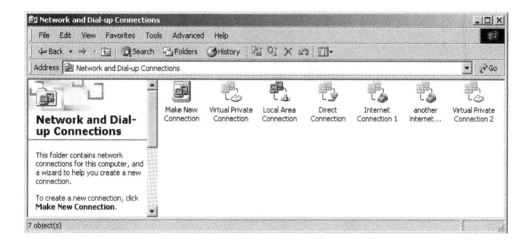

Vocabulary

Review the following terms in preparation for the certification exam.

Term	Description
API	An Application Programming Interface is a set of routines that provide an application with the ability to request and perform services provided and performed by a computer's operating system.
ATM	Asynchronous Transfer Mode is a high-speed, connection-oriented, fixed-sized packet protocol with data transfer speeds ranging from 25 to 622 Mbps.
BDC	A Backup Domain Controller is a computer running Microsoft Windows NT 4.0 or earlier that maintains a copy of the domain's directory database.
DHCP	The Dynamic Host Configuration Protocol is a networking protocol that provides dynamic configuration of IP addresses for client computers. It ensures that address conflicts do not occur and provides centralized management of address allocation.
DNS	The Domain Name System is a hierarchical naming system that maps domain names to IP addresses as well as the reverse. The DNS provides a mechanism by which a computer can query remote systems based upon a name rather than an IP address.
HCL	The Hardware Compatibility List is provided by Microsoft on their Web site on the Windows 2000 operating system page.

Term	Description
IP	The Internet Protocol is a routable protocol belonging to the TCP/IP suite. IP is responsible for packet addressing and routing, as well as deconstructing and later reconstructing of IP packets.
IPX/SPX	A combination of two network protocols native to the Novell Netware product. The Internetwork Packet Exchange works on the network layer to provide packet addressing and routing controls within and between networks. The Sequenced Packet Exchange protocol works on the transport layer to ensure that all packets are received error-free and in their correct order.
L2TP	Layer 2 Tunneling Protocol encapsulates Point-to-Point frames to be sent over IP, X.25, Frame Relay, or ATM networks.
LAN	A Local Area Network is a collection of computers connected on a network and in close physical proximity to each other so that devices such as a router are not required for interconnectivity.
LANE	Local Area Network Emulation is a service consisting of a set of protocols that provide a mechanism by which existing Ethernet and Token Ring LAN services are emulated on an ATM network.
Mbps	A communications speed measurement indicating millions of bits transferred per second.
MMC	The Microsoft Management Console is an application that serves as a framework that hosts various administrative consoles providing access to respective administrative items.
NetBEUI	The NetBIOS Enhanced User Interface is a Microsoft network protocol usually used in small Local Area Networks (LANs). It is the Microsoft implementation of the NetBIOS standard.
NetBIOS	The Network Basic Input/Output System is an Application Programming Interface (API) used by computers on a LAN. It provides a set of functions that provide access to low-level network services.

Term	Description
NIC	A Network Interface Card is an adapter card that provides the mechanism by which a computer can communicate with a network.
OU	An Organizational Unit is an Active Directory container object that provides a mechanism by which users, groups, computers, printers, and other organizational units are placed.
PDC	A Primary Domain Controller is a computer running Microsoft Windows NT 3.51 or 4.0 that is the primary storehouse for domain data including the directory database.
PPP	The Point-to-Point Protocol is an industry-standard set of Internet protocols that facilitates dial-up networking.
RID	The Relative Identifier identifies an account or group and is a part of a Security Identifier (SID). They are unique to the domain in which the entity was created.
SAM	Security Accounts Manager is a Windows 2000 service that maintains user information. It is used during the logon process.
SID	A Security Identifier is a unique name that identifies a user, group of users, or a computer.
TCP/IP	The Transmission Control Protocol/Internet Protocol is a set of software protocols for networking that is widely used on the internet. The TCP/IP protocol provides a communication medium across interconnected networks with diverse hardware platforms and operating systems.
VPN	A Virtual Private Network is a logically constructed WAN that uses existing public transmission mediums. A VPN allows an organization to emulate a private WAN connection.
WAN	A Wide Area Network is a network that connects resources and users from distinct locations that may be separated geographically.
WINS	Windows Internet Name Service is a software service that maps IP addresses to computer names permitting users to access resources by name rather than IP address.

In Brief

If you want to...	Then do this...
Use the Computer Management utility	1. From the **Start** menu, choose **Settings**. 2. Select **Control Panel**, and double-click **Administrative Tools**. 3. Double-click **Computer Management**.
Verify TCP/IP settings	From the command prompt, type **IPCONFIG /ALL**.
Upgrade a computer currently running Microsoft Windows NT 3.5 to Windows 2000	You must first upgrade the computer to Microsoft Windows NT 3.51 or 4.0, before you can upgrade it to Windows 2000.
Return your domain to its original pre-upgrade state	1. Remove all computers running Windows 2000 from the production environment. 2. Promote the offline BDC to PDC and bring it online. 3. The new PDC will then replicate its data to any remaining Microsoft Windows NT 4.0 BDCs and return the domain to its original state.

If you want to...	Then do this...
Verify TCP/IP connectivity, using the PING command	• Ping 127.0.0.1 (loop back address) to verify that TCP/IP was installed correctly • Ping the IP address of your local host to verify the local host was added correctly • Ping the IP address of the default gateway to ensure that it is functioning correctly • Ping the IP address of a remote host to verify that you can communicate through a router
Switch to native mode	You switch to native mode by using the Active Directory Domains and Trusts Microsoft Management Console (MMC) snap-in.

Lesson 4 Activities

Complete the following activities to better prepare you for the certification exam.

1. Discuss the recommended domain upgrade sequence.

2. Describe the requirements for switching to native mode.

3. Discuss how to return a domain to its original, pre-upgrade state.

4. Describe how to verify TCP/IP connectivity after the upgrade.

5. State why you should consider switching to native mode.

6. Explain the effect on Microsoft Windows NT 4.0 groups caused by upgrading your PDC.

7. State why you should upgrade your BDCs as soon as possible.

8. Discuss reasons for remaining in mixed mode.

9. What factors should you consider when determining the upgrade order of BDCs?

10. Describe why you cannot add a Microsoft Windows NT 4.0 domain controller to a domain in native mode.

Answers to Lesson 4 Activities

1. The recommended domain upgrade sequence is to first upgrade your account domains and then your resource domains.

2. Before you can switch to native mode, you must upgrade all domain controllers to Windows 2000 and determine that there is no longer a need to support downlevel domain controllers.

3. If your domain upgrade fails for any reason, you can return to the original state by performing the following in order:

    1. Remove all computers running Windows 2000 from the production environment.

    2. Promote the offline BDC to PDC and bring it online.

    3. The new PDC will then replicate its data to any remaining Microsoft Windows NT 4.0 BDCs and return the domain to its original state.

4. You can use the PING command to verify that TCP/IP is installed correctly, the local host was added correctly, the default gateway is functioning correctly, and that you can communicate through a router. To perform these tests, ping the following:

    *   127.0.0.1 (loop back address)

    *   The IP address of your local host

    *   The IP address of the default gateway

    *   The IP address of a remote host

5. Native mode is the preferred mode of operation. There are many benefits derived from native mode. Under native mode, your overall network functionality is enhanced, new group types specific to native mode become available, and you can use universal groups and new group nesting features.

6. When you upgrade your PDC, there is no immediate effect on groups. Your local and global groups under Microsoft Windows NT 4.0 become your local and global groups under Windows 2000.

7. You should upgrade your BDCs as soon as possible to minimize the impact of having Microsoft Windows NT 4.0 BDCs that do not support Windows 2000 features.

8. You may decide to remain in mixed mode if you find that you have applications running on BDCs that require Microsoft Windows NT 4.0 and are not Windows 2000 compatible.

You could decide to remain in mixed mode to maintain the ability to return to a Microsoft Windows NT 4.0 environment.

You may wish to remain in mixed mode if you cannot provide adequate security to BDCs that will become Windows 2000 domain controllers.

9. When determining the upgrade order of BDCs, you should consider the following factors:

- Presence of applications that require Microsoft Windows NT 4.0

- Presence of services that require Microsoft Windows NT 4.0

- Hard disk space availability

- Hardware compatibility

- Hardware upgrade needs

- Physical accessibility

- Key network services

BDCs that are more physically accessible or provide key network services should be considered prime candidates for an early upgrade.

10. mode does not provide support for pre-Windows 2000 replication. You cannot have any domain controllers in your domain that are running anything other than Windows 2000.

Lesson 4 Quiz

These questions test your knowledge of features, vocabulary, procedures, and syntax.

1. What happens to local groups on the PDC when you switch to native mode?
    A. They become domain universal groups.
    B. They become nested domain local groups.
    C. They become domain local groups.
    D. There is no change to local groups.

2. What are the effects of switching to native mode?
    A. It is a one-way path; you cannot switch back.
    B. It is done automatically when the last BDC is upgraded.
    C. It allows you to have Microsoft Windows NT 4.0 BDCs in your domain.
    D. It activates Active Directory.

3. What should you check to verify your TCP/IP configuration?
    A. IP address settings
    B. DNS and WINS settings
    C. Native Mode switch
    D. Default Gateway Settings

4. What are the requirements for running in mixed mode?
    A. All BDCs have been upgraded to Windows 2000 Server.
    B. All clients have been upgraded to Windows 2000 Professional.
    C. Kerberos v5 authentication has been disabled.
    D. The PDC has been upgraded to Windows 2000 Server.

5. What is the upgrade path for a computer running Microsoft Windows NT Server 3.1?

   A. Directly to Windows 2000 Advanced Server

   B. Directly to Windows 2000 Server

   C. First to Windows 2000 Professional and then to Windows 2000 Server

   D. First to either Microsoft Windows NT 3.51 or 4.0 then to Windows 2000 Server

6. From which operating systems can you upgrade directly to Windows 2000 Advanced Server?

   A. Windows 98

   B. Microsoft Windows NT Server 3.51

   C. Microsoft Windows NT Server 4.0

   D. Microsoft Windows NT Advanced Server versions 3.1

7. When can you upgrade the forest root domain?

   A. You can upgrade the forest root at any time.

   B. You must upgrade the forest root first.

   C. You can upgrade the forest root only after you upgrade subordinate domains.

   D. You must upgrade the forest root after you upgrade all member domains.

8. How are transitive trusts created when you install Active Directory on a PDC of a child domain?

   A. They must be manually configured.

   B. They are created between the child domain and the parent domain.

   C. They are created automatically.

   D. They are created between all children domains and the parent domain.

9. What roles are created when you establish the forest root domain by upgrading the first PDC?

   A. Domain naming master for the entire forest

   B. PDC emulator for the entire forest

   C. Infrastructure master for the entire forest

   D. Schema operations master for the entire forest

10. What are the reasons for developing a recovery plan?

    A. To provide continuity of services should a domain controller upgrade fail

    B. To prevent the accidental loss of data

    C. To ensure that the domain does not become orphaned should the PDC upgrade fail

    D. To ensure that a domain can be rolled back to its original state

Answers to Lesson 4 Quiz

1. Answer C is correct. When you convert to native mode, your local groups on the PDC become domain local groups.

    Answers A, B, and D are incorrect. Universal groups are a new feature of Windows 2000 and are the simplest form of group. Group nesting is a feature that allows you to extend the basic group. Neither universal groups nor group nesting are implemented automatically.

2. Answer A is correct. Once you switch to native mode, you cannot switch back to mixed mode.

    Answers B, C, and D are incorrect. Switching to native mode does not occur automatically. Once you are in native mode, you cannot have any domain controllers that are not running Windows 2000. You can use Active Directory in mixed mode, however some of the functionality will be limited.   3. Answers A, B, and D are correct. You should check the IP, DNS and WINS settings as well as the default gateway configurations.

    Answer C is incorrect. Running in native mode versus mixed mode has no effect on your TCP/IP configuration.

4. Answer D is correct. When the domain PDC has been upgraded to Windows 2000, the domain defaults to mixed mode.

    Answers A, B, and C are incorrect. You do not need to upgrade all BDCs to Windows 2000, nor do you need to upgrade all clients or disable Kerberos authentication.

5. Answer D is correct. To upgrade a computer running Microsoft Windows NT Server 3.1, you must first upgrade to either Microsoft Windows NT 3.51 or v4.0 before you can upgrade to Windows 2000 Server.

    Answers A, B, and C are incorrect. You cannot directly upgrade a computer running Microsoft Windows NT Server 3.1 to Windows 2000 Server or Advanced server. Upgrading directly to Windows 2000 Professional is also not possible.

6. Answer C is correct. You can upgrade directly from Microsoft Windows NT Server 4.0 to Windows 2000 Advanced Server.

    Answers A, B, and D are incorrect. You cannot upgrade to Windows 2000 Advanced Server from Windows 98 or 95, Microsoft Windows NT Server 3.51 or Microsoft Windows NT Advanced Server 3.1.

7. Answer B is correct. You must upgrade the forest root first.

    Answers A, C, and D are incorrect. You cannot upgrade the forest root at any time. The first domain that you upgrade becomes the forest root, therefore, you cannot upgrade a domain to the forest root if any other domain has already been upgraded.

8. Answers B and C are correct. During the Active Directory installation on a PDC of a child domain, transitive trusts are automatically created between a child domain and the parent domain.

    Answers A and D are incorrect. The transitive trusts do not need to be configured manually, nor are they created between children domains.

9. Answers A and D are correct. The forest root domain computer assumes the roles of domain naming master and schema operations master for the entire forest.

    Answers B and C are incorrect. Every domain in the forest will have a PDC emulator and an infrastructure master.

10. Answers A, B, C, and D are correct. You need to develop a recovery plan to prevent the accidental loss of data and to provide a mechanism by which you can roll back the upgrade in the case of a catastrophic failure. Part of your recovery plan should include adding a BDC to a domain with only a PDC so that the domain will not become orphaned should the PDC upgrade experience failure. You must also consider continuity of service should a domain controller upgrade experience difficulties or failure.

Lesson 5: Network Upgrade Strategies

Two of the most important goals that you can have during your migration are to ensure network functionality during the upgrade and to minimize the impact that network changes will have on productivity. Upgrading from a Microsoft Windows NT 4.0 to a Windows 2000 network environment can provide you with many benefits including improved manageability, security, availability, and scalability. Your upgrade plan needs to address achieving these benefits while maintaining consistent network operations.

You need to examine your existing network services and develop a strategy to ensure their reliability during the upgrade. You also need to determine how the upgrade will affect your existing network security and develop a strategy that maintains the desired security during the upgrade. Finally, you need to define a strategy to regulate network traffic during the upgrade to optimize network performance.

After completing this lesson, you should have a better understanding of the following topics:

- Network Services

- Replication

- Authentication

- Security Standards

- Resource Access Components

Network Services

When you upgrade a domain, several network services will be affected. You need to carefully plan the domain upgrade to ensure that changes to these services will not impact your ability to maintain reliable network connectivity and functionality.

Maintaining Network Services during an Upgrade

Perhaps the largest risk during a domain upgrade is the potential for interruptions to network operations. The upgrade will affect many network services whose function is vital to the organization.

You need to examine how you will replicate Domain Name System (DNS) data in your Windows 2000 network. This knowledge will help you provide reliable DNS naming services during the upgrade.

Another necessity is to determine how Network Basic Input/Output Service (NetBIOS) names are used. This knowledge will help you to examine the potential for removing Windows Internet Name Service (WINS) services after the upgrade.

Besides, you have to identify the normal interruptions to Dynamic Host Configuration Protocol (DHCP) server services that will occur during the upgrade. This knowledge will help you to maintain and maximize reliability during the upgrade.

You need a plan that provides a mechanism to maintain Microsoft Windows NT 4.0 Local Area Network (LAN) Manager (NTLM) protocol replication after you have implemented the Windows 2000 File Replication Service (FRS).

- You also need to develop a plan and strategy for the following situations:
- Maintaining Routing and Remote Access Service (RRAS) support during the upgrade
- Transitioning from Microsoft Windows NT 4.0 System Policies to Windows 2000 Group Policy
- Transitioning from Microsoft Windows NT 4.0 logon scripts to Windows 2000 Group Policy

Reliable DNS Services

Request For Comment (RFC) 2052 defines a new DNS resource record. The Service (SRV) resource record specifies the location of specific protocol and domain servers. Windows 2000 relies on DNS using SRV records as a locator service. Windows 2000 DNS SRV records are shown in Figure 5.1. Clients use the service to locate, among others, the following important Windows 2000 services:

- Domain controllers
- Global Catalog servers
- Kerberos Key Distribution Center (KDC) servers
- Lightweight Directory Access Protocol (LDAP)

Figure 5.1 SRV Resource Records

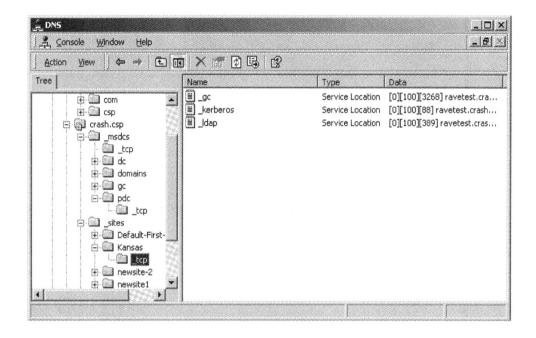

To provide the required support for SRV resource records, it is essential to migrate the Microsoft Windows NT 4.0 DNS service to Windows 2000 DNS as quickly as possible.

 Note: If there are any non-Windows DNS servers in your network, they must be upgraded to support SRV records prior to promoting the first domain controller in the first domain.

When you upgrade the primary DNS server to Windows 2000, you gain the ability to enable the configuration of zones to accept SRV resource record registrations and the benefit of dynamic updates of resource records. You also gain these benefits when you switch the primary zone to be hosted on a Windows 2000 server.

Note: If even one DNS server is not upgraded to Windows 2000, you must manually add the SRV records required by Active Directory.

DNS zones hosted on a Windows 2000 domain controller can be configured to be Active Directory integrated. If you have any DNS domains that will contain Active Directory resource records, then it is recommended that you employ Active Directory integrated zones.

 Note: Active Directory integrated zones can only be implemented on domain controllers.

If you wish to use DNS on a member server, then it can only be a primary or secondary DNS server.

When planning your network upgrade, you must factor in the upgrading of Microsoft Windows NT 4.0 DNS services to Windows 2000 DNS services. You should also plan to move a write-enabled copy of the DNS zone data to Windows 2000. You can upgrade your DNS servers in two ways. You can upgrade the existing Microsoft Windows NT 4.0 server that contains the DNS primary zone to Windows 2000, configuring the zone for dynamic updates, or you can perform the following actions:

- Install a new Windows 2000 server
- Configure the new server as the secondary DNS server for the existing zone
- Do the zone transfer
- Reverse roles so that the new server becomes the primary DNS server
- Configure the zone for dynamic updates

Tip: To take advantage of secure dynamic updates and multimaster writes, convert the DNS zone to Active Directory integrated after upgrading the DNS service to Windows 2000.

When you enable dynamic updates, you no longer have to manually update the zone database when there are changes to the domain for which a name server has authority. Dynamic DNS (DDNS) allows name servers and clients within the network to automatically update the zone database file as illustrated in Figure 5.2.

Figure 5.2 DDNS Updates

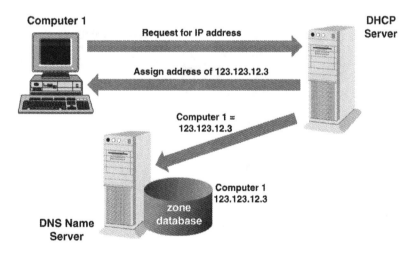

SRV records will appear as generic resource records in the Microsoft Windows NT 4.0 DNS Manager interface. Queries to the Microsoft Windows NT DNS manager for SRV resource records will succeed.

You need to consider the following factors to help minimize the impact of a domain upgrade on DNS services:

- DNS tools are platform-specific

- Active Directory integrated zones cannot be replicated between domains

- Microsoft Windows NT 4.0 and Windows 2000 DNS servers can be masters for each other

You cannot manage Microsoft Windows NT 4.0 DNS with the Windows 2000 DNS management tool—you must use the Microsoft Windows NT 4.0 DNS management tool to manage Microsoft Windows NT DNS. Likewise, you must use the Windows 2000 DNS management tool to manage Windows 2000 DNS. You cannot run the Microsoft Windows NT DNS tool on a Windows 2000 server nor can you run the Windows 2000 DNS management tool from Microsoft Windows NT 4.0. This is illustrated in Figure 5.3.

Figure 5.3 DNS Is Platform-Specific

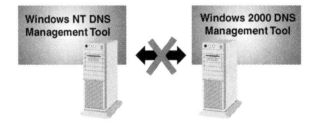

If one of your requirements is to host zones on DNS servers in different domains, you will need to configure the DNS servers as secondary DNS zones in domains other than the local domain.

You can use a Microsoft Windows NT 4.0 DNS server as a master server for Windows 2000 DNS servers. The reverse is also true—you can use a Windows 2000 DNS server as a master server for Microsoft Windows NT 4.0 DNS servers.

Reliable NetBIOS Resolution Services

One of the features of NetBIOS is that it provides a naming service. NetBIOS names uniquely identify clients and resources. The use of NetBIOS names and their resolution is supported in Microsoft Windows NT 4.0 by WINS. While a Windows 2000 network does not require WINS, you should continue its use until you are certain that all computers and applications on the network can operate without referencing NetBIOS names or using the NetBIOS name resolution services.

Neither NetBIOS name resolution or the WINS support for NetBIOS name resolution are affected by an upgrade to Windows 2000. However, during the first restart of a newly upgraded computer, WINS will fail. During the first restart, WINS will automatically convert its database into a newer version of the database. WINS will function properly and maintain all previous records and replication configurations after the database conversion is completed.

Tip: You can use Toolsets from either Microsoft Windows NT 4.0 or Windows 2000 to manage WINS servers.

During your upgrade planning, you should consider removing WINS. If NetBIOS is no longer required on the network, NetBIOS name resolution requests must not be to be sent to the WINS server. As long as WINS is employed, only registrations and release requests can be sent to the WINS server.

You need to determine NetBIOS dependencies during your migration and upgrade planning. If all computers and applications on a network that has been completely migrated to Windows 2000 can function without using NetBIOS naming services, you can discontinue WINS. Maintaining WINS can cause unnecessary network traffic caused by the following processes:

- WINS replication

- NetBIOS name registration

- Registrations sent to WINS servers

- Releases sent to WINS servers

Note: Clients will continue to broadcast NetBIOS name registrations and releases if they have enabled NetBIOS over Transmission Control Protocol/Internet Protocol (TCP/IP).

If you plan to remove WINS services from the network, ensure that NetBIOS over TCP/IP is disabled on all clients. To do so, refer to the documentation for the respective client operating systems.

To determine if WINS is required in your network to support NetBIOS name resolution, use the Performance console administrative tool for a Windows WINS server as illustrated in Figure 5.4.

Figure 5.4 Performance Console Administration

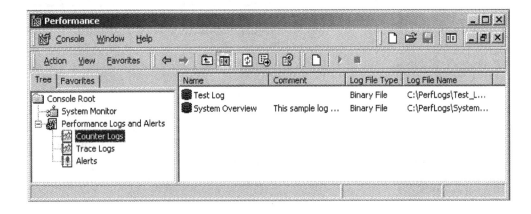

Using the Performance console administrative tool, you will need to examine the following counters:

- Windows Internet Name Service Server: Total Number of Registrations/Sec

- Queries/Sec

- Successful Queries/Sec

You determine the total number of unique and group registrations that are received per second by using the Windows Internet Name Service Server: Total Number of Registrations/Sec counter. If this counter indicates that the registrations are zero, you should consider removing the WINS server. A zero value in this counter tells you that no clients are registering names with the WINS server.

A zero value in the Queries/Sec counter indicates that NetBIOS name resolution is no longer occurring. The Queries/Sec counter tells you the rate at which the WINS server receives NetBIOS name resolution queries.

Note: A non-zero value in the Queries/Sec counter indicates a need for continuing WINS functionality.

You determine the rate at which the WINS server successfully resolves NetBIOS queries using the Successful Queries/Sec counter. You need to contrast the value in this counter with the value of the Queries/Sec counter. A zero value in the Successful Queries/Sec counter indicates that no NetBIOS names are being successfully resolved on the WINS server. If both counters have a value of zero, then the WINS server is not resolving NetBIOS names. If both of these counters are non-zero, then NetBIOS name resolution is taking place on the WINS server.

Warning: If the value of the Successful Queries/Sec counter is less than the value of the Queries/Sec counter, then you may have a problem that must be resolved.

If there are far fewer successful queries taking place then queries, either the necessary servers are not registering, or your WINS replication topology has problems that are preventing replication of NetBIOS records to all WINS servers.

Reliable DHCP Server Services

Windows 2000 Active Directory requires the use of the TCP/IP protocol on the network. DHCP automatically configures clients with TCP/IP addresses and configuration information. You can use a

Microsoft Windows NT 4.0 DHCP server to provide dynamic address assignment services to Windows 2000 clients and servers as well as other down-level clients and servers.

When you upgrade a DHCP server, the DHCP service provided by that server will be interrupted because the server will be unable to provide DHCP-assigned addresses to clients. The server will also fail to renew leases during the upgrade.

 Note: You must provide backup for DHCP services when DHCP servers are upgraded.

During a DHCP server upgrade, dynamically assigned Internet Protocol (IP) addresses will not be distributed. When you upgrade a Microsoft Windows NT 4.0 server, the DHCP server database will automatically be converted to a newer database version. The DHCP server will temporarily register errors in the system log until the conversion is complete.

When you are planning the upgrade of a domain that uses DHCP Server services, you should plan for the following actions:

- Providing backup DHCP services
- Defining an Active Directory authorization process

You must provide a backup DHCP server to renew DHCP leases that expire during the upgrade because the DHCP server being upgraded will be unable to provide DHCP-assigned addresses. After the upgrade is completed, the DHCP server will be unable to service DHCP requests until a member of the Enterprise Admins group authorizes the server in Active Directory. Authorizing the DHCP server in Active Directory prevents unauthorized DHCP servers from being implemented on the network and the assignment of unapproved TCP/IP addresses to clients.

 Note: You must authorize upgraded DHCP servers in Active Directory after you complete their upgrade.

Remote Access Service

You will need to develop a strategy for supporting remote access services during the upgrade. The Microsoft Windows NT 4.0 Routing and Remote Access Service (RRAS) is used to provide users with the capability of remote access to the network. A Microsoft Windows NT 4.0 remote access server will continue to function in the same manner after it has been upgraded to Windows 2000. However, it is a good idea to upgrade your RRAS servers early in the upgrade process.

While both Remote Access Service (RAS) and RRAS services will be unaffected during the upgrade, if the network employs down-level remote access servers then RAS connectivity could be intermittent and sometimes fail. This is the main issue during a domain upgrade. When one or more Microsoft Windows NT 4.0 domain controllers have been upgraded and down-level remote access servers are still present in the network, then the interoperability of remote access services in the mixed environment may cause legitimate dial-in users to be denied remote access.

 Note: Do not confuse the terms mixed mode and mixed environment. A mixed environment is a Windows 2000 domain that contains pre-Windows 2000 clients or servers. Such a domain can be in either mixed mode or native mode. A mixed mode domain is a domain that allows Windows 2000 domain controllers and Microsoft Windows NT 4.0 Backup Domain Controllers (BDCs) to coexist.

Microsoft Windows NT 4.0 RAS and RRAS use the LocalSystem account to determine if a user has dial-in permissions or if any other dial-in settings have been configured, such as callback phone numbers. A service logs on with NULL credentials when it logs on as LocalSystem, meaning the service does not provide a user name or password. In a Windows 2000 domain, this can cause problems. Active Directory, by default, will not accept NULL session queries for object attributes. Unless you relax Active Directory security or only install RAS or RRAS services on a BDC, dial-in connectivity could be intermittent. This is because user dial-in authentication will fail if a Windows 2000 domain controller performs the authentication.

Note: It is impossible to configure a RAS or RRAS server so that it will only contact a BDC for authentication.

While your network has a mixed environment, remote users can be authorized successfully if you use a Microsoft Windows NT 4.0 member server as the RAS or RRAS server, and it contacts a Microsoft Windows NT 4.0 BDC to determine the user's dial-in properties. This process is identical to the remote user authentication process in a Microsoft Windows NT 4.0 domain.

 Note: You cannot guarantee that a member server will contact a Microsoft Windows NT 4.0 BDC instead of a Windows 2000 domain controller.

If you use a Microsoft Windows NT 4.0 BDC as a RAS or RRAS server, it will successfully authorize remote users using its local Security Accounts Manager (SAM) database. However, if you also have Windows 2000 RRAS servers in the domain, there is no way to guarantee that the user will contact the Microsoft Windows NT 4.0 BDC RAS or RRAS server when dialing in.

Due to these limitations, it is important to plan in advance to ensure that reliable remote access is operational during the upgrade. You want your Microsoft Windows NT RAS or RRAS server to retrieve properties reliably while you are operating in a mixed Active Directory environment. Your upgrade plan must address the following issues:

● Using the built-in account Everyone

● Upgrading Microsoft Windows NT 4.0 RAS and RRAS servers as soon as possible

You can grant permissions to read user object attributes to the built-in account Everyone. This can be done regardless of the domains mode, either mixed or native. You can accomplish this when you are upgrading the first domain controller. While configuring the Active Directory Installation wizard, you can select Permission compatible with pre-Windows 2000 server as illustrated in Figure 5.5. When you do this, you add the Everyone account to the Pre-Windows 2000 Compatible Access local group.

Figure 5.5 Active Directory Installation Wizard

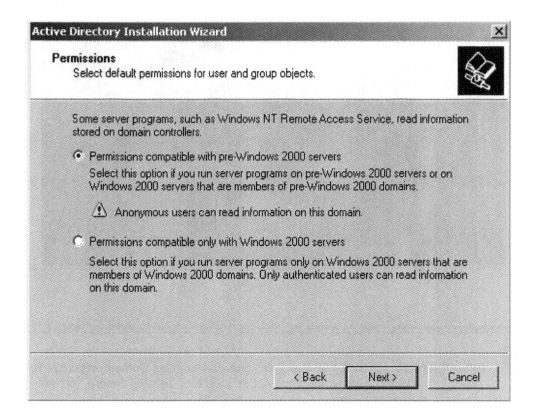

If you have already upgraded the first domain controller, you can manually add the Everyone account to the Pre-Windows 2000 Compatible Access local group. To accomplish this task, you would type the command **net localgroup "Pre-Windows 2000 Compatible Access" Everyone /add** as shown in Figure 5.6.

Figure 5.6 Command Line Everyone Account Addition

 Warning: When you use the Everyone group, you relax domain security. You must understand the impact on Active Directory security before you employ this method.

The best approach is one that minimizes the need to relax domain security. You should plan to upgrade all Microsoft Windows NT 4.0 RAS and RRAS servers as soon as possible so that you do not need to authenticate users from NULL sessions. Dial-in users will be reliably authorized once you have upgraded all remote access servers.

Note: You can configure Windows 2000 remote access servers uniformly if you use Remote Authentication Dial-In User Service (RADIUS) servers.

If your organization has multiple remote access servers, then it may prove difficult to upgrade them all at the same time so that you avoid the need to relax domain security. Carefully consider your options when planning your upgrade.

Group Policy and System Policy Interaction

You need to define a strategy for migrating from Microsoft Windows NT 4.0 System Policies to Windows 2000 Group Policies. System policies do not automatically migrate to Windows 2000. If you upgrade a Microsoft Windows NT 4.0 client that is managed by a Windows 2000 server, the upgraded client will only receive Active Directory Group Policy settings.

When a Microsoft Windows NT 4.0 domain controller authenticates a client, System Policies are applied. However, when a Windows 2000 domain controller authenticates the client, Group Policy is applied. If the user and computer accounts are located in different types of domains, then you need to consider some additional factors.

Tip: Group Policies are never applied to Microsoft Windows NT 4.0 clients.

Your upgrade plan should address your goals for policy application. You need to determine the best method for migrating Microsoft Windows NT 4.0 System Policy settings. Your migration options include the following:

- Migrating the current System Policy settings using the GPOLMIG.EXE resource kit utility
- Processing both Group Policy and System Policy in a mixed environment

System Policies are not written to the \Software\Policies tree and will persist in the registry because not all policies outside of the tree are removed when a user logs off from the network. Microsoft

Windows NT 4.0 System Policies can be removed from the network once all client computers have been migrated to Windows 2000. System Policies are removed by deleting the file NTCONFIG.POL from the NETLOGON share of a Windows 2000 domain controller. Figure 5.7 illustrates the NETLOGON share. Once you have deleted the file, the File Replication Service (FRS) will ensure that the file is deleted from all other domain controllers in the domain.

Figure 5.7 Windows 2000 NETLOGON Share

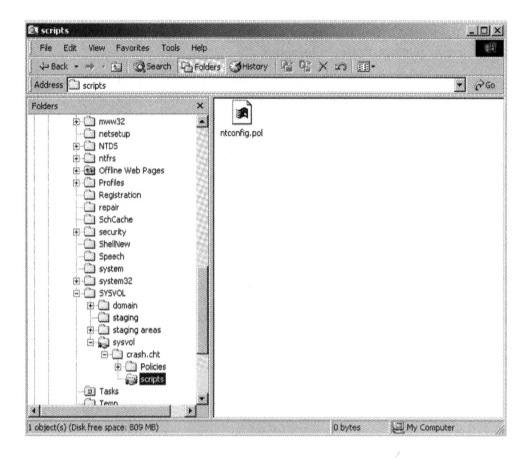

Windows 2000 Server FRS is automatically configured to replicate the System Volume (SYSVOL) to every domain controller. If you modify any logon script stored in SYSVOL on any domain controller, that change is replicated to other domain controllers in multiple-master fashion. This process is illustrated in Figure 5.8.

Figure 5.8 FRS Process

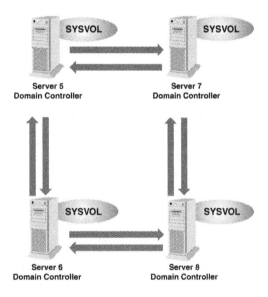

Server 5
Domain Controller

Server 7
Domain Controller

Server 6
Domain Controller

Server 8
Domain Controller

Working with Logon Scripts

Your upgrade plan must define a strategy for migrating Microsoft Windows NT 4.0 logon scripts to Windows 2000 Group Policy. When a Windows NT 4.0 domain controller is upgraded, there is no effect on user-based logon scripts stored on the NETLOGON share of the controller. The scripts will be available when a client authenticates. FRS will synchronize the contents of the NETLOGON folder with all Windows 2000 domain controllers. If you wish to synchronize the contents of this folder with domain controllers in a domain that has not been upgraded, you will need to bridge the LAN Manager replication service with FRS.

Migrating and Applying Logon Scripts

User-based logon scripts that are stored in the NETLOGON share will continue to be processed by down-level clients. A Windows 2000 client will run user-assigned logon scripts located in the NETLOGON share and any scripts assigned to the user or the computer through Group Policy. Logon scripts assigned through Group Policy to Windows 2000 clients are applied at the following levels:

- Site

- Domain

- Organizational Unit (OU)

Group Policy cannot be applied to users. Since this is the case, you may need to use non-Group Policy logon scripts. You can replace or augment user-based scripts with Group Policy scripts. You may wish to consider the following Group Policy logon scripts:

- Logon

- Logoff

- Startup

- Shutdown

The Logon script is applied before the shell is applied to the user. The Logoff script is applied when the user logs off the computer and before the logon screen is displayed. The Startup script is applied to computers and is run before the Windows logon screen is displayed. After the user has logged off the computer, the Shutdown script is applied when the computer is shut down.

 Note: Group Policy logon scripts are stored in the SYSVOL folder, which is replicated between domain controllers. Group Policy scripts are only applied to Windows 2000 clients.

The Windows 2000 Windows Script Host processes MS-DOS-based logon files. MS-DOS batch files are commonly used in user-based logon scripts. The Windows Scripts Host also processes files that are not limited by the syntax of MS-DOS batch files including the following:

- Microsoft Visual Basic Scripting Edition (VBScript)
- JScript

Replication

You need to consider the effect of an upgrade on replication services. Windows 2000 does not support LAN Manager replication, so you need to develop a strategy for coexisting with the File Replication Service (FRS) during the upgrade.

Planning for LAN Manager Replication

Logon scripts, System Policies, and other data types are replicated by the LAN Manager replication service for Microsoft Windows NT 4.0 servers. Windows 2000 supports the same functionality through FRS. LAN Manager replication service and FRS are distinct services, each having a different configuration.

LAN Manger replication service uses a single server to host an export directory. This server is typically a domain controller. The contents of the directory are imported to an import folder by any number of domain controllers or member servers. This process is illustrated in Figure 5.9.

Figure 5.9 LAN Manager Replication Process

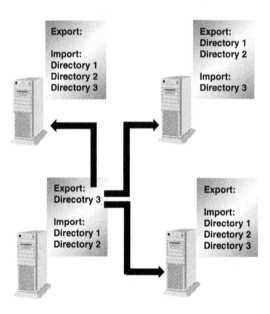

FRS configures all domain controllers to host a replicated SYSVOL automatically. Any changes made to the contents of SYSVOL are automatically replicated to all other domain controllers in the domain in multimaster fashion.

Tip: SYSVOL can only be hosted by domain controllers.

An export server that has not yet been upgraded will continue to replicate the contents of its export directories to import servers that have not been updated. LAN Manager replication services are removed from Microsoft Windows NT 4.0 domain controllers as they are upgraded. The LAN Manager replication service is fully removed from the domain when the last Microsoft Windows NT 4.0 computer is upgraded to Windows 2000.

Note: Although you have Microsoft Windows NT 4.0 domain controllers in a domain that are authenticating clients and are configured to provide logon scripts and System Policies, it is important to maintain LAN Manager replication services.

Planning for Replication Services Integration

You need to ensure that clients reliably receive any required logon scripts and System Policies, regardless of the authenticating domain controller's operating system version. Integrating LAN Manager replication service with FRS will accomplish this task as well as ensure that all updates are propagated to all domain controllers in the domain.

Your upgrade plan must define a method to reliably provide logon scripts and System Policies to clients during the upgrade. To do so, you need to integrate LAN Manager replication service and FRS using the following tasks:

- Identify all Microsoft Windows NT 4.0 import and export servers

- Create a bridge between the Microsoft Windows NT 4.0 scripts directory and the Windows 2000 NETLOGON share

- Maintain the bridge between replication systems

- Reconfigure the LAN Manager replication service during the upgrade

- Decommission the bridge between the replication systems when the upgrade is complete

The first step is to identify all Microsoft Windows NT 4.0 import and export servers. If an export server is also the Primary Domain Controller (PDC), then you will need to move the export services to another computer. You can then upgrade the PDC while continuing to replicate scripts and policies to domain controllers that have not yet been upgraded via LAN Manager replication.

Warning: If your export server is a BDC, you must ensure that it is the last BDC to be upgraded.

If you upgrade a BDC that is the export server before you upgrade other BDCs, then you must redefine the export server for LAN Manager replication.

You will next need to create a bridge between the Microsoft Windows NT 4.0 scripts directory and the Windows 2000 NETLOGON share. You will find a file in the Windows 2000 resource kit, LBRIDGE.CMD, which keeps the NETLOG share in Windows 2000 synchronized with the Microsoft Windows NT 4.0 export server. With this tool, you can copy files from the Windows 2000 NETLOGON share, located within SYSVOL, into the Microsoft Windows NT 4.0 export directory structure. Files are not copied in the opposite direction. Microsoft Windows NT 4.0 holds commonly replicated scripts and system policies in the following folders:

- systemroot\system32\repl\export\scripts

- systemroot\system32\repl\import\scripts

 Note: The contents of the Windows 2000 NETLOGON share will replace the contents of the Microsoft Windows NT 4.0 export directory.

During this time, changes to logon scripts and System Policies cannot be made at a Microsoft Windows NT 4.0 export server. You should make administrators of affected systems aware of this change as part of your upgrade plans.

You can configure the LBRIDGE.CMD script to use either xcopy or robocopy. Robocopy is another utility found in the Windows 2000 Resource Kit. It is the preferred utility to use because it can determine if files have been deleted in the source folder. If a script has been deleted from the source folder, it will be deleted in target folders.

You need to maintain this bridge between replication systems during the upgrade. You should configure the LBRIDGE.CMD script to run every two hours in Scheduled Tasks in the Windows 2000 Control Panel. This is illustrated in Figure 5.10.

Figure 5.10 LBRIDGE.CMD Script Schedule

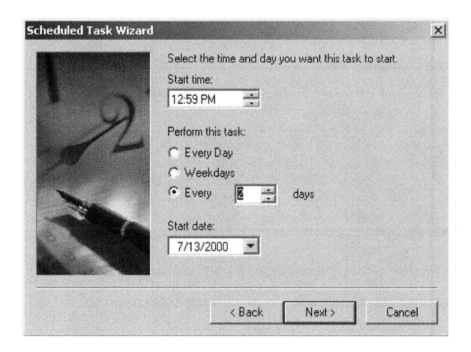

As your upgrade proceeds, you will need to reconfigure LAN Manager replication. When you upgrade an import server to Windows 2000, you will need to remove the upgraded server from the list of servers to which the export server replicates.

Planning for Replication Upgrade Traffic

You need to plan carefully to minimize the impact of Active Directory replication traffic over slow links during a domain upgrade. Controlling replication traffic is one method of maintaining network performance during the upgrade.

 Note: Include definitions for all required sites and subnets for the network in your Active Directory design plan.

You use sites to control Active Directory replication. You must plan to create your sites, subnets, and site links after you install the first domain controller in the forest. The creation of sites after the first domain controller in the forest is installed provides you with a mechanism to minimize the impact of the upgrade-related replication traffic during your migration. Once you have associated the sites with their respective subnets, an upgraded domain controller will automatically be placed in the correct site. The placement is based on the controller's IP address. By scheduling and configuring replication between sites, you can effectively control upgrade-related replication traffic.

 Tip: Carefully defining site boundaries is key to managing replication traffic.

You can create the sites, subnets, and site links that are defined in your Active Directory design after you have upgraded the first domain controller in the forest. By creating these objects early in the upgrade process, you ensure that the replication traffic related to the domain upgrade is controlled by the site topology.

After creating sites and subnets, you link the subnets to the proper sites. Once this has been accomplished, all further upgrades will automatically place the upgraded domain controller within the predetermined site. Defining site links allows replication to occur between sites as soon as domain controllers are installed at the site.

Note: A newly created Windows 2000 domain controller sends all replication information in compressed format. The compressed format is used even if the replication occurs between domain controllers in the same site.

While Microsoft Windows NT 4.0 domain controllers that are configured to authenticate clients and provide logon scripts and System Policies are still present in the domain, it is important to maintain LAN Manager replication.

Authentication

One result of upgrading a domain to Windows 2000 is the availability of multiple authentication methods. In an upgraded domain, Windows 2000 authentication is available in addition to LAN Manager and NT LAN Manager (NTLM) authentication. Your organization may wish to optimize the network for Windows 2000 authentication.

Planning for Authentication Traffic

Understanding the network servers used during the authentication process is key to optimizing the network for Windows 2000 authentication. You can ensure that authentication performance is maintained by locating these services so that they are locally accessible to clients on the network.

Authentication and Network Services

- The authentication process of site-aware users employs one or more of the following network services:

- DHCP server

- DNS server

- Domain controller

- Global Catalog (GC) server

The absence of any of these services at a remote site may result in a failed authentication. Another potential consequence of not having all the authentication services available at a remote site is an authentication that succeeds using cached credentials from a previously successful authentication.

Authentication Optimization

Logon traffic will be affected by the upgrade. When planning to minimize the effect, you should consider the following actions:

- Deploying all sites and subnets in your Active Directory design
- Placing a domain controller in each site with clients that are Active Directory-aware
- Placing a Global Catalog server at remote sites
- Providing WINS servers for legacy clients not running Directory Service (DS) client software

When you deploy all sites, all domain controllers are placed into the appropriate site based on their IP address. Clients that are site-aware will be able to authenticate with local domain controllers that exist in their site. A site-aware client is a computer running Windows 2000 or Windows 95 or 98 with the DS client installed.

To ensure that authentication for all site-aware clients will occur in the client's local site, you should place a domain controller in each site where these clients reside. Placing a domain controller in each such site also ensures that the site-aware clients will register any changes to Active Directory with a local domain controller.

When you place a Global Catalog server at a remote site, you ensure that the clients at that site receive full logon authentication. Client membership in universal groups cannot be determined without a Global Catalog server. A client logging in when no Global Catalog server is present may be given an incomplete access token or may be granted logon access with cached credentials.

 Note: If you are deploying Active Directory in a single, native mode domain, a Global Catalog server is not required to determine universal group membership. All membership data will be stored in the local domain partition of Active Directory.

At remote sites where a local domain controller does not yet exist, a WINS server will be required to allow authentication by domain controllers at remote subnets. WINS allows clients at remote sites to connect to domain controllers. As an alternative, you can populate the LMHOSTS configuration file with domain controller information.

Authenticating Network Services

You need to carefully plan the placement of authenticating network services for a site to optimize the authentication process.

DHCP Server

The DHCP server provides IP addresses to requesting client computers. The IP addresses are used to determine the site in which a client computer is located.

DNS Server

The DNS server provides Service (SRV) resource records that are used to determine a domain controller that is located in the requesting client's local site.

Domain Controller

A Windows 2000 domain controller located at a remote site provides local access to Active Directory for authentication. The remote Windows 2000 domain controller also provides access to any updates.

Global Catalog Server

An authenticating domain controller in native mode determines universal group membership by contacting a Global Catalog server when building the access token. If the user logon name is in the form of a User Principal Name (UPN), the authenticating domain controller will query the Global Catalog server to determine the domain and account with which the UPN is associated.

Security Standards

It is vital that you define a comprehensive strategy to maintain security during your domain upgrade. Upgrading to Windows 2000 affects nearly every aspect of the network's security infrastructure. To take advantage of new Active Directory features, you need to alter or reorganize the following items:

- User accounts

- Group accounts

- Trust relationships

- Security templates

 Note: Microsoft Windows NT Service Pack 4 introduced security templates with the Security Configuration Editor.

Maintaining Security during an Upgrade

To maintain security during an upgrade, you must consider the following factors in your migration plans:

- Migrating resource access components

- Migrating trust relationships

- Planning for security policy application

- Defining a strategy to maintain user profiles

- Supporting clients

Your domain upgrade strategy must include maintaining and managing security levels during the upgrade.

Maintaining Resource Security

Access to resources is provided by Discretionary Access Control Lists (DACLs) under both Microsoft Windows NT 4.0 and Windows 2000. Due to the way that the components of resource access are maintained, a Windows 2000 upgrade should not affect access to resources. No additional planning should be necessary.

Your migration plan needs to address migrating trust relationships. You need to define methods that will translate existing trust relationships into Active Directory domains. By default, Windows 2000 trusts are two-way and transitive in nature. Old Microsoft Windows NT 4.0 trust relationships are translated into new relationships within the Active Directory domain structure during the upgrade. When you upgrade a domain and join it to the forest, the existing one-way trusts in the Microsoft Windows NT 4.0 domain are automatically reinterpreted and implemented, as Windows 2000 transitive trusts.

Depending upon the order in which your domains are upgraded and the parent-child domain relationships in the Active Directory domain hierarchy, some of the Windows NT 4.0 one-way trusts become two-way transitive trusts while others will become transitive shortcut trust relationships. This is illustrated in Figure 5.11.

Figure 5.11 Trust Relationships Migration

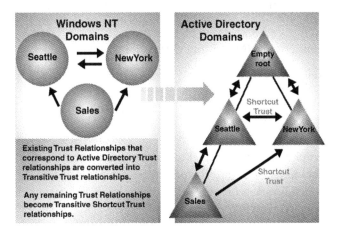

An existing trust relationship that maps to a default Active Directory trust relationship will be converted into a transitive trust relationship. Any remaining trust relationship will be converted into a transitive shortcut trust relationship. Some   one-way trusts in a Microsoft Windows NT 4.0 domain were created to help authentication performance. This type of trust is not one of the default Windows 2000 forest trusts, and so it will be represented as a shortcut trust in Windows 2000.

Two-way transitive trusts will be established between an upgraded child domain and its parent when the child domain is upgraded. A domain that is upgraded, as the root of a separate tree, will also be linked by a two-way transitive trust. Any existing one-way trust that does not map to a default Windows 2000 trust relationship will be maintained but will be reinterpreted as a shortcut trust. No additional steps to migrate trust relationships are required.

 Note: Default transitive trust relationships established between domains in a forest cannot be deleted. However, you can delete shortcut trusts.

Establishing Security Policy Application

Predefined default security templates are used by Windows 2000 for newly installed computers. You do not need to apply additional security settings to increase the base security for new computers running Windows 2000. The configuration settings in the default security templates define the following items:

- New Technology File System (NTFS) file permissions

- Registry permissions

- Registry configuration entries

- User rights

The default security templates are not applied to servers and domain controllers that are upgraded to Windows 2000. You should include steps to apply these templates in your upgrade plan. By applying these templates, you take advantage of new security features while maintaining consistency between upgraded and newly installed servers.

Computers with a new install of Windows 2000 will have a higher default security configuration than computers that have been upgraded. You should consider applying the basic templates to all upgraded computers to maintain consistent security across the domain. You should also consider using the default security templates to enhance domain security even if the newly installed domain controller is not part of an upgraded domain.

To ensure that security templates are consistent across all computers running Windows 2000 and that domain security is optimized, your upgrade plan should address the following factors:

- Identifying the proper security template for each server role

- Determining a method to deploy the proper basic security template

- Ensuring continued long-term application of the basic security template

You need to identify and apply the proper security template for each server role. This ensures that the security settings are consistent between upgraded computers and computers with a new installation of Windows 2000.

 Note: The file BASICDC.INF is the basic security template for domain controllers. The file BASICSV.INF is the basic security template for servers.

You need to define a method of deploying the proper basic security template. One way you can apply the basic security template to an upgraded computer is by using the Security Configuration and Analysis snap-in in the Microsoft Management Console (MMC), as illustrated in Figure 5.12.

Figure 5.12 MMC Security Configuration and Analysis

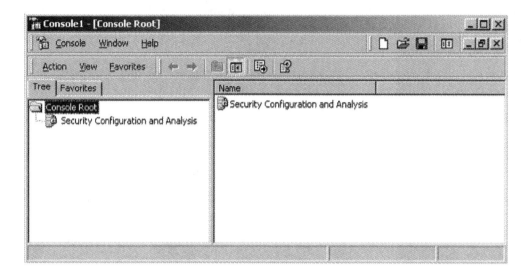

Another method you can use to apply the basic security template to an upgraded computer is to import the basic template into the Default Domain Controllers Policy for Group Policy. The Group Policy snap-in is shown in Figure 5.13.

Figure 5.13 Group Policy Snap-in

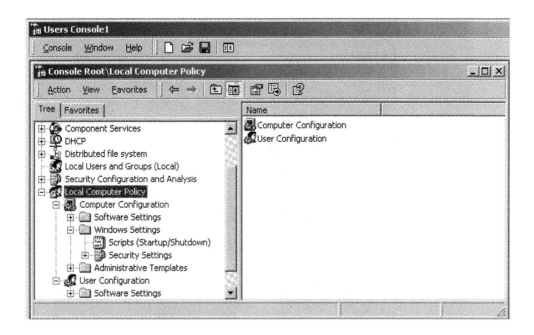

Figure 5.14 illustrates importing a security template using the Import Policy form.

Figure 5.14 Import Security Template

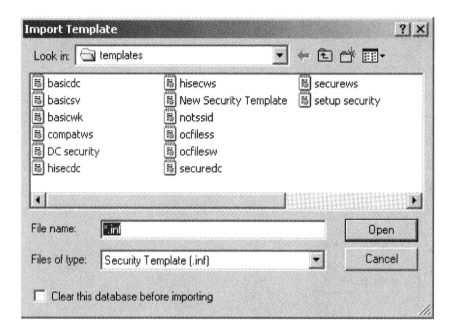

One way to apply the basic security templates directly to upgraded computers is by using the Security Configuration Toolset. Another method is to deploy these security policies within the Group Policy object framework. The Security Templates console is illustrated in Figure 5.15.

Figure 5.15 Security Templates Console

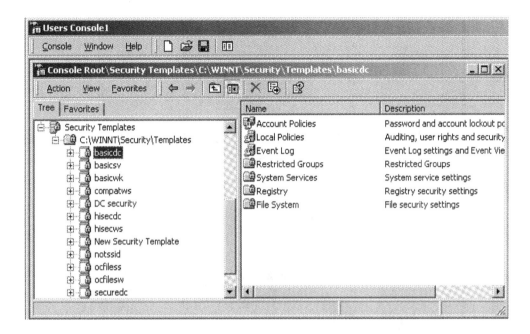

You need to ensure the continuing long-term application of the basic security template. You can ensure that any settings in Group Policy take precedence over local settings that are configured on a computer running Windows 2000 by applying the basic template through Group Policy. Group Policy takes precedence over local security settings. Due to the order in which Group Policies are processed, Group Policy will take precedence over a Windows 2000 computer's local settings.

Resource Access Components

During the domain upgrade, you need to maintain the following resource access components:

- Security Identifiers (SIDs)
- Group membership
- Share permissions and New Technology File System (NTFS) permissions

- Registry permissions

- Trust relationships

During a domain upgrade, all user and group SIDs are maintained. The only instances that a primary SID will change are listed in the following:

- When an account is moved between domains

- During a restructure

- When security principal is deleted and recreated with the same name

The use of a SID in identifying resources is illustrated in Figure 5.16.

Figure 5.16 Resource Access through a SID

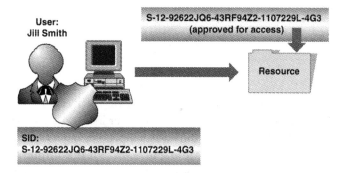

All user accounts will retain the same group membership attributes after the upgrade is completed. All NTFS and share permissions will be maintained with the same groups and users referenced within the DACL during the upgrade. All registry permissions will be maintained as well. Any trust that exists with other down-level Microsoft Windows NT 4.0 domains will continue to be recognized by upgraded domain controllers.

Managing Resource Access

In a Microsoft Windows NT 4.0 domain, you cannot add user accounts and groups that are in resource domains to the DACLs for resources that are located in account domains. You are prevented from doing so by the nature of the one-way trust relationships in a Microsoft Windows NT 4.0 domain.

When you upgrade to a Windows 2000 domain, the one-way trust relationships are translated into two-way trust relationships. Permissions and administrative group memberships are not altered during the upgrade. However, the new two-way transitive trust relationships allow administrators to access accounts that they could not previously access. When a Microsoft Windows NT 4.0 domain is upgraded, the newly implemented transitive trusts allow users and groups from any domain in the forest to be recognized by any member computer in the forest and to be included in groups or DACLs.

The change in the trust relationships will not affect the previous security assignments. However, users and groups will now be able to be assigned access to resources that were not accessible with the one-way trust relationships inherent in Microsoft Windows NT 4.0.

You can prevent any security assignments from changing by auditing memberships in all administrative groups to ensure that no new accounts have been added to the memberships. If you maintain membership in administrative groups, you prevent any users without administrative privileges from suddenly gaining these new access privileges. You should also review the important resources in DACLs. Reviewing your DACLs for all resources would be time-prohibitive. Instead, focus on key resources for the organization. If you concentrate on the key resources, you can confirm that security for those resources has not been compromised during or after the upgrade.

Vocabulary

Review the following terms in preparation for the certification exam.

Term	Description
BDC	A Backup Domain Controller is a computer running Microsoft Windows NT 4.0 or earlier that maintains a copy of the domain's directory database.
DACL	A Discretionary Access Control List is part of an object's security descriptor that grants or denies access to the object by specific users or groups.
DDNS	Dynamic Domain Name System is a service that allows clients with a dynamically assigned address to register directly with a server running the DNS service. It also allows such clients to update the DNS table dynamically.
DHCP	The Dynamic Host Configuration Protocol is a networking protocol that provides dynamic configuration of IP addresses for client computers. It ensures that address conflicts do not occur and provides centralized management of address allocation.

Term	Description
DS	Directory Service client software is a Windows 95 or 98 add-on that makes Windows 95 or 98 computers Active Directory-aware.
FRS	The File Replication Service is used by distributed file systems to synchronize content, and by Active Directory Sites and Services to replicate topological and Global Catalog information between domain controllers.
GC	The Global Catalog is a highly optimized Active Directory service that stores directory information from all source domains in a single location. Users submit queries to the GC to obtain information about objects in the network regardless of their physical or logical location.
IETF	The Internet Engineering Task Force is a large, open community of network designers, operators, researchers, vendors, and others concerned with the evolution of the architecture of the Internet.
IP	The Internet Protocol is a routable protocol belonging to the TCP/IP suite. IP is responsible for packet addressing and routing as well as deconstructing and later reconstructing of IP packets.

Term	Description
JScript	Java Script is a cross-platform programming language from Sun Microsystems that can be used to create animations and interactive features.
KDC	A Key Distribution Center is a network service that is used to supply session tickets and temporary session keys used in the Kerberos authentication protocol. Under Windows 2000, the KDC uses Active Directory to manage sensitive account information for user accounts.
LAN	A Local Area Network is a collection of computers connected on a network and in close physical proximity to each other so that devices such as a router are not required for interconnectivity.
LDAP	The Lightweight Directory Access Protocol is a directory service protocol that runs directly over TCP/IP. LDAP is the primary access protocol for Active Directory.
mixed environment	A mixed environment is a Windows 2000 domain that contains pre-Windows 2000 clients or servers. The domain can be in either mixed or native mode.
mixed mode	Mixed mode is the default domain mode setting for Windows 2000 domain controllers. It allows Microsoft Windows NT 4.0 and Windows 2000 domain controllers to coexist in a network.
MMC	The Microsoft Management Console provides a common structure in which administrative tools (snap-ins) can run.

Term	Description
NetBIOS	The Network Basic Input/Output System is an Application Programming Interface (API) used by computers on a LAN. It provides a set of functions that provide access to low-level network services.
NTLM	Microsoft Windows NT LAN Manager is a security protocol used for pass-through network authentication, remote file access, and authenticated Remote Procedure Call (RPC) connections to earlier versions of Windows.
NTFS	New Technology File System is a file system that is designed for Windows 2000 and supports many features, such as file system security, Unicode, recoverability, and long file names.
OU	An Organizational Unit is a logical container within a domain. You use an OU to organize objects for easier administration and access.
PDC	A Primary Domain Controller is a computer running Microsoft Windows NT 3.51 or 4.0 that is the primary storehouse for domain data including the directory database.
RADIUS	The Remote Authentication Dial-in User Service provides authentication and accounting services for distributed dial-up networking.

Term	Description
RAS	The Remote Access Service is a Microsoft Windows NT 4.0 service that provides remote networking access. It is used by system administrators who must monitor and manage network servers at remote locations as well as by remote users to access the network.
RFC	A Request For Comment is a document published by the Internet Engineering Task Force (IETF) requesting comments on a proposed standard affecting network protocols, programs, and concepts.
RPC	A Remote Procedure Call is a message-passing facility allowing a distributed application to call services available on network machines. RPC is used during remote administration of computers.
RRAS	The Routing and Remote Access Service is a service that provides remote access through telephone lines or Virtual Private Networks (VPNs). RRAS under Windows 2000 is also a full-feature software router.
SID	A Security Identifier is a unique name that identifies a user, group of users, or a computer.
site-aware client	A site-aware client is a computer running Windows 2000 or Windows 95 or 98 with the DS client installed.

Term	Description
SRV	A Service resource record is used in a zone to register and locate TCP/IP services. It is used in Windows 2000 to locate domain controllers for Active Directory services.
SYSVOL	The System Volume stores the server's copy of the domain's public files. These files are replicated between all domain controllers in a domain.
TCP/IP	The Transmission Control Protocol/Internet Protocol is a set of software protocols for networking that are widely used on the Internet. The TCP/IP protocol provides a communication medium across interconnected networks with diverse hardware platforms and operating systems.
UPN	A User Principal Name consists of a user account name and a domain name that identify the user's logon name and the domain in which the user's account is located.
VBScript	The Visual Basic Scripting language is based on the Visual Basic programming language, but it is similar to JScript and much simpler.

Term	Description
VPN	A Virtual Private Network is a logically constructed WAN that uses existing public transmission mediums. A VPN allows an organization to emulate a private WAN connection.
WINS	Windows Internet Name Service is a software service that maps IP addresses to computer names permitting users to access resources by name rather than IP address.

In Brief

If you want to...	Then do this...
Import a security template into a security database	1. In the **Security Configuration and Analysis** console, right-click **Security Configuration and Analysis**. 2. Open or create a working security database. 3. Choose **Import Template** and then select a security template file. 4. Choose **Open**.
To integrate LAN Manager replication service and FRS during an upgrade	Complete the following tasks: • Identify all Microsoft Windows NT 4.0 import and export servers • Create a bridge between the Microsoft Windows NT 4.0 scripts directory and the Windows 2000 NETLOGON share • Maintain the bridge between replication systems • Reconfigure the LAN Manager replication service during the upgrade
Create and maintain a bridge between LAN Manager replication service and FRS	Configure the LBRIDGE.CMD script to run every two hours in Scheduled Tasks in the Windows 2000 Control Panel
Manually add the Everyone account to the Pre-Windows 2000 Compatible Access local group	Type the command **net localgroup "Pre-Windows 2000 Compatible Access" Everyone /add**

If you want to...	Then do this...
Grant the built-in account Everyone permissions to read user object attributes	While configuring the Active Directory Installation wizard, choose Permission compatible with pre-Windows 2000 server.
Determine if NetBIOS name resolution is taking place on the WINS server	Examine the Successful Queries/Sec and Queries/Sec counters in the Performance console administrative tool. If both counters have a value of zero, then the WINS server is not resolving NetBIOS names.
Disable NetBIOS on a Windows 2000 client	From within the WINS property page, choose Advanced TCP/IP Settings for a network adapter, and then select Disable NetBIOS over TCP/IP.

Lesson 5 Activities

Complete the following activities to better prepare you for the certification exam.

1. Discuss why robocopy is the preferred utility to use with LBRIDGE.CMD.

2. Describe the largest risk during a domain upgrade.

3. Describe how an SRV record is used.

4. Define when you would want to employ Active Directory integrated zones.

5. Describe how to upgrade Microsoft Windows NT 4.0 DNS services to Windows 2000 DNS services.

6. Describe the conditions necessary to discontinue the use of WINS.

7. Describe how to determine if NetBIOS name resolution is taking place on a WINS server.

8. Discuss the effect of a Windows 2000 domain upgrade on Microsoft Windows NT 4.0 trusts.

9. List the resource access components that you will need to maintain during the domain upgrade.

10. Describe the definitions provided by the configuration settings in the default security templates.

Answers to Lesson 5 Activities

1. Robocopy is the preferred utility to use because it can determine if files have been deleted in the source folder. If a script has been deleted from the source folder, it will be deleted in target folders.

2. Perhaps the largest risk during a domain upgrade is the potential for interruptions to network operations.

3. The Service (SRV) resource record specifies the location of specific protocol and domain servers. Windows 2000 relies on DNS using SRV records as a locator service. Clients use the service to locate important Windows 2000 services including the following:

    - Domain controllers

    - Global Catalog servers

    - Kerberos Key Distribution Center (KDC) servers

    - Lightweight Directory Access Protocol (LDAP)

4. If you have any DNS domain that will contain Active Directory resource records, then it is recommended that you employ Active Directory integrated zones.

5. There are two ways in which you can upgrade your Microsoft Windows NT DNS servers. You can upgrade the existing Microsoft Windows NT 4.0 server that contains the DNS primary zone to Windows 2000, configuring the zone for dynamic updates or you can perform the following actions:

    - Install a new Windows 2000 server

    - Configure the new server as the secondary DNS server for the existing zone

    - Accomplish the zone transfer

    - Reverse roles so that the new server becomes the primary DNS server

    - Configure the zone for dynamic updates

6. While a Windows 2000 network does not require WINS, you should continue its use until you are certain that all computers and applications on the network can operate without referencing NetBIOS names or using the NetBIOS name resolution services.

7. You determine if NetBIOS name resolution is taking place on the WINS server by examining the Successful Queries/Sec and Queries/Sec counters in the Performance console administrative tool. If both counters have a value of zero, then the WINS server is not resolving NetBIOS names.

8. When you upgrade to a Windows 2000 domain, the Microsoft Windows NT 4.0 one-way trust relationships are translated into two-way, transitive trust relationships.

9. During the domain upgrade, you need to maintain the following resource access components:

    - Security Identifiers (SIDs)

    - Group membership

    - Share permissions and NTFS permissions

    - Registry permissions

    - Trust relationships

10. The configuration settings in the default security templates define the following items:

    - NTFS file permissions

    - Registry permissions

    - Registry configuration entries

    - User rights

Lesson 5 Quiz

These questions test your knowledge of features, vocabulary, procedures, and syntax.

1. What is the effect on user-based logon scripts stored on the NETLOGON share when a Window NT 4.0 domain controller is upgraded?

    A. The scripts will be available when a client authenticates

    B. The scripts are migrated to Group Policy

    C. There is no effect

    D. FRS will synchronize the contents of the NETLOGON folder with all Windows 2000 domain controllers

2. What will happen during the first restart of a newly upgraded computer?

    A. WINS will fail

    B. WINS will replicate its services on the upgraded computer

    C. WINS will launch the Active Directory installation wizard

    D. WINS will automatically convert its database into a newer version of the database

3. When a Microsoft Windows NT 4.0 domain is upgraded, what will the newly implemented transitive trusts allow?

    A. Free access to any resource associated with a non-Windows server

    B. Users and groups from any domain in the forest to be recognized by any member computer in the forest

    C. Administrators to access accounts that they could not previously access

    D. Users and groups from any domain in the forest to be included in groups or DACLs

4. What is the name of the file that is the basic security template for domain controllers?

    A. BASICSV.INF

    B. DCSECURE.INF

    C. DCSECTMP.INF

    D. BASICDC.INF

5. What is the purpose of the SRV record?

    A. Specify the location of specific protocol and domain servers

    B. Indicate the services that a user has permission to access

    C. Maintain a service history record

    D. Provide administrators with an easy to use maintenance tool

6. Where can Active Directory integrated zones be implemented?

    A. Only on member servers in a child domain

    B. Only on domain controllers

    C. Only on the PDC emulator

    D. On any DNS server in the network

7. What is a site-aware client?

    A. A non-Windows DNS server with SRV and DDNS support

    B. A client computer with a static IP address

    C. A computer running Windows 2000 or Windows 95 or 98 with the DS client installed

    D. A client computer that provides LDAP services

8. Under what conditions is a Global Catalog server not required?

    A. You remove all non-Windows 2000 clients from the network

    B. You deploy a resource only subnet

    C. You deploy Active Directory in a single, native mode domain

    D. You deploy a domain with a single domain controller

9. When should you upgrade your LAN Manager export server if it is a BDC?

    A. You must upgrade it before you upgrade any other BDC

    B. You must upgrade it simultaneously with all other BDCs

    C. You must promote it to PDC before you upgrade it

    D. You must ensure that it is the last BDC to be upgraded

10. What is the default nature of Windows 2000 trusts?

    A. One-way

    B. Transitive

    C. Two-way

    D. Implicit

Answers to Lesson 5 Quiz

1. Answers A, C, and D are correct. When a Window NT 4.0 domain controller is upgraded, there is no effect on user-based logon scripts stored on the NETLOGON share of the controller. The logon scripts will be available when a client authenticates. FRS will synchronize the contents of the NETLOGON folder with all Windows 2000 domain controllers.

    Answer B is incorrect. The scripts are not automatically migrated to Group Policy.

2. Answers A and D are correct. During the first restart of a newly upgraded computer, WINS will fail but it will also automatically convert its database into a newer version of the database.

    Answers B and C are incorrect. WINS will not replicate itself nor will it launch the Active Directory Installation Wizard.

3. Answers B, C and D are correct. When a Microsoft Windows NT 4.0 domain is upgraded, the newly implemented transitive trusts will allow users and groups from any domain in the forest to be recognized by any member computer in the forest and to be included in groups or DACLs. The new trusts will also allow administrators to access accounts that they could not previously access.

    Answer A is incorrect. Free access to resources is never permitted by default in a Windows 2000 network environment.

4. Answer D is correct. The file BASICDC.INF is the basic security template for domain controllers.

    Answers A, B and C are incorrect. BASICSV.INF is the basic security template for servers. The other two files are fictitious.

5. Answer A is correct. The Service (SRV) resource record specifies the location of specific protocol and domain servers.

    Answers B, C and D are incorrect. A SRV record does not indicate user access permissions, maintain a service history record nor provide an easy-to-use maintenance tool for system administrators.

6. Answer B is correct. Active Directory integrated zones can only be implemented on domain controllers.

    Answers A, C and D are incorrect. Active Directory integrated zones cannot be implemented on member servers nor on non-Windows 2000 DNS servers in the network. Active Directory integrated zones are not limited to the PDC emulator.

7. Answer C is correct. A site-aware client is a computer running Windows 2000 or Windows 95 or 98 with the DS client installed.

    Answers A, B and D are incorrect. Upgrading a non-Windows DNS server with SRC and DDNS support does not make the computer site-aware. Computers with static IP addresses or that provide LDAP services are site-aware only if they are running Windows 2000 or have the DS client installed.

8. Answer C is correct. If you are deploying Active Directory in a single, native mode domain, a Global Catalog server is not required to determine universal group membership. All membership data will be stored in the local domain partition of Active Directory.

    Answers A, B and D are incorrect. Removing all non-Windows 2000 clients from the network will not remove the requirement for a Global Catalog server. As long as your network is in mixed mode or has more than one domain, you will need a Global Catalog server. Deploying a resource only subnet or having a single domain controller does not remove the need for a Global Catalog server.

9. Answer D is correct. If your LAN Manager export server is a BDC, you must ensure that it is the last BDC to be upgraded

    Answers A, B and C are incorrect. You do not need to promote your LAN Manager export server to a PDC before upgrading it. You should not upgrade it before you upgrade any other BDC nor should you upgrade it simultaneously with other BDCs.

10. Answers B and C are correct. By default, Windows 2000 trusts are transitive and two-way in nature.

    Answers A and D are incorrect. Windows 2000 trusts are not one-way or implicit by default.

Lesson 6: User Profiles and Trust Relationships

Your domain upgrade plan must address maintaining the current standards of the existing network environment. You will need to ensure that user profiles are maintained and that client support is uninterrupted. To accomplish this, your upgrade plan must address those issues that relate to the network user and the environment in which that user works on a day-to-day basis. It is important for you to understand Windows 2000 trust relationships and how they apply to network, performance and reliability. In this regard, you must evaluate your current application programs that are critical to your organization. Planning ahead will ensure that your organization's operations are not interrupted or degraded during the upgrade.

After completing this lesson, you should have a better understanding of the following topics:

- User profiles
- Client support
- Trust relationships
- Application upgrades
- Directory information
- Network performance

User Profiles

Your domain upgrade plan must define a strategy that maintains current user profiles. In Windows NT 4.0 and in Windows 2000, user profiles store configuration information for individual users. The information stored in these profiles includes the following:

- Configuration information

- Registry settings

- User associated files

During a domain upgrade, the Security Identifiers (SIDs) of user accounts in the domain will not change. Since SIDs remain constant, the accessibility to both local and roaming user profiles are maintained during the upgrade. Therefore, it is not necessary to add further planning tasks to your design structure to support user profiles during the upgrade.

Maintaining Local Profiles

A local user profile ensures that when a user logs onto a client computer, the user always receives his or her individual desktop settings and connections. Local profiles provide an individual environment for each user of that computer. When a desktop setting is modified, the user profile changes when the user logs off. The next time the user logs onto the computer, the user's recent desktop settings will be restored. This concept is illustrated in Figure 6.1.

Figure 6.1 User Profiles

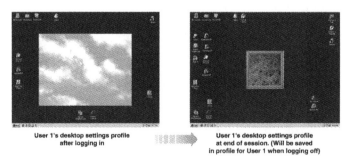

User 1's desktop settings profile
after logging in

User 1's desktop settings profile
at end of session. (Will be saved
in profile for User 1 when logging off)

After you upgrade a Windows NT 4.0 computer to Windows 2000, the Windows NT 4.0 local user profile is stored in the systemroot\profiles\%username% folder as shown in Figure 6.2.

Figure 6.2 Windows 2000 User Profile Directory

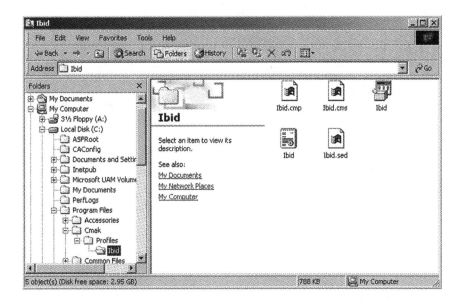

A computer that is upgraded from Windows 95 or Windows 98 will store local profile information in the C:\Documents and Settings\%username% folder as shown in Figure 6.3.

Figure 6.3 Windows 95/98 User Profile Directory

During the upgrade to Windows 2000, all permissions assigned to the local profile folders are maintained.

Managing Roaming Profiles

Within an organization, a user might work at multiple computers or multiple locations. Roaming profiles support these users. A roaming profile resides on a network server so it is always available to the user, no matter where the user logs into the domain. A roaming profile, like a local profile, restores the desktop settings and connections to the user. However, the roaming profile is available to the user, no matter where he or she logs on.

When a user logs on, the roaming user profile is copied from the network server to the client computer and the profile settings are then applied to that computer. The first time a user logs on from a computer, all the user specific documents and settings are copied to that computer. If the user logs on from the same computer later, the contents of the locally stored user profile are compared to the roaming user profile. Any changes are replicated to the local computer. However, items that have not changed are not copied to the new computer, which reduces replication traffic and speeds the logon process.

When a user changes settings during a session, the changes are copied back to the server where the roaming profile is stored when the user logs off. This process is shown in Figure 6.4.

Figure 6.4 Maintaining Roaming User Profiles

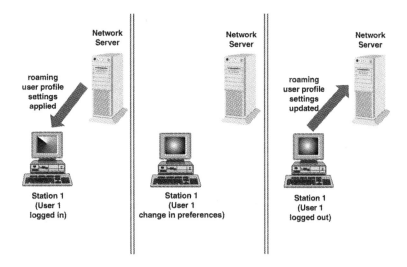

When using Windows NT 4.0, roaming user profiles are configured in an individual user's property pages. When the Primary Domain Controller (PDC) is upgraded to Windows 2000, the roaming user profiles migrate to Windows 2000 security properties. After the upgrade, the roaming user profiles are available from either a Windows NT 4.0 or Windows 2000 client. As shown in Figure 6.5, any settings that are Windows 2000-specific will be ignored on a Windows NT 4.0 system, and Windows NT 4.0-specific settings will be ignored on a Windows 2000 system.

Figure 6.5 Roaming User Profile Platform Specific Settings

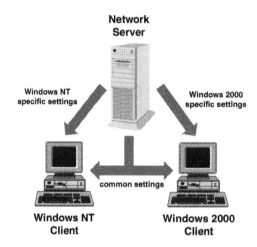

Since roaming profile settings are platform specific, the user who logs onto one or more Windows NT 4.0 clients will receive the same profile each time he or she logs on to a Windows NT 4.0 computer. The same user can log onto Windows 2000 clients and may have a different desktop on the Windows 2000 computer then on a Windows NT 4.0 computer. Every time users log on to a Windows 2000 client, they will receive the same Windows 2000 profile. Users can maintain the same profiles whether they log on at a Windows NT 4.0 client or a Windows 2000 client.

Supporting Clients during an Upgrade

Your domain upgrade plan must include a strategy that minimizes the impact on users with roaming profiles. These users must be notified when the server that maintains their profiles is upgraded. They will need to know that any changes they have made during this time will not be maintained. They also need to be informed that they should not log onto the network from a computer they have not used before. If they do so, they will be presented with the default desktop and connection settings for that computer. None of their modifications will be restored and any changes they make to their desktop or connection settings on the new computer will not be maintained. This concept is shown in Figure 6.6.

Note: Roaming user profiles are unavailable during a server upgrade.

Figure 6.6 Unavailable Roaming Profiles

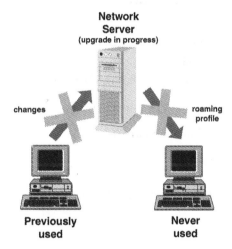

After an upgrade is completed, a user's roaming profile and local profile will again be accessible to that user.

Maintaining Security during an Upgrade

It is important to note that the user profile, regardless of whether it is local or roaming, does not contain security-specific data since the profile does not contain the user's password. This means that the inaccessibility of a user's roaming profile during the server upgrade will have no impact on overall network security. However, it could mean that several network connections are not available to that user.

Client Support

Several Active Directory features are not available to Windows 95, Windows 98, and Windows NT 4.0 clients that are supported by Windows 2000 Professional. When you upgrade your network to Windows 2000, Windows 95, Windows 98, and Windows NT 4.0 clients are not automatically enhanced to take advantage of these features. However, you can upgrade Windows 95 and Windows 98 clients to take advantage of some of the Active Directory features by installing Directory Services (DS) client software.

Supporting DS Client Functionality

If you have Windows 95 or Windows 98 client computers that you cannot upgrade to Windows 2000 because of hardware compatibility issues, you can still use these computers and take advantage of Active Directory services by installing DS client software. DS client software supports many Active Directory features and allows the client to take advantage of the following aspects:

● Use the fault-tolerant Distributed File System (DFS)

● Change a password on any domain controller

● Search Active Directory services

Note: You must install Internet Explorer 4.01 or later and enable the Active Desktop component on Windows 95 client computers before you install the DS client software. If you do not install Internet Explorer, the DS client setup wizard will not run.

Deploying DS Client Software

You can deploy the DS client software to client computers by using the Microsoft Systems Management Server (SMS) to create separate installation packages for the DS client on Windows 95, Windows 98, and Windows NT 4.0 computers. Through SMS, the installation packages will be sent only to client computers that have the matching operating system installed.

Trust Relationships

Windows NT 4.0 networks employ one-way non-transitive trusts. A one-way trust relationship is non-transitive. This means that if domain "A" trusts domain "B," domain "B" does not automatically trust domain "A" (Figure 6.7). Explicit one-way trust relationships are manually created. In a large network environment, many one-way trusts are created and maintained.

Figure 6.7 Windows NT 4.0 One-way Non-transitive Trusts

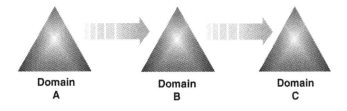

Domain A   Domain B   Domain C

To provide connectivity with down-level domains, Windows 2000 Active Directory supports Windows NT 4.0 one-way non-transitive trusts. These trusts are also used in a Windows 2000 network to optimize communication with domains in other trees (Figure 6.8).

Figure 6.8 One-Way Non-transitive Trusts Between Domains in Separate Trees

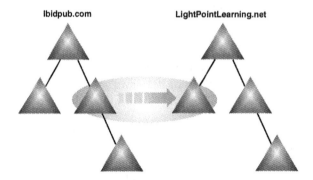

In a two-way trust relationship, if domain "A" trusts domain "B," then domain "B" trusts domain "A." In a transitive trust relationship, if domain "A" trusts domain "B" and domain "B" trusts domain "C," then domain "A" trusts domain "C" as well. Therefore, in a two-way transitive trust relationship, if domain "A" trusts domain "B" and domain "B" trusts domain "C," then not only will domain "A" trust domain "C," but domain "C" will also trust domain "A" (Figure 6.9).

Figure 6.9 Windows 2000 Two-way Transitive Trusts

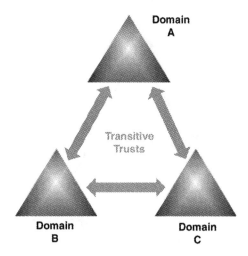

The default relationship in Windows 2000 is a two-way transitive trust. It is the default relationship between parent and children domains within a tree, as well as between the top-level domains in a forest. Trust relationships are maintained automatically between domains in a tree.

When you create a new child domain, a two-way transitive trust is automatically established with the parent domain. Since the trust is two-way and transitive, the new child domain automatically trusts all the other domains in the tree and they trust the new child domain. This means that any user in any domain of the tree can access a resource to which they have been granted permissions, regardless of where the domain of the tree is located, as shown in Figure 6.10.

Figure 6.10 Accessing Windows 2000 Resources in a Tree

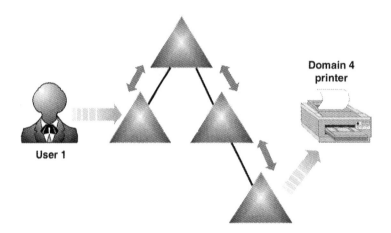

During your upgrade, any Windows NT 4.0 trusts that can be mapped to a default Windows 2000 trust are converted automatically into a transitive trust relationship. Any existing one-way trusts that do not map to a default Windows 2000 trust are maintained and converted into a shortcut trust. A shortcut trust, sometimes called a cross-link trust, is an explicit one-way transitive trust relationship.

Managing Trust Relationships

When a user in one domain requests access to a network resource in another domain in the tree, the domain controller in the user's domain must communicate with the domain controller of the resource's tree. If the two domains are not in a parent-child relationship, then the communication must be routed through additional domain controllers residing higher in the tree's domain hierarchy, that are between the user's domain and the resource's domain. This is illustrated in Figure 6.11.

Figure 6.11 Resource Authentication across a Tree

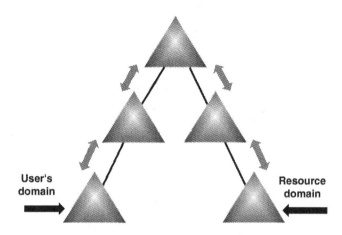

Each additional hop that the authentication traffic takes will increase the likelihood of an error. In addition, each hop represents additional authentication traffic in the tree and may have to traverse slow links. In this situation, you can reduce network authentication traffic by creating shortcut trusts between any two domains in the tree. When you create shortcut trusts, the domains can now communicate directly with each other as shown in Figure 6.12.

Figure 6.12 Shortcut Trusts in a Tree

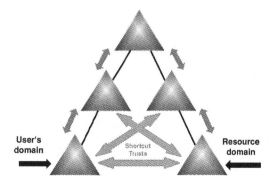

If you have a forest with multiple trees, each tree root domain has the default two-way transitive trust relationship with the root of the forest. Recall that all tree root domains are considered to be the children of the root domain of the forest. This means that authentication traffic from one tree to another must pass through the forest root unless you create shortcut trusts between the tree root domains. If you have two or more trees in the forest that regularly communicate with each other, you might consider implementing shortcut trusts between them.

Shortcut trusts must be maintained, just like the Windows NT 4.0 trust relationships. It is preferable not to use them unless there is a specific reason for doing so. You can use them to fix documented problems or when you have a lot of traffic between peer domains in a tree or between a domain in one tree and a domain in another tree with resulting slow authentication times.

Application Upgrades

Before you perform your domain upgrade, you need to determine whether your server applications will be fully functional after the upgrade. You must know in advance how server applications will behave in a Windows 2000 environment.

Some server applications may not function correctly in a Windows 2000 network. Through testing, you can determine if an application requires the underlying operating system of Windows NT 4.0. Some applications must be hosted on a Windows NT 4.0 Backup Domain Controller (BDC). These applications can operate in a mixed-mode Windows 2000 domain environment, however you will not be able to switch the domain to native mode unless you can upgrade the application to run under Windows 2000.

Some network applications, as well as some line-of-business applications, might be affected by a domain upgrade. Your domain upgrade plan must define specific processes to determine the compatibility of applications with Windows 2000.

Performing Upgrade Tests

It is advisable to test all applications for functionality and interoperability in a Windows 2000 domain before you begin a domain upgrade. Tests must not be performed in the production environment, but rather in your test lab, followed by a pilot program before they are moved into the production environment. This concept is illustrated in Figure 6.13. Your organization may depend upon these applications to function and any disruption of the services provided by these applications could be extremely costly.

Figure 6.13 Application Migration Path

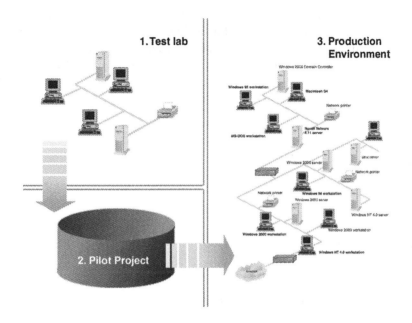

The pilot program is especially important as it emulates the production environment. Tests run in the pilot program will evaluate the performance of how an application will perform in the production environment. Pilot program testing will uncover problems not usually found in a test lab environment.

If you discover that an application does not run under Windows 2000, you should contact the application vendor to determine if a service pack or newer version of the product is available. Many application vendors provide upgrades, service packs, or new releases of their products that function correctly in a Windows 2000 environment.

If an application does not run under Windows 2000 and no service pack, upgrade or new release of the product is available, and then you must determine if the application can be moved to a Windows NT 4.0 member server. If a required application must run on a Windows NT BDC, then you cannot upgrade that computer to Windows 2000, and your domain cannot move to native mode. However, if the application can be moved to a member server, the Windows 2000 domain can then be switched to native mode.

Testing all applications available on your network can be a very large task. You might want to consider selecting a manager to develop a test plan and a methodology for testing and monitoring the test process. You should address application testing early in your upgrade plans, so you have sufficient time to address any issues that arise during the testing procedure. Your upgrade plan should cover the following tasks:

- Generating an application inventory
- Creating a method to prioritize applications
- Defining a testing methodology
- Creating the test environment
- Scheduling the tests
- Creating a test plan
- Defining a method for tracking and reporting
- Coordinating and consulting with application experts
- Monitoring and reporting the test progress

It is recommended that you compile a list of the applications as well as information about the applications that you will use after the upgrade. Your list could contain one or several of the following items:

- The application name and version
- The application's vendor name
- The current status of the application
- The number of users of the application
- The business unit that uses the application
- The importance of the application to the organization
- The application's platform

- Client or server-based application versions

- Location of application components

- Web application site addresses

- Application installation requirements

- Names and phone numbers of support personnel

You must test your applications in the environment where you wish to deploy them. You will need to test the installation of the applications, as well as how they run in your target environment. You will also need to mirror the way the applications are used, testing the features and the configurations that will be employed in the upgraded network.

You should consider using several of the following types of tests:

- Log on as a user and test specific scenarios needed to accomplish business tasks

- Log on as different users who are members of a group that use the application

- Apply group policy to the application and to the system

- Test different combinations of applications

- Run several applications simultaneously for a prolonged period of time

- Test automated tasks in Microsoft Office applications that use Visual Basic for Applications (VBA)

- Test applications to verify support for long file names and embedded periods

- Test the use of large files including graphics

- Test word processing applications with extensive editing of documents

- Test development environments

- Test custom controls

- Test the hardware interfaces, such as scanners, printers and other plug and play devices

- Test terminal services on a terminal services server.

- Test with multiple users running the same application

Since Windows 2000 uses new techniques and technologies, several applications could experience problems in the following areas:

- System file protection

- Robust heap checking

- Enumeration of fonts

- Enumeration of hardware devices

- Changed registry keys

- Version checking

- Windows Messaging Service

- File input/output security

 Warning: You must resolve any application incompatibilities before you perform an upgrade of any system related to the problem application.

Directory Information

When you upgrade a Windows NT 4.0 PDC to Windows 2000, the existing user attributes are migrated to Active Directory at the time the Active Directory installation wizard is run. User attributes are stored in the Security Accounts Manager (SAM) database. Several Windows NT 4.0 applications increase the number of attributes stored in the SAM database beyond the number provided in User Manager for Domains. For example, Microsoft Exchange Server v5.5 extends user attributes with Exchange mailbox attributes. You can ease the migration to Windows 2000 by populating Active Directory with these attribute values to take advantage of the additional information.

Using Existing Directory Information

You can use the Active Directory Connector (ADC) to migrate user attributes to Active Directory. The ADC allows you to easily map Microsoft Exchange Server attributes to Active Directory, which enhances the Active Directory (Figure 6.14).

The ADC allows you to populate Active Directory user object attributes with mailbox attributes from Microsoft Exchange Server v5.5. You can also extend the attribute set for Active Directory user objects by modifying the Active Directory schema using ADC.

Figure 6.14 Active Directory Connector

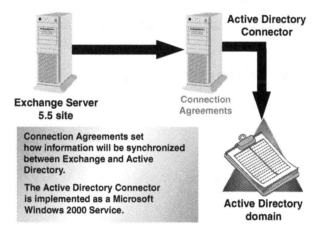

Active Directory Connector

Exchange Server 5.5 site

Connection Agreements

Connection Agreements set how information will be synchronized between Exchange and Active Directory.

The Active Directory Connector is implemented as a Microsoft Windows 2000 Service.

Active Directory domain

Using ADC, you can extend the Active Directory schema to include attributes from Exchange Server 5.5 that by default are not included as Active Directory attributes. ADC is an Active Directory-integrated application that allows configuration of connection agreements between Active Directory Organizational Units (OUs) and Recipient containers in Exchange Server. You can use these connection agreements to perform the following tasks:

- Share directory information between Exchange and Active Directory

- Synchronize directory information between Exchange and Active Directory

- Define the mapping of mailbox attributes to Active Directory attributes

Network Performance

You will want to create a strategy to maintain network performance during the domain upgrade. You can manage Active Directory replication and authentication traffic by carefully defining your sites and site boundaries. However, you need to consider Windows 2000 trust relationships and how they work, to ensure that network performance is maximized both during and after the upgrade. You must maintain user access to resources and applications so that these services are not interrupted or made unavailable during the upgrade.

 Note: Network performance is not just the speed at which the network operates, but includes its functionality as well.

Maintaining Network Performance

To ensure that your network does not disrupt its existing services, you can perform the following tasks:

- Thoroughly test applications

- Carefully evaluate and plan your domain hierarchy

- Judiciously apply shortcut trusts

- Carefully plan how you will migrate applications

- Test not only the applications, but also the application migration plan itself

- Organize your domain hierarchy in a manner that minimizes authentication and replication traffic over slow links

- Examine your perceived need for shortcut trusts and consider the impact on maintenance that such trusts mandate versus the benefit employing shortcut trusts provides by reducing domain or forest authentication traffic

Vocabulary

Review the following terms in preparation for the certification exam.

Term	Description
ADC	The Active Directory Connector is a synchronization agent that ensures that the two directories, Active Directory and Exchange Server 5.5 directory service, remain consistent.
BDC	A Backup Domain Controller is a computer running Windows NT 4.0 Server that receives a copy of the domain's directory database in a Microsoft Windows NT 4.0 Server domain.
child domain	For DNS and Active Directory, a child domain is located in the namespace tree directly beneath another domain name (the parent domain).
cross-link trust	Another name for a Shortcut Trust, it is a two-way trust that is explicitly created between two domains in different domain trees within a forest and optimizes the inter-domain authentication process. A shortcut trust can be created only between Windows 2000 domains in the same forest.
DC	A Domain Controller is the server that authenticates domain logons and maintains the security policy and the master database for a domain.
DFS	The Distributed File System is a Windows 2000 service that consists of software that resides on network servers and clients. It transparently links shared folders located on different file servers into a single namespace. The benefit is improved load sharing and data availability.
DS	Directory Services client software allows Windows 95 and Windows 98 client computers to take advantage of Windows 2000 Active Directory features.

Term	Description
one-way trust	A trust relationship where only one of the two domains trusts the other domain. All one-way trusts are non-transitive.
OU	An Organizational Unit is a logical container within a domain. You use an OU to organize objects for easier administration and access.
parent domain	For DNS and Active Directory, domains located in the namespace tree directly above other domain names (child domains).
PDC	A Primary Domain Controller is a computer running Windows NT 4.0 server that authenticates domain logons and maintains the directory database for a domain in a Microsoft Windows NT 4.0 Server domain.
SAM	Security Accounts Manager is a Windows 2000 service used during the login process that maintains user information.
schema	A description of the object classes and attributes stored in Active Directory. For each object class, the schema defines what attributes an object class must have, what additional attributes it may have, and what object class can be its parent.
SID	A Security Identifier is a unique name that is used to identify a user who has logged on to a Windows NT 4.0 or Windows 2000 security system. A SID can be used to represent an individual user, a group of users, or a computer.

Term	Description
shortcut trust	A shortcut trust is a two-way trust that is explicitly created between two domains in different domain trees within a forest and optimizes the inter-domain authentication process. A shortcut trust can be created only between Windows 2000 domains in the same forest. They are transitive.
SMS	The Microsoft Systems Management Server is a part of the Windows BackOffice suite of products. SMS includes inventory collection, diagnostic, and deployment tools that can automate the task of upgrading software on client computers. SMS can also be used to manage software licenses and to monitor computers and networks.
transitive trust	A trust relationship among domains, where if domain A trusts domain B and domain B trusts domain C, then domain A trusts domain C.
trees	A set of domains connected to each other through transitive bi-directional trusts. Trees share the same configuration, schema and global catalog. The domains in a tree form a hierarchal contiguous namespace.
two-way trust	A trust relationship where both of the domains in the relationship trust each other. In a two-way trust relationship, each domain has established a one-way trust with the other domain. Two-way trusts can be transitive or non-transitive. All two-way trusts between Windows 2000 domains in the same domain tree or forest are transitive.
VBA	Visual Basic for Applications is a programming environment that is designed specifically for creating application macros. It is the standard macro language in the Microsoft Office suite of products.

In Brief

If you want to...	Then do this...
Ensure application functionality and availability	Thoroughly test all critical applications in a test lab. Further testing in a pilot project is recommended since the pilot environment will mirror your production environment to a much larger degree than the test lab is capable of.
Migrate user attributes from Exchange Server v5.5	User the Active Directory Connector to automate the migration of user attributes and to modify the Active Directory schema to accommodate the new user attributes.
Employ down level clients that can take advantage of Active Directory features.	Upgrade Windows 95 and Windows 98 client computers with the Directory Services (DS) client software.
Reduce network traffic between users and resources located in different domains in the forest	Use explicit one-way, non-transitive shortcut trusts between the domains.

Lesson 6 Activities

Complete the following activities to prepare for the certification exam.

1. Discuss why a pilot program is an important component of your upgrade plans.

2. Describe how to upgrade a Windows 98 client to support Active Directory features and the value this represents.

3. Define a shortcut trust and state its purpose.

4. Describe how you extend the Active Directory schema to include Exchange Server version 5.5 attributes.

5. the effect on user attributes when you upgrade the PDC.

6. Describe the consequences of having a required application that must run on a BDC.

7. Define a local user profile and its use.

8. Describe a roaming profile.

9. Describe the ADC.

10. Discuss application verification.

Answers to Lesson 6 Activities

1. The pilot program is an important component in your migration plans because the pilot project mimics the production environment. Tests made in the pilot program can be used to discover problems related to your network configuration that would not be found in the test lab.

2. A Windows 98 client computer can take advantage of Active Directory services by installing the DS client software. DS client software supports many Active Directory features and provides the Windows 98 client with the ability to do the following:

   - Use the fault-tolerant Distributed File System (DFS)

   - Change a password on any domain controller

   - Search Active Directory services

3. A shortcut trust, sometimes called a cross-link trust, is an explicit one-way transitive trust relationship used between domains in separate branches of a tree, or from a domain in one tree to a domain in another tree, to reduce authentication traffic.

4. Use the Active Directory Connector (ADC) to extend the Active Directory schema to include attributes from Exchange Server 5.5 that are not included as Active Directory attributes by default.

5. When you upgrade a Windows NT 4.0 Primary Domain Controller (PDC) to Windows 2000, the existing user attributes are migrated to Active Directory when the Active Directory installation wizard is run.

6. If a required application must run on a Windows NT 4.0 Backup Domain Controller (BDC), then you cannot upgrade that computer to Windows 2000, and your domain cannot move to native mode.

7. A user local profile ensures that when a user logs onto a client computer, the user always receives their individual desktop settings and connections.

8. A roaming profile is a user profile that resides on a network server so that it is available to the user, no matter where the user logs into the domain from. A roaming profile, like a local profile, is used to restore desktop settings and connections to the user. The roaming profile is available to the user regardless of where they are on the network, in contrast to the local profile, which resides on a single computer.

9. ADC is an Active Directory-integrated application that allows connection agreements to be configured between Active Directory Organizational Units (OUs) and Recipient containers in Exchange Server.

10. To verify applications, you must test your applications in the environment in which you wish to deploy them. You need to test the installation of the applications as well as how they run in your target environment. You also need to mirror the manner in which the applications will be used, testing features and configurations that will be employed in the upgraded network.

Lesson 6 Quiz

These questions test your knowledge of features, vocabulary, procedures, and syntax.

1. Where are user accounts stored in Windows 2000?

    A. Active Directory schema

    B. SYSVOL

    C. SAM database

    D. C:\WinNT\Users and Computers

2. Where are local user profiles configured under Windows NT 4.0?

    A. The SAM database

    B. In an individual user's property pages

    C. In the system32 directory

    D. At the client workstation under control panel

3. What happens to roaming user profiles when the PDC is upgraded to Windows 2000?

    A. They will migrate to Windows 2000 security principal properties

    B. They will become part of the Active Directory schema

    C. They will be converted into shortcut trusts

    D. They will be converted into local profiles

4. What tool is used to extend the Active Directory schema to incorporate attributes from Exchange Server 5.5?

    A. System Information snap-in

    B. Active Directory Users and Computers

    C. ADC

    D. DS client software

5. What is another name for a shortcut trust?

    A. A transitive trust

    B. A two-way trust

    C. A one-way transitive trust

    D. A cross-link trust

6. What information is stored in a user profile?

    A. Configuration information

    B. User associated files

    C. Registry settings

    D. The user's password

7. What is the default trust relationship in Windows 2000?

    A. A one-way explicit trust

    B. A two-way non-transitive trust

    C. A two-way transitive trust

    D. A one-way transitive trust

8. Where should you test critical applications?

    A. On an upgraded member server

    B. In a test lab

    C. On an isolated workstation before the workstation is upgraded

    D. In a pilot project

9. When you test an application, what are you trying to determine?

    A. Functionality in a Windows 2000 environment

    B. Usefulness in a Windows 2000 environment

    C. Interoperability in a Windows 2000 environment

    D. Need for the application in a Windows 2000 environment

10. What happens when you create a new child domain?

    A. A two-way, transitive trust is automatically established with the parent domain

    B. An explicit trust between peer children domains is automatically generated

    C. The new child domain automatically trusts all other domains in the tree

    D. All domains in the tree automatically trust the new child domain

Answers to Lesson 6 Quiz

1. Answer C is correct. User attributes are stored in the Security Accounts Manager (SAM) database

   Answer A is incorrect. The Active Directory schema is a model for objects stored in Active Directory.

   Answer B is incorrect. No user information is stored in SYSVOL.

   Answer D is incorrect. The data is not stored in C:\WinNT\Users and Computers.

2. Answer B is correct. Under Windows NT 4.0, roaming user profiles are configured in an individual user's property pages.

   Answer A is incorrect. Roaming user profiles are not configured in the SAM database.

   Answer C is incorrect. Roaming user profiles are not configured nor stored in the system32 directory.

   Answer D is incorrect. You cannot configure roaming user profiles from the client workstation's control panel.

3. Answer A is correct. When the PDC is upgraded to Windows 2000, the roaming user profiles will migrate to Windows 2000 security principal properties.

   Answer B is incorrect. The Active Directory schema is used to define objects that are stored in Active Directory; it is not used to store any user profiles.

   Answer C is incorrect. Roaming profiles are not converted into shortcut trusts.

   Answer D is incorrect. Roaming user profiles will not be converted into local user profiles.

4. Answer C is correct. Using ADC, you extend the Active Directory schema to include attributes from Exchange Server 5.5 that are not included as Active Directory attributes by default.

   Answer A is incorrect. You cannot extend the Active Directory schema using the System Information MMC Active Directory snap-in.

   Answer B is incorrect. You cannot use Active Directory Users and Computers to extend the Active Directory schema.

Answer D is incorrect. DS client software is used to provide Active Directory functionality to Windows 95 and Windows 98 client computers.

5. Answer D is correct. A shortcut trust is sometimes called a cross-link trust.

    Answer A is incorrect. A shortcut trust is not transitive in nature.

    Answer B is incorrect. A shortcut trust is not a two-way trust.

    Answer C is incorrect. A shortcut trust is one-way in nature but it is not transitive.

6. Answers A, B and C are correct. The information stored in a user profile will include configuration information, registry settings and user-associated files.

    Answer D is incorrect. The user profile will not contain the user's password.

7. Answer C is correct. The default relationship in Windows 2000 is a two-way transitive trust. It is the default relationship between parent and children domains within a tree as well as between the top-level domains in a forest.

    Answer A is incorrect. You can create one-way explicit trusts under Windows 2000, but this type of trust is not the default trust relationship.

    Answer B is incorrect. The default relationship is two-way, but it is transitive in nature.

    Answer D is incorrect. The default relationship in Windows 2000 is not one-way in nature.

8. Answers B and D are correct. You should first test applications in a test lab. Once you are sure that they are Windows 2000 compatible in the test lab, move the test into a pilot project that mirrors your production environment to detect problems that may be related to your network infrastructure.

    Answer A is incorrect. You should not test applications on a member server. Not all applications will be executed from member servers. You must test applications in the environment in which they will run.

    Answer C is incorrect. Testing applications on an isolated workstation before it is upgraded will accomplish nothing.

9. Answers A and C are correct. When you test an application, you are determining the application's functionality and interoperability in a Windows 2000 domain before you begin your domain upgrade.

Answer B is incorrect. You are not determining the applications usefulness. If the application were not useful in the first place, it would not have been deployed in the network to begin with.

Answer D is incorrect. You are not determining the need for the application. The application's users determine its need.

10. Answers A, C and D are correct. When you create a new child domain, a two-way, transitive trust is automatically established with the parent domain. Because the trust is two-way and transitive, the new child domain automatically trusts all other domains in the tree and they trust the new child domain.

    Answer B is incorrect. An explicit trust between peer children domains is never automatically generated.

Lesson 7: Domain Restructuring

If your domain model is outdated or no longer supports your organization's business needs, you should consider a domain restructure. A domain restructure entails a complete redesign of your organization's existing domain environment. One of the most important things you will need to understand is how a domain restructure will affect security principals. You will also need to move users and resources from your Microsoft Windows NT 4.0 source domain into the Microsoft Windows 2000 target domain. You may also need to move users or resources from one Windows 2000 domain in a forest to a Windows 2000 domain in another forest. To accomplish these tasks, you must develop a domain restructure strategy and create a restructure plan.

After completing this lesson, you should have a better understanding of the following topics:

- Domain restructure strategy

- Domain restructure components

- Domain restructuring methodologies

Domain Restructure Strategy

Performing a domain restructure gives you an opportunity to redesign your domain environment to better meet the needs of your organization. This is in contrast to a domain upgrade, which maintains the existing domain structure. The difference between a domain upgrade and a domain restructure is illustrated in Figure 7.1.

Figure 7.1 Domain Upgrade vs. Domain Restructure

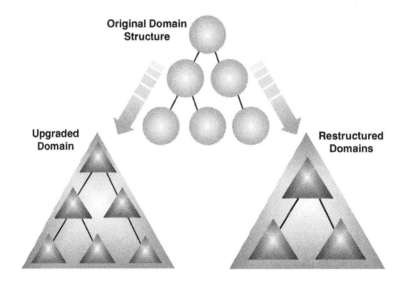

You have two restructuring choices: an inter-forest and an intra-forest restructuring. In an inter-forest restructure, you copy security principals from a Windows NT 4.0 domain to a Windows 2000 domain or from a Windows 2000 domain from one forest into a Windows 2000 domain in another forest, as shown in Figure 7.2.

Figure 7.2 Copying Security Principals in an Inter-Forest Restructure

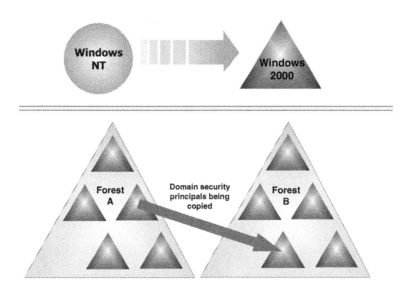

In an intra-forest restructure, you move security principals from one Windows 2000 domain to another Windows 2000 domain in the same forest as shown in Figure 7.3.

Figure 7.3 Moving Security Principals in an Intra-Forest Restructure

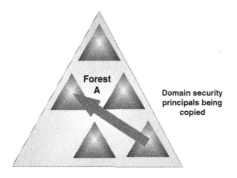

When you restructure your domain, you might need to employ inter-forest copy operations as well as intra-forest move operations.

 Note: Restructuring a Windows NT 3.51 domain involves several specific issues that are beyond the scope of this document.

Creating a Domain Restructure Strategy

You should create a domain restructure strategy that ensures that your network continues to function properly during the restructure. You must also ensure that your Microsoft Active Directory services design defines a domain hierarchy that matches your organization. When you plan for your restructure, you define how you will achieve that goal.

- To create a restructure strategy, consider the following tasks:

- Determine the order of restructure within a domain

- Identify and perform domain post-restructure tasks

You should identify and perform domain pre-restructure tasks to ensure the integrity of security principal information. If for some reason you must roll back to the source environment, you will have to reconstruct the pre-restructure security principal information. It is important to document any decisions you make regarding the restructure to assist in your rollout of a successful domain migration and to provide a rollback path.

To ensure that source group membership and resource Discretionary Access Control Lists (DACLs) are migrated intact, you should pre-define the order of restructuring within the domain.

You will want to identify and perform tasks after the restructure that ensure that all users retain their logon capability and access to resources.

Note: You must ensure continuity of network service and application availability during a migration rollout.

Evaluating a Domain Restructure Strategy

It is essential to ensure that your domain restructure strategy defines a structure that satisfies the business needs of your organization. The restructure should not adversely impact the performance of your network and it is suggested that you must assess your domain restructure strategy to ensure these goals are met.

When evaluating your restructure strategy, the following pre-restructure tasks must be addressed:

- Examine the existing domain environment to identify obsolete components

- Evaluate the existing domain to help in the selection of a restructure methodology

- Document the existing domain to ensure existing services and resource access is maintained during the restructure

- Choose a restructure methodology that meets your Active Directory design goals

- Ensure your domain restructure methodology meets your migration goals

- If you select inter-forest restructuring, prepare to deploy the target environment

- Develop a recovery plan

- Select migration tools appropriate for your restructure methodology

- Identify and document existing security principal details to ensure that they can be reconstructed if needed

- Decide how to migrate security principal details

Note: To prevent accidental data loss during the restructure, it is imperative you develop a recovery plan. This plan must also address the possible need to roll back to the pre-restructured Windows NT 4.0 environment.

By examining and documenting your current domain model, you can identify obsolete network components. Domain management in the new environment can be simplified by removing outdated domains and security principals. A thorough understanding of your current environment will aid you in the selection of a restructure methodology. To arrive at the ideal network environment, you may need to abandon your existing domain model and begin with an entirely new infrastructure that better meets the requirements of your business.

You may be able to achieve the ideal environment by upgrading existing account domains to join a parallel environment while you eliminate obsolete resource domains. Finally, examining and documenting your current domain model will help to ensure that existing network services remain intact and access to resources is maintained during the restructure.

When you examine your existing domain structure, as shown in Figure 7.4, you should plan to include the following tasks:

- Identify the current domain model

- Document all one-way and two-way trust relationships

- Identify all applications that run on domain controllers

- Identify the services that run on domain controllers and their configurations

Figure 7.4 Documenting Your Existing Domain Structure

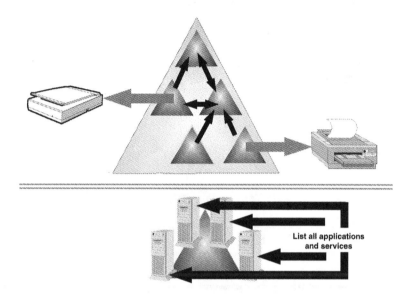

You must document the number of domains and the functions that they perform in your existing environment. You should establish the reason that a particular domain was originally created. If your organization required multiple account domains to ensure scalability, or multiple resource domains to segregate administrative access, you may be able to replace these domains with a single Active Directory domain as illustrated in Figure 7.5. You also need to ensure that migrated users retain access to resources in trusted domains.

Figure 7.5 Combining Multiple Accounts and Resource Domains

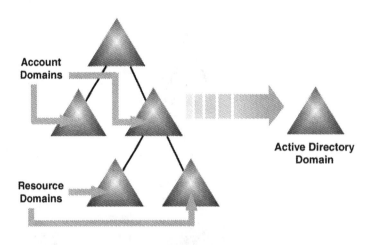

 Note: You must create trusts in the target domain that mirror trusts in the resource domain.

When you identify applications that run on Windows NT 4.0 domain controllers, you must plan to test them to ensure that they are compatible with Windows 2000. Any applications that are incompatible with Windows 2000 must be either upgraded or moved to a different domain so that they do not prevent the source domain from being decommissioned.

Services that run on a domain controller will not be available during the migration of that domain controller. You will need to ensure there are backups to the services provided by these domain controllers, and these are in place before the domain controllers are migrated.

Domain Restructure Components

An important factor to consider when planning your domain restructure tasks, is that the components that control domain security and access to resources are in place. In addition, you need to understand these components and how they are used in your network environment.

During your restructure, you will be moving security principals into Active Directory. You must be familiar with the effect moving security principals will have on the security of the domain and on resource access.

Understanding Key Components of Domain Security and Resource Access

Domain security, under both Windows NT 4.0 and Windows 2000, depends upon Security Identifiers (SIDs). A SID is a domain-specific identifier that is used by the operating system to distinguish security principals. Examples of a security principal include the following:

- Users
- Groups
- Computers

A user views a security principal by its name, however, the operating system maps the name to a SID for the following purposes:

- Logon authentication
- Permissions assignment
- Resource authorization

When a user logs on to the system, he or she presents the system with credentials, which includes a username and password. The user is then authenticated and granted an access token, if the credentials match those stored on record. The access token consists of a list of SIDs identifying the user and the groups that the user is a member of. It also contains the system rights granted to the user, and is the key that enables the user to gain access to network resources.

System administrators define access permission to resources by using Discretionary Access Control Lists (DACLs). DACLs contain the following information:

- User SIDs

- Group SIDs

- Access permissions granted to each security principal

When a user attempts to access a resource, the user's access token and the type of access requested by the user are compared with the SIDs and permissions listed in the DACL of the resource. If the SIDs and access rights match, the user is granted access permissions to the resource as defined in the DACL.

 Note: A SID is specific to a domain.

There is only one way to move or copy a security principal between domains. You must create a new security principal in the target domain, which assigns a new SID to the object. Under downlevel operating systems, you had to search the source domain and any trusting domains for references to an object's old SID and then add the object's new SID to all resource DACLs to grant resource access to the newly created security principal. Fortunately, this task is made easier under Windows 2000 because of an Active Directory service attribute called sIDHistory.

 Note: You can only populate the sIDHistory attribute in a Windows 2000 domain operating in native mode.

The sIDHistory attribute of a security principal object is used to store the former SID of the restructured security principal. Access to resources by that security principal is ensured after restructuring by this value, even on systems that predate Windows 2000 and Active Directory. As part of the migration process, the sIDHistory attribute is updated with the former SID of the migrated object. This concept is illustrated in Figure 7.6.

Figure 7.6 The sIDHistory Attribute and the Original SID Object

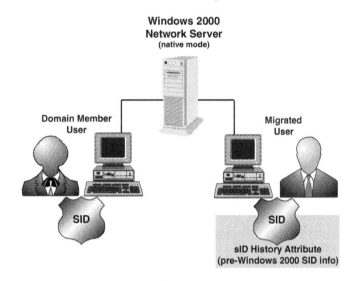

A user's primary SID and all the entries in the user's sIDHistory are added to the user's access token when the user logs on with a migrated account. Groups are also security principals with sIDHistory attributes. When a user logs on, the sIDHistory of all the groups the user is a member of are also added to the user's access token.

 Note: A migration operation that depends upon using the sIDHistory attribute must target a restructured native-mode domain.

Domain Restructuring Methodologies

The major component of determining a restructure methodology is the decision of when to restructure the domain. You can choose to restructure your domain during any of the following times:

- Post upgrade

- Post migration

- Instead of upgrade

The most common approach is to restructure during a second phase in a Windows 2000 migration plan. The restructure then takes place after the domain has been upgraded to Windows 2000. The advantage in this approach is that the upgrade will address many of the less complex migration issues. For example, the groups of domains where the trust relationships are for the most part correct or where there are no outstanding administrative issues. The restructure goals, in this case, would be to rework the domain structure to reduce complexity, or to incorporate resource domains into the forest in a secure manner.

The post migration restructure is one in which a general domain redesign is accomplished in a pure Windows 2000 environment. Such a restructure could occur several years after the migration to accommodate organizational changes, corporate acquisitions or if the current domain structure becomes outdated.

You may decide to perform the migration instead of an update, if you find your current domain structure or directory services infrastructure will not allow you to take advantage of Active Directory. Another reason to perform a migration would be that you do not want to jeopardize the stability of the current production environment during the migration. In either case, the preferred migration path would be to design and build the ideal forest, isolated from the production environment. In this way, you ensure that your organization can conduct business normally while you develop and test the pilot environment, which eventually would become the production environment.

After you have completed the pilot project, you then begin to migrate a small number of users, groups and resources into the pilot and begin the actual restructure. Once this has been completed successfully, you can then transition the pilot program to a staged migration into the new Windows 2000 environment. When you have completed the migration, you can then decommission the old domain structure and re-deploy any remaining resources.

You can use one of two fundamental methods to employ a domain restructure. You can employ an inter-forest restructure or an intra-forest restructure. During an inter-forest restructure, accounts are copied from a Windows NT 4.0 domain to a Windows 2000 domain or they are copied from a Windows 2000 domain in one forest to a Windows 2000 domain in another forest. During an intra-forest restructure, security principals are moved between two Windows 2000 domains in the same Active Directory forest.

Creating a Domain Restructure Plan

If you choose to restructure rather than upgrade your domain, you will perform an inter-forest restructure. You use an inter-forest restructure methodology when you restructure after you have completed a migration and you relocate security principals between Windows 2000 forests. In this later case, the restructure is sometimes referred to as a "prune and graft" and may reflect a corporate merger or acquisition.

An intra-forest restructure is the most common restructure scenario in two-phased migrations where an organization chooses to restructure after a full upgrade from a Windows NT 4.0 domain model. Another reason to employ an intra-forest restructure is to answer the need for a more complex Active Directory structure after a corporate reorganization.

Your domain restructure plan will depend upon the method that you employ and must address all issues related to that method.

Planning Inter-Forest Restructure Scenarios

You can plan an inter-forest restructure when you perform one of the following:

* Restructure a Windows NT 4.0 account domain

* Restructure a Windows NT 4.0 resource domain

* Restructure between two Windows 2000 forests

Restructuring Windows NT 4.0 Account Domains

When you restructure a Windows NT 4.0 account domain, you incrementally copy users and groups from a Windows NT 4.0 account domain to a parallel Windows 2000 Active Directory environment. The Active Directory environment works in tandem with the existing Windows NT 4.0 network, while reflecting the proposed Active Directory design. In this situation, you copy user, global, and shared local group accounts from the source Windows NT 4.0 domain into a pristine Windows 2000 environment, as illustrated in Figure 7.7. Since two copies of the environment exist, this methodology requires duplicate hardware and is more expensive, but it also ensures that you can recover from problems discovered during the migration.

The original accounts remain untouched during the process. When you restructure an account domain in this manner, existing security is preserved until the cloned accounts access is fully tested using the migrated sIDHistory attribute. You can decommission the Windows NT 4.0 domain after all users and groups have been copied to Active Directory, the environment has been thoroughly tested, and the new accounts are in use.

Figure 7.7 Copying An Account Domain to a Windows 2000 Domain

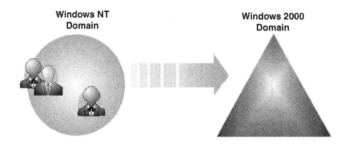

Restructuring Windows NT 4.0 Resource Domains

Another scenario in an inter-forest restructure is restructuring resource domains. You can reduce the number of domains as well as the administrative cost of managing trust relationships, by moving Windows NT 4.0 resource domains into a Windows 2000 Organizational Unit (OU). An OU is a container object that contains other objects such as users, groups, computers or even other OUs. This concept is illustrated in Figure 7.8.

Figure 7.8 Moving a Resource Domain into a Windows 2000 OU

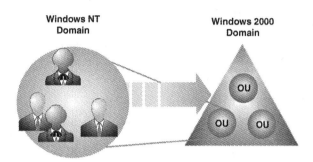

When you restructure a Windows NT 4.0 resource domain, you employ both copying and moving techniques. Computer accounts for workstations and member servers can be moved or copied to the target domain. You must clone shared local groups that reside on a Windows NT 4.0 domain controller to the target domain.

Restructuring Between Two Windows 2000 Forests

Once you have completed your pilot program, you can use inter-forest restructuring to cut accounts and resources from the pilot Active Directory forest and paste then into the production environment forest. In this situation, you are copying from one forest into another. You can employ this technique to move users, groups, computers or resources from a source domain in one organization's forest to a target domain in another organization's Active Directory Forest. This concept is illustrated in Figure 7.9.

Figure 7.9 Copying Between Two Windows 2000 Forests

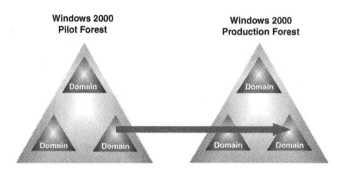

 Note: You cannot merge the schemas of separate Active Directory forests, which means that you cannot truly combine forests.

Since you will be cloning security principals, which is a security-sensitive operation, you must prepare the appropriate target environment before you begin your inter-forest restructure. Your restructure plan must take into consideration the requirements that must be met for an inter-forest restructure.

If you plan to employ the sIDHistory attribute, your target domain must be a native-mode Windows 2000 domain. The user that performs the restructure operation must have administrative privileges in both the source and target domains and must be a member of Domain Admins in the target domain (Figure 7.10).

Figure 7.10 Required Administrative Privileges

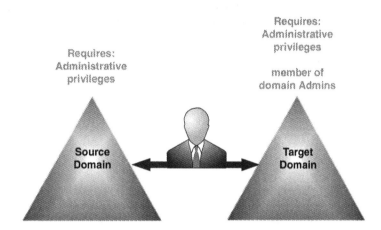

For the restructure, you will need to enable account auditing on both the source and target domains. You will also need to create an empty local group in the source domain, whose name is the source domain's name with "$$$" appended, for example ibidpub$$$, for auditing purposes. To enable account auditing in a Windows NT 4.0 domain, enable *success* and *failure* Group Management auditing on the Primary Domain Controller (PDC). To enable account auditing in a Windows 2000 domain, enable audit account management on the Default Domain Controllers Policy (Figure 7.11).

Figure 7.11 Account Auditing Is Required

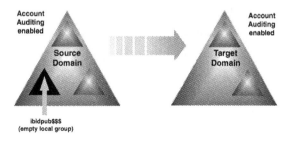

Note: To enable an inter-forest restructure, the source domain controller's registry must contain the following registry entry:HKEY_LOCAL_MACHINE | System | CurrentControlSet | Control | Lsa | TcpipClientSupport: REG_DWORD:0X1

This is a not a default registry entry.

In addition to the requirements of an inter-forest restructure, there are also some restrictions. The source domain controller must be one of the following:

- A Windows NT 4.0 PDC

- A Windows 2000 PDC Emulator (native or mixed mode domain)

The source domain in an inter-forest restructure cannot be in the same forest as the target domain. The SID of the source object cannot already exist in the target forest as a primary account SID or in the sIDHistory attribute of any other account. The source object must be a user account or a security-enabled group. A security-enabled group includes the following:

- Global groups

- Windows NT 4.0 shared local groups

- Windows 2000 domain local groups

The following objects cannot be migrated:

- Build-in groups

- Accounts with well-known SIDs

- Accounts with well-known Relative Identifiers (RIDs)

Finally, any migration tool that you use must be run on the target domain controller. Unless you use Windows Terminal Services to run the tools remotely, you will need physical access to the target computer.

Planning Intra-Forest Restructuring on Security Principals

Your organization is not static. People who work in one division or location of the company may move into another role or location, requiring an account to be moved between domains. The needs of the business may change over time and may result in changes to the design of the forest. For example, you may find that you can merge domains in order to create a smaller Active Directory infrastructure, which prompts a post-migration, intra-forest as illustrated in Figure 7.12.

Figure 7.12 Inter-forest Restructuring

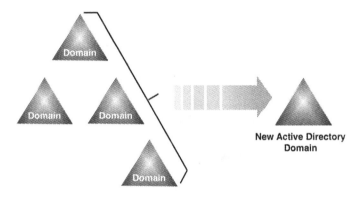

In an intra-forest restructure, the only operation that you can perform is to move security principals between Windows 2000 domains. When you move a security principal under Windows 2000, a certain amount of risk is present. The move operation deletes the source account. This means that you cannot perform a rollback. When you delete an object, its SID is permanently retired and cannot be re-assigned.

Moving Security Principals

Moving security principals is a security-sensitive operation. Because of this, there are some specific requirements that must be met before you can perform an intra-forest restructure.

The restructure operation consists of moving a security principal from a Windows 2000 domain into another Windows 2000 domain in the same forest as shown in Figure 7.13. The target domain must be a native-mode Windows 2000 domain.

Figure 7.13 Moving Security Principals

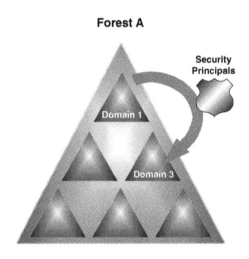

 Note: Like an inter-forest restructure, to enable an intra-forest restructure, the source domain controller's registry must contain the following registry entry, and it is not a default registry entry:HKEY_LOCAL_MACHINE | System | CurrentControlSet | Control | Lsa | TcpipClientSupport: REG_DWORD:0X1

The user who performs the restructuring operations must have administrative rights in both the source and target domain. In addition, auditing must be enabled in both domains.

Like an inter-forest restructure, there are restrictions on an intra-forest restructure. The source domain must be a Windows 2000 domain and must reside in the same forest as the target domain. You can only move user or security-enabled groups, computers or OUs.

If the source object's SID already exists in the target domain as either a primary account SID or as a member of the sIDHistory attribute of an account, you cannot move it.

 Note: Since built-in groups have known SIDs and RIDs, you cannot move a built-in account.

You can run migrations tools on either the source or target domain controller, but administrative shares must exist on the computer where the Active Directory Migration Tool (ADMT) is running as well as on any computer where the ADMT must install an agent.

Vocabulary

Review the following terms in preparation for the certification exam.

Term	Description
ADMT	The Active Directory Migration Tool is a tool provided by Microsoft to assist in the migration process.
DACL	A Discretionary Access Control List is a part of an object's security descriptor. It defines the access rights of users and groups to the object and can only be modified by the owner of the object.
inter-forest restructure	During an inter-forest restructure, you copy security principals from a Windows NT 4.0 domain to a Windows 2000 domain or from a Windows 2000 domain in one forest to a Windows 2000 domain in another forest
intra-forest restructure	In an intra-forest restructure, you move security principals from one Windows 2000 domain to another Windows 2000 domain in the same forest
OU	An Organizational Unit is a container object that contains other objects such as users, groups, computers or even other OUs.
PDC	A Primary Domain Controller is a computer running Windows NT 4.0 server that authenticates domain logons and maintains the directory database for a domain in a Microsoft Windows NT 4.0 Server domain.
RID	A Relative Identifier is a part of a SID and is used to identify an account or group. A RID is unique to in a domain in which the account or group reside.
Security Principal	An entity that is assigned a security identifier. Security principals include users, groups and computers.
SID	A Security Identifier is a domain-specific identifier that is used by the operating system to distinguish security principals.
sIDHistory	The sIDHistory attribute of a security principal object is used to store the former SID of the restructured security principal

In Brief

If you want to...	Then do this...
Enable account tracking in Windows NT 4.0	To enable account auditing in a Windows NT 4.0 domain, enable *success* and *failure* Group Management auditing on the Primary Domain Controller (PDC).
Enable account tracking in Windows 2000	To enable account auditing in a Windows 2000 domain, enable audit account management on the Default Domain Controllers Policy.
Set the required registry entry in a source domain to enable restructure.	Set the following registry entry: HKEY_LOCAL_MACHINE | System | CurrentControlSet | Control | Lsa | TcpipClientSupport: REG_DWORD:0X1

Lesson 7 Activities

Complete the following activities to better prepare you for the certification exam.

1. Discuss the requirements for an intra-forest restructure.

2. Describe the restrictions on an intra-forest restructure.

3. Describe the requirements for an inter-forest restructure.

4. Discuss the restrictions on an inter-forest restructure.

5. Detail the use of the sIDHistory attribute.

6. Define an inter-forest restructure.

7. Describe an intra-forest restructure.

8. Describe the conditions under which you would perform an intra-forest restructure.

9. Define the conditions under which you would perform an inter-forest restructure.

10. Describe how the operating system uses a SID.

Answers to Lesson 7 Activities

1. The requirements for an intra-forest restructure include the following:

   - The target domain must be a Windows 2000 native-mode domain

   - The source domain controller must have the required registry entry

   - The user who performs the restructuring operations must have administrative rights in both the source and target domain

   - Auditing must be enabled in both domains

2. The restrictions on an intra-forest restructure are the following:

   - The source domain must be a Windows 2000 domain and must reside in the same forest as the target domain

   - You can only move user or security-enabled groups, computers or OUs

   - You cannot move a built-in account

   - If the source object's SID already exists in the target domain as either a primary account SID or as a member of the sIDHistory attribute of an account, you cannot move it

   - You can run migrations tools on either the source or target domain controller

   - Administrative shares must exist on the computer where the Active Directory Migration Tool (ADMT) is running as well as on any computer where the ADMT must install an agent

3. The requirements of an inter-forest restructure include the following:

   - If you plan to use the sIDHistory attribute, the target domain must be a native-mode Windows 2000 domain

   - The source domain controller's required registry entry must be set

   - The user who performs the restructuring operations must have administrative rights in both the source and target domain

   - Auditing must be enabled in both domains

   - A local group, *sourcedomainname$$$*, must be created in the source domain

4. The restrictions on an inter-forest restructure include the following:

   - The source domain controller must be the PDC or PDC emulator

   - The source and target domains must not be in the same forest

   - The source objects must be user accounts or security-enabled groups

   - The SID of the source object cannot already exist in the target domain

   - Objects with well-known SIDs or RIDs cannot be migrated

   - Migration tools must be run on the target domain controller

5. The sIDHistory attribute of a security principal object is used to store the former SID of the restructured security principal.

6. An inter-forest restructure occurs when you copy Windows NT 4.0 accounts or resource domains into a Windows 2000 Active Directory environment. An inter-forest restructure also occurs when you move accounts and resources between two Windows 2000 forests.

7. You perform an inter-forest restructure when you move security principals between two Windows 2000 domains in the same Active Directory forest.

8. If you select to restructure rather than upgrade your domain, you will perform an inter-forest restructure.

9. An intra-forest restructure is the most common restructure scenario in two-phased migrations in which an organization chooses to restructure after a full upgrade from a Windows NT 4.0 domain model. Another reason to employ an intra-forest restructure is to answer the need for a more complex Active Directory structure after a corporate reorganization.

10. A SID is a domain-specific identifier that is used by the operating system to distinguish security principals.

Lesson 7 Quiz

These questions test your knowledge of features, vocabulary, procedures, and syntax.

1. What type of operation do you perform when you copy security principals from a Windows NT 4.0 domain into a Windows 2000 domain?

    A. Inter-forest restructure

    B. Intra-forest restructure

    C. Domain upgrade

    D. You cannot copy security principals

2. What type of operation do you perform when you move security principals between Windows 2000 domains in the same forest?

    A. Inter-forest restructure

    B. Intra-forest restructure

    C. Domain upgrade

    D. You cannot move security principals

3. What is required for you to be able to perform an intra-forest restructure?

    A. Administrative rights on the source domain

    B. Administrative rights on the target domain

    C. Membership is Domain Admins in the target domain

    D. Membership in all groups that are moved

4. What is required for you to be able to perform an inter-forest restructure?

    A. Administrative rights on the source domain

    B. Administrative rights on the target domain

    C. Membership is Domain Admins in the target domain

    D. Membership in all groups that are moved

5. What does the operating system use to authenticate users in downlevel domains?

    A. SID

    B. RID

    C. The sIDHistory attribute

    D. The user's password

6. What are the restrictions on using the sIDHistory attribute?

    A. The target domain must be in mixed-mode

    B. The source domain must be a native-mode Windows 2000 domain

    C. The target domain must be a native-mode Windows 2000 domain

    D. The source domain cannot be upgraded

7. What types of information are stored in an object's DACL?

    A. The objects access rights

    B. User SIDs

    C. Group SIDs

    D. Access permissions granted to each security principal

8. What happens to the SID of a deleted object?

    A. The SID is cleared and can be re-used at a later time

    B. The SID is transferred to the objects sIDHistory attribute

    C. The SID is permanently retired and cannot be re-assigned

    D. The SID is stored in case the object is re-created

9. What types of groups are security-enabled groups?

    A. Global groups

    B. Resource groups

    C. Windows NT 4.0 shared local groups

    D. Windows 2000 domain local groups

10. What types of objects cannot be migrated?

    A. User objects

    B. Build-in groups

    C. Accounts with well-known SIDs

    D. Accounts with well-known RIDs

Answers to Lesson 7 Quiz

1. Answer A is correct. You perform an inter-forest restructure when you copy security principals from a Windows NT 4.0 domain into a Windows 2000 domain

    Answer B is incorrect. You do not perform an intra-forest restructure when you copy objects from a Windows NT 4.0 domain.

    Answer C is incorrect. You do not copy security objects during an upgrade.

    Answer D is incorrect. You can perform a copy operation.

2. Answer B is correct. You perform an intra-forest restructure when you move security principals between two Windows 2000 domains in the same forest.

    Answer A in incorrect. You do not perform an intra-forest restructure when you move security principals.

    Answer C is incorrect. You do not move objects during an upgrade.

    Answer D is incorrect. You can move security principals.

3. Answers A and B are correct. You must have administrative rights on both the source and target domains to perform an intra-forest restructure.

    Answer C is incorrect. You do not have to be a member of Domain Admins in the target domain.

    Answer D is incorrect. You do not have to be a member of a group to be able to move it.

4. Answers A, B, and C are correct. You must have administrative rights on both the source and target domains to perform an intra-forest restructure and you have to be a member of Domain Admins in the target domain.

    Answer D is incorrect. You do not have to be a member of a group to be able to move it.

5. Answer C is correct. The sIDHistory attribute is used to authenticate users in downlevel domains.

    Answer A is incorrect. The SID of an object may change when migrated and is not used for downlevel authentication.

    Answer B is incorrect. The RID of an object is not used for authentication in downlevel domains.

Answer D is incorrect. The user's password may be changed and cannot be used for downlevel authentication.

6. Answer C is correct. The target domain must be a native-mode Windows 2000 domain.

   Answer A is incorrect. The target domain must not be a mixed-mode domain.

   Answer B is incorrect. The source domain does not have to be a native-mode Windows 2000 domain.

   Answer D is incorrect. The source domain can be an upgraded domain.

7. Answers B, C and D are correct. A DACL contains user and group SIDs as well as the access permissions assigned to each security principal.

   Answer A in incorrect. A DACL does not store the access rights of the object to which it is attached but rather the access rights of other objects to the object.

8. Answer C is correct. When you delete an object, its SID is permanently retired and cannot be reassigned.

   Answer A is incorrect. The SID can never be used again in the domain.

   Answer B is incorrect. The SID is not transferred to the object's sIDHistory attribute. After the object is deleted, it has no sIDHistory attribute. A Windows NT 4.0 object does not have a sIDHistory attribute.

   Answer D is incorrect. The SID cannot be re-assigned to an object even if it is re-created. The SID is permanently retired.

9. Answers A, C, and D are correct. Security-enabled groups include Global groups; Windows NT 4.0 shared local groups, and Windows 2000 domain local groups.

   B is incorrect. Resource groups are not security-enabled groups.

10. Answers B, C and D are correct. You cannot migrate Build-in groups, accounts with well-known SIDs, or accounts with well-known RIDs.

    Answer A is incorrect. User objects can be migrated.

Lesson 8: Security Principals and Restructure Tools

When you plan a domain restructure, you have the opportunity to re-design your network infrastructure to better match your organization's needs. In most cases, the resulting structure will have fewer but larger domains. Windows 2000 provides native functionality to enable a domain restructure. You can move security principals from one domain to another while you maintain access to resources. In addition, you can move domain controllers from one domain to the other, without re-installing the operating system.

With Windows 2000, Microsoft provides a set of tools to assist you in your domain migration. These tools have been tested in many domain migration scenarios.

After completing this lesson, you should have a better understanding of the following topics:

- Security principals
- Domain security
- Domain restructure tools

Security Principals

A security principal is a user, group or computer that has been assigned a security identifier. The security identifier determines access rights and privileges to resources on the network. Under Windows 2000, you can manage user security principals through Active Directory.

Depending upon the type of migration you choose, you can either copy or move security principals. You should understand the implications of moving or cloning users, global and universal groups, computers, local group accounts and local groups.

If you perform an inter-forest restructure, you will need to consider the following tasks:

- Close users
- Clone universal groups

- Clone global groups

- Clone domain local groups

- Clone local groups

- Move computer accounts

If you create an intra-forest restructure, you will need to complete the following tasks:

- Move users

- Move global groups

- Move domain local groups

- Move closed sets

- Move computers

- Move local accounts

- Move domain controllers

Cloning Security Principals

The most common operations in an inter-forest restructure are cloning or copying security principals. You create a clone when you copy account properties into a Windows 2000 native-mode domain. During the cloning process (Figure 8.1), you copy the account properties from one of the following types of domains:

- A Windows NT 4.0 domain

- A Windows 2000 domain in a separate forest

Figure 8.1 Cloning Source and Target Domain Types

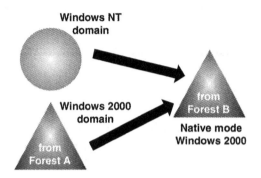

When you clone an object, the cloned object has a different primary Security Identifier (SID) than the original object. The SID of the original object can be stored in the sIDHistory attribute of the clone.

For the clone to have the same access rights to network resources that were available to the source account, you must populate the sIDHistory attribute with the SID of the source account. However, the access rights will depend upon construction of the appropriate trusts from the resource's domains to the clone's account domain.

 Note: You cannot clone objects between domains in the same forest.

Microsoft provides the Active Directory Migration Tool (ADMT) and ClonePrincipal tools to facilitate cloning security principals. When you use these tools, you have the option of migrating the SID into the sIDHistory attribute.

One of cloning's primary advantages is that it does not cause disruptions in the existing production environment. When you clone a user, it is placed into a parallel environment. This allows users to log on to Active Directory using their cloned account while you maintain the ability to rollback to the source account if necessary. You can fall back to the source account from the production environment, until you decommission the source domain.

Note: You can only clone between domains in separate forests.

Cloning Users

When you clone a user, the user automatically becomes a member of Domain Users. If you add the SID of the original account to the sIDHistory attribute of the new account, the user retains access to resources of the source environment.

To clone users in an inter-forest restructure, you can use either the ClonePrincipal utility or the ADMT. The ClonePrincipal utility automatically disables the source accounts. As shown in Figure 8.2, you can configure the ADMT to disable the source or target account.

Figure 8.2 Configuring the ADMT

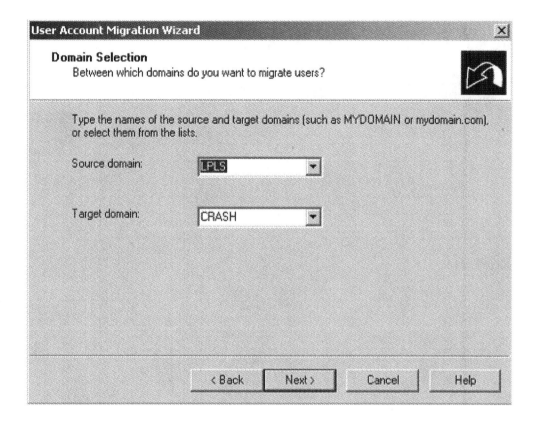

If you have already cloned global or universal groups, then cloned users that were members of those groups are automatically restored to those groups in the target domain. If you clone the groups after the users, the membership of the cloned users is automatically restored when the groups are cloned.

 Note: Not all source account properties are copied during the cloning operation.

Cloning users with the ADMT is illustrated in Figure 8.3.

Figure 8.3 Cloning Users with the ADMT

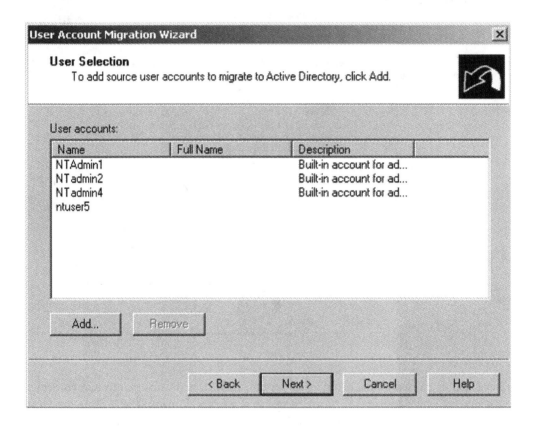

Cloning Global and Universal Groups

When you clone a global or universal group, the source object's primary SID is retained as a sIDHistory value in the new cloned account. If a global or universal group's members have been cloned, then membership in the cloned group is restored to reflect the membership in the source account. If you choose to clone the users later, their membership in the groups will be restored at that time. If the source domain is a Windows 2000 domain, then this is also true for nested groups.

You can merge multiple source groups into a single target group during the cloning operation. This allows you to combine global groups when restructuring multiple Windows NT 4.0 account domains into a single Windows 2000 domain.

During your inter-forest restructure, you can use ClonePrincipal or the ADMT to clone group accounts. Using the ADMT is illustrated in Figure 8.4.

Figure 8.4 Cloning Groups with ADMT

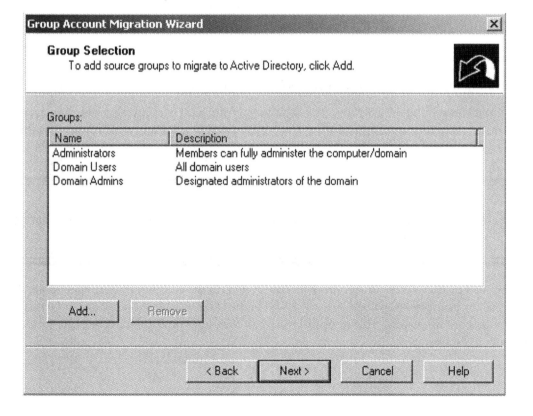

Migrating Computers and Local Group Accounts

You should understand the implications of migrating computers and local-group accounts. When you carry out an inter-forest restructure, you will need to migrate both workstation and member server computer accounts.

 Note: Computer accounts cannot be cloned. They must be moved to the target domain.

You can move computer accounts using any of the following methods:

- Remotely, using the ADMT
- Remotely, using the NETDOM migration utility
- Manually configuring each computer to join the target domain

Local group accounts and their properties are a part of the local Security Accounts Manager (SAM) database. As such, they are migrated when the computer on which they reside is joined to the target domain.

 Note: Local groups are unaffected by a computer migration. Their SIDs do not need to be changed.

Local groups provide access to resources that are found on the computer where they reside. During the migration, permissions granted to local groups in the Discretionary Access Control Lists (DACLs) of resources are maintained. If appropriate trusts to the target domain are created, resource access continues to function properly.

Tip: If a local group contains members from trusted domains, then you will need to create trusts between the target domain and any domain in which those members reside.

Cloning Local Groups on Domain Controllers

A shared local group is a group for which the following rules are true:

- It resides on a Windows NT 4.0 Primary Domain Controller (PDC)

- It is shared between the PDC and all Backup Domain Controllers (BDCs) in the same domain

Membership in a shared local group can consist of accounts from any trusted Windows NT 4.0 or Windows 2000 domain. When a shared local group is cloned, the following events occur:

- The sIDHistory of the former account is retained

- A domain local group is created on the target domain

Note: When the target domain is in native-mode, cloned shared local groups are converted to domain local groups.

The recommended migration tool for cloning shared local groups is the ADMT tool. It is the easiest to use and provides a comprehensive method to migrate local groups. When you use the ADMT tool to clone a shared local group, it copies the local group and populates its membership automatically, provided the member accounts are migrated simultaneously. Using the ADMT to clone a shared local group is illustrated in Figure 8.5.

Figure 8.5 Cloning a Shared Local Group with ADMT

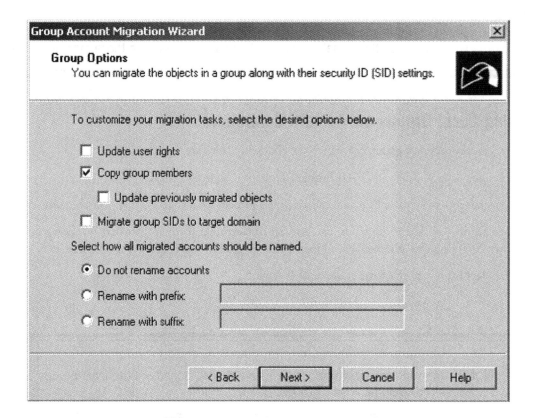

Tip: You can use ClonePrincipal to clone shared local groups however, retaining group membership is a much more complex operation.

You must establish the appropriate trusts to ensure that resource permissions granted to the cloned local group will function. If the shared local group contains members from additional trusted domains, you must define a trust between the target domain where the clone account resides, and the domain in which the group members reside.

Tip: You can use the NETDOM and ADMT utilities to identify and establish the appropriate trusts when you clone shared local groups.

Moving Domain Controllers

You can migrate domain controllers after you clone the following to the target domain:

- Users

- Groups

- Computer accounts

Note: Domain controllers cannot be cloned.

During the migration, domain controllers must be moved. When you move a domain controller, you decommission the source domain. Moving domain controllers is one of the final steps in an inter-forest domain restructure.

If the domain controller to be migrated is a Windows NT 4.0 PDC or BDC, you can move the computer in either of the following ways:

- Upgrade the domain controller to Windows 2000 Server

- Reinstall the server as a Windows NT 4.0 member server

If you elect to upgrade the domain controller to Windows 2000 Server, you can configure the computer to join the target domain when you run the Active Directory Installation wizard.

If you choose to reinstall the server as a Windows NT 4.0 member server, the server's computer account can be moved in the same method all other computer accounts are moved. Once the server becomes a member of the target domain, it can be maintained as a member server or it can be promoted as a replica domain controller that supports the target domain.

Warning: You must always upgrade the PDC first.

To move a Windows 2000:domain controller, you must demote it to a member server. The member server can then join the target domain. You may also move the account using the NETDOM or ADMT utilities in the same manner in which other computer accounts are moved.

Tip: If you decide to reinstall an application server BDC as a member server, you must ensure all the application data is backed up prior to reinstalling the operating system. You will restore this data once the reinstall is completed.

Moving Security Principals

During an intra-forest restructure, you move security principals between two Windows 2000 domains in the same Active Directory forest. You may find that you need to perform an intra-forest restructure if a user transfers from one division in the organization to another. Changes in your organization's business needs may also influence your decision to perform an intra-forest restructure. The only migration operation possible in an intra-forest restructure is a move.

When you move a security principal, the source account is deleted. There is a certain amount of risk involved when you move security principals from one domain to another. When you move a security principal, the move creates a new, identical account in the destination domain and deletes the account from the source domain. However, the new object does not have the same SID as the original object.

Warning: After you move a security principal, you cannot return to the original account if any problems occur because it is permanently deleted!

You must ensure that access permissions are maintained during the intra-forest restructure. This is accomplished by a constraint applied by the underlying Application Programmer Interface (API) of the migration tools called a *closed set*. Blocks of accounts that are moved at the same time constitute a closed set.

You can use either the MoveTree or ADMT migration tools to move security principals. Using the ADMT tool to move security object is illustrated in Figure 8.6. Both of these tools provide the ability to retain the source account SID in the target account's sIDHistory attribute, which provides continued access to resources.

Figure 8.6 Moving Security Principals with ADMT

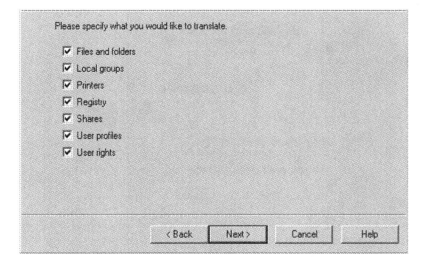

Tip: You cannot clone in an intra-forest migration. Cloning would cause two security principals to be associated with a single SID.

Using Closed Sets to Move Users and Global Groups

A global group can only contain members from its own domain. All members of a global group must be moved when the global group is moved.

When you move a global group, the primary SID of the group is retained in the new group object's sIDHistory attribute. If you move a user between domains, any global groups that the user is a member of, must be moved at the same time as shown in Figure 8.7. This maintains resource permissions assigned to the global group while preserving group membership.

Figure 8.7 Moving Global Groups When You Move Users

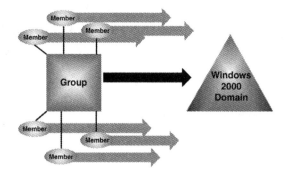

When you move a global group, all of its members must also be moved at the same time, using a closed-set. This concept is illustrated in Figure 8.8.

Figure 8.8 Moving Users When You Move Global Groups

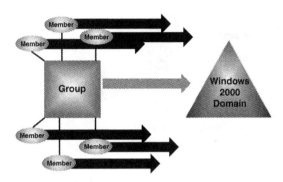

In a Windows 2000 native-mode domain, global groups may contain other global groups. For each nested group, all members must be moved in closed-set fashion.

Using Closed Sets to Move Domain Local Groups

There are several consequences to moving domain local groups. Windows 2000 domain local groups are only valid in the domain where they were created.

You may choose to merge two or more domains in an effort to simplify your Active Directory domain hierarchy. When you do this, you move Windows 2000 domain local groups and the domain controllers on which they reside into a target domain. If a domain local group is moved independently of its members, then any reference in a source domain's resource DACL to the group will be irresolvable. To prevent this, you should use closed sets.

You will need to retain resource access and preserve group membership during the migration. All domain controllers in the domain containing resource DACLs that reference the domain local group must be moved at the same time you move the domain local group. Likewise, all domain local groups referenced in DACLs on a domain controller's resources must be moved at the same time that the domain controller is moved. This concept is shown in Figure 8.9.

Figure 8.9 Moving Domain Local Groups

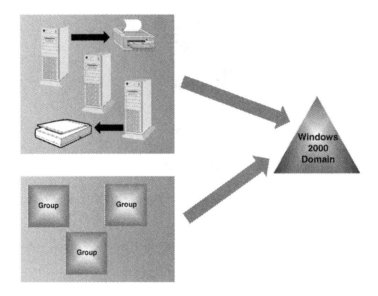

Moving Closed Sets

Moving closed sets between Windows 2000 domains during an intra-forest restructure can be a particularly challenging task for the following reasons:

- Depopulating and repopulating large groups can be very time consuming
- The smallest closed set may be the entire source domain

Fortunately, there are some alternative approaches, as follows:

- Create parallel groups
- Leverage universal groups
- Reconsider your migration strategy

When you create parallel groups, instead of moving groups, you should create them in the target domain. Additional steps are required, as the parallel group will not contain the sIDHistory of the source group. The additional steps are as follows:

- The new group membership must be defined

- All resources in the enterprise that contain DACLs that reference the original group must be modified to include permissions for the parallel group

- The created permissions must match the permissions of the source global group

An alternative is to change the group type of the groups to be moved to universal. Universal groups can be safely moved because they have scope across the entire forest. This will retain their membership and access to resources. The group types can be changed back to their original type after the restructure is completed.

 Warning: Membership in universal groups is stored in the global catalog and is replicated throughout the entire forest.

The use of closed sets is not imposed by the action of cloning or copying security principals. Cloning can only be used when copying accounts between forests. To avoid the restrictions and complications of moving closed sets, you may elect to reconsider your migration strategy. You can avoid using closed sets if you restructure directly from an existing Windows NT 4.0 domain or a separate Windows 2000 forest.

Moving Computers and Local Accounts

When you move a computer account in an intra-forest restructure, you carry out the same functions as when you move computer accounts in an inter-forest restructure. When you relocate workstations or member servers between domains, they will always take their own SAM database with them.

When you transfer a computer account in an intra-forest restructure, local user accounts are unaffected. Local group accounts are defined on a workstation or member server and move with the computer. They are not affected by the move. A local group containing accounts from trusted domains will also remain unaffected by the move.

Local groups provide access to resources on the local computer on which they reside. During the move, all permissions granted to local groups in the DACLs of resources on the moved computer will be maintained. If the appropriate trusts to the target domain already exist, then resource access continues to function correctly.

 Note: If a local group contains members from trusted domains, then you must create trusts between the target domain and the domains in which those members reside.

You can move computer accounts in the following ways:

- ADMT

- NETDOM

- Manually by a user at the local computer

Domain Security

A critical concern when moving security principals into Active Directory is the effect that the move will have on domain security and resource access. You need to be familiar with how Windows NT 4.0 and Windows 2000 manage security issues.

Understanding Domain Security

Domain security under both Windows NT 4.0 and Windows 2000 depends upon Security Identifiers (SIDs). A SID is a domain-specific identifier used by the operating system to distinguish security principals. A security principal can be one of the following:

- User

- Group

- Computer

A security principal is displayed as a name to the user. However, the names are mapped to SIDs by the operating system to perform the following:

- Logon authentication

- Assignment of permissions

- Authorization of resources

When a user logs on, he or she is validated with a set of credentials that includes a username to the system. The system verifies that the credentials match with the appropriate set of credentials that the system maintains on record. If the credentials match, the user is authenticated and is granted an access token, which is a key that enables the user to access network resources. The token consists of a list of SIDs identifying the user, as well as the groups to which the user belongs and the various system rights that are granted to the user.

Each resource has an associated DACL defining the resource's access permissions. The DACL contains user and groups SIDs as well as access permissions to be granted to each security principal. The system compares the DACL list with the access token of a user requesting access to the resource. If a group or user SID is found, the type of request is then verified. If the SIDs and the access type match, then the user is granted access to the resource. This concept is illustrated in Figure 8.10.

Figure 8.10 Verifying Access Rights to a Resource

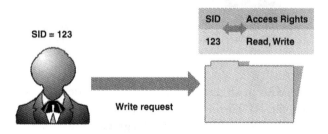

You can only move or copy a security principal between domains. To accomplish this you must create a new object in the target domain. Recall that a SID is domain specific, so when you create the new security principal in the target domain, a new SID is assigned to the object. In a down-level domain, you have to search all resource DACLs in the source domain and all trusting domains for references to the old SID and replace them with the new SID. This potentially daunting task is shown in Figure 8.11.

Figure 8.11 Replacing SIDs in Downlevel Domains

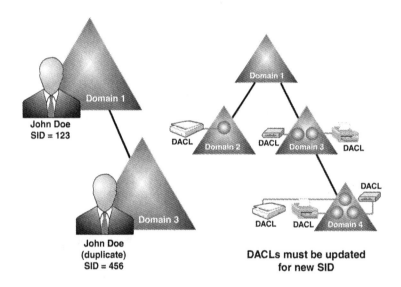

The task of updating all DACLs in all resource domains is considerably easier under Windows 2000. Active Directory employs the sIDHistory service attribute that maintains the original SID of an object. Its value ensures that access to resources can be granted after the restructure.

Tip: The sIDHistory attribute can only be used in a native-mode Windows 2000 domain.

The value of the sIDHistory attribute is appended to a user's access token when he or she logs on. The same is true that the sIDHistory attribute values are appended from each group where the user is a member. This ensures that access to resources is uninterrupted both during and after the migration.

Domain Restructure Tools

Microsoft and third-party software vendors provide several tools to help administrators in migrating from Windows NT 4.0 domains to Windows 2000 domains. These tools can also simplify restructuring a Windows 2000 forest. The migration tools that you can use to manage your restructure are as follows:

- Active Directory Migration Tool (ADMT)

- ClonePrincipal

- NETDOM

- LDP

- MoveTree

Comparing Domain Restructure Tools

Some tasks that you must perform during your restructure can be executed by more than one tool. In deciding which tool to use, compare the user interface against the command-line interface and determine which you prefer. In some cases, one tool may be chosen over another.

Active Directory Migration Tool

The ADMT is a Microsoft Management Console (MMC) wizard-based interface that is licensed from Mission Critical Software. The ADMT facilitates both inter-forest and intra-forest migrations.

The ADMT is a comprehensive migration tool. You can use the ADMT to move or copy user accounts, groups, and computer accounts from one domain to another while automatically populating the sIDHistory attribute of any migrated security principal.

By redefining permissions on source resources that have not yet been migrated, you can use ADMT to resolve file, directory, and share security issues related to the accounts that have been copied. You can use ADMT to analyze the impact of the migration both before and after the migration occurs. This tool also provides a mechanism to verify your migration scenario before you perform the actual migration.

Following are several key features of ADMT:

- Reporting

- Fallback capability

- Localized

- Support of multiple migration scenarios

Using ADMT reporting, you can generate pre-defined reports on the following:

- Migrated users and computers

- Expired computer accounts

- Accounts that are referenced in DACLs

- Naming conflicts

Many operations can be reversed providing fallback to an original state using the ADMT's fallback capabilities. The tool is localized into Windows 2000 server languages. It supports inter-forest restructures, the cloning of security principals and resources from a Windows NT 4.0 domain or a Windows 2000 domain to a Windows 2000 native-mode domain in a different forest. The tool also supports moving security principals and resources between Windows 2000 domains in the same forest, an intra-forest restructure.

ClonePrincipal Tool

ClonePrincipal is a Microsoft migration tool consisting of a suite of sample Microsoft Visual Basic scripts you can use to copy users and groups from a Windows NT 4.0 or Windows 2000 domain to a Windows 2000 native-mode domain. The tool allows you to perform the copy operations without impacting your existing production environment. ClonePrincipal retains access to resources in the source environment by populating the sIDHistory attribute of cloned accounts.

As shown in Figure 8.12, ClonePrincipal provides the following preset scripts:

- Sidhist.vbs
- Clonepr.vbs
- Clonegg.vbs
- Cloneggu.vbs
- Clonelg.vbs.

Figure 8.12 ClonePrincipal Preset Scripts

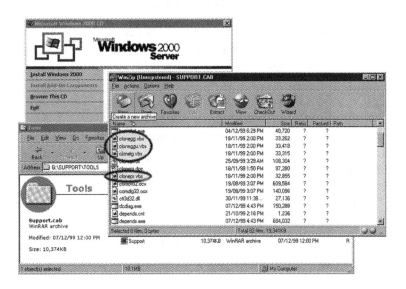

Sidhist.vbs copies the SID of a source principal to the SIDHistory of an existing destination principal.

Clonepr.vbs copies the properties of a source principal and the source SID to the SIDHistory of the destination object. If the destination principal exists, then both destination SAM name and the distinguished name (DN) must refer to the same object. The destination principal does not need to pre-exist.

Clonegg.vbs clones all global groups in a domain. It will clone well-known accounts, such as Domain Guests but will not clone built-in accounts, such as Backup Operators.

Cloneggu.vbs clones all global groups and users in a domain. This also includes well-known accounts but excludes built-in accounts.

Glonelg.vbs clones all local groups in a domain. This includes well-known groups but excludes built-in accounts.

 Note: ClonePrincipal files are found in the \support\tools folder of the Windows 2000 Server CD-ROM.

ClonePrincipal provides sample scripts that you can modify depending on the needs of your organization. The scripts are easily customized and can be combined. They can also be used in conjunction with other command-line migration tools using Visual Basic Scripting.

NETDOM Utility

NETDOM is a command-line utility you can use to facilitate both intra-forest and inter-forest restructure operations. It can query a domain for trust relationships and it can automatically create new trust relationships. You can use NETDOM as part of an automated migration script. The NETDOM utility is useful in an environment in which the existing trust relationships are unclear.

Using NETDOM, you can perform the following tasks:

- Securely join a computer running Windows 2000 to a Windows NT 4.0 or Windows 2000 Organizational Unit (OU)

- Add, remove or query client computer accounts

- While maintaining the primary SID, move an existing computer account from one domain to another

- Establish trust relationships

- Verify and reset secure channels for BDCs, domain replicas, and member clients and servers

- View and list trust relationships between Windows NT 4.0 and Windows 2000 domains as well as between two Windows 2000 domains

You can use NETDOM to establish both one-way and two-way trusts relationships for Windows NT 4.0 domains, Windows 2000 parent and child domains in a domain tree, and for the Windows 2000 portion of a trust link to a Kerberos realm.

LDP Graphical Tool

The LDP graphical tool is an Active Directory administrative tool whose interface is much like that of Windows Explorer. It allows a user to perform Lightweight Directory Access Protocol (LDAP) operations against any LDAP-compatible directory, such as Active Directory.

LDAP operations include the following command functions:

- Connect

- Bind

- Search

- Modify

- Add

- Delete

Administrators can use LDP to view objects and their attributes stored in Active Directory, such as security descriptors and replication metadata. This information is useful in troubleshooting as it allows the user to identify whether objects have been migrated or replicated between domain controllers.

MoveTree Utility

MoveTree is a command-line utility that moves Active Directory objects between domains in a single forest during an intra-forest migration. The following Active Directory objects can be moved using the MoveTree utility:

- OUs

- Users

- Groups

MoveTree preserves access to resources after a group, user, or computer is moved from one Windows 2000 domain to another by using the sIDHistory attribute.

 Note: MoveTree only works if the target domain is a native-mode Windows 2000 domain.

MoveTree can only move global groups as a closed set of groups in the source domain. This restriction makes MoveTree a tool of limited functionality in most migration scenarios.

Vocabulary

Review the following terms in preparation for the certification exam.

Term	Description
ADMT	The Active Directory Migration Tool is a wizard based Microsoft Management Console (MMC) interface that can be used to facilitate inter-forest and intra-forest restructures. It is licensed from Mission Critical Software.
ClonePrincipal	A set of Visual Basic scripts that are used to copy users and groups while populating the sIDHistory attribute. The scripts can be modified to suite the needs of your organization.
DACL	A Discretionary Access Control List is part of an object's security descriptor that is used to grant or deny access to the object by specific users or groups.
Distinguished Name	Every object in Active Directory has a distinguished name that is used to uniquely identify the object. It contains the name of the domain in which the object resides as well as the complete path through the container hierarchy to the object.

Term	Description
MMC	The Microsoft Management Console is a framework that hosts administrative consoles and provides some commands and tools for authoring consoles.
MoveTree	A command-line tool used in intra-forest restructures to move Active Directory objects between domains in a single forest.
NETDOM	A command line utility used to manage Windows 2000 domains and trust relationships. It is also used to facilitate inter-forest and intra-forest migration operations.
MoveTree	A command line tool used to facilitate intra-forest migration operations. It provides a mechanism by which security principals can be moved between domains in the same Active Directory forest.
OU	An Organizational Unit is an Active Directory container object in which users, groups, computers, printers and other organizational units are placed.
SAM	Security Accounts Manager is a Windows 2000 service used during the login process that maintains user information.
SID	A Security Identifier is a domain-specific identifier that is used by the operating system to distinguish security principals.
TCP/IP	The Transmission Control Protocol/Internet Protocol is a set of software protocols for networking that are widely used on the internet. The TCP/IP protocol provides a communication medium across interconnected networks with diverse hardware platforms and operating systems.

In Brief

If you want to...	Then do this...
Allow a clone the same access rights to network resources that were available to the source account.	You need to populate the sIDHistory attribute with the SID of the source account.
Clone a user	Use either the ADMT or ClonePrincipal migration tool.
Clone a global or universal group	Use either the ADMT or ClonePrincipal migration tool.
Migrate a computer	Use either the ADMT or NETDOM migration tool.
Move a security principal	Use either the ADMT or MoveTree migration tool.
Move a computer account	Use ADMT, NETDOM or do it manually at the local computer.

Lesson 8 Activities

Complete the following activities to prepare for the certification exam.

1. Describe the types of pre-defined reports you can generate with ADMT.

2. Define the restriction limits the functionality of MoveTree has in most restructure scenarios.

3. Define a security principal.

4. Discuss an advantage of cloning.

5. Describe the operations in an inter-forest restructure.

6. List the tools available to help manage a domain restructure.

7. A number of types of restructure are supported by the ADMT. List them.

8. Explain the conditions where you can use the sIDHistory attribute.

9. Describe the operations in an intra-forest restructure.

10. Contrast an inter-forest restructure with an intra-forest restructure.

Answers to Lesson 8 Activities

1. Using ADMT reporting, you can generate pre-defined reports for the following:

   - Migrated users and computers

   - Expired computer accounts

   - Accounts that are referenced in DACLs

   - Naming conflicts

2. The restriction that MoveTree can only move global groups as a closed set limits the functionality of MoveTree in most migration scenarios.

3. A security principal is a user, group or computer that has been assigned a security identifier.

4. One of the primary advantages to cloning is that it does not cause disruptions in the existing production environment. Another advantage is that cloning provides a mechanism for a secure fallback.

5. If you perform an inter-forest restructure, you will need to perform the following tasks:

   - Close users

   - Clone universal groups

   - Clone global groups

   - Clone domain local groups

   - Clone local groups

   - **Move computer accounts**

6. The available migration tools that you can use to manage your domain restructure are as follows:

   - Active Directory Migration Tool (ADMT)

   - ClonePrincipal

   - NETDOM

   - Ldp

   - MoveTree

7. The ADMT supports inter-forest restructures, the cloning of security principals and resources from a Windows NT 4.0 domain or a Windows 2000 domain to a Windows 2000 native-mode domain in a different forest, as well as intra-forest restructures, moving security principals and resources between Windows 2000 domains in the same forest.

8. The sIDHistory attribute can only be used in a native-mode Windows 2000 domain.

9. If you are performing an intra-forest restructure, you will need to perform the following operations:

    - Move users

    - Move global groups

    - Move domain local groups

    - Move closed sets

    - Move computers

    - Move local accounts

10. An inter-forest restructure involves copying security objects from a Windows NT 4.0 or Windows 2000 source domain to a Windows 2000 target domain. An intra-forest restructure involves moving security objects from one Windows 2000 domain to another Windows 2000 domain in the same Active Directory forest.

Lesson 8 Quiz

These questions test your knowledge of features, vocabulary, procedures, and syntax.

1. What is the purpose of the sIDHistory attribute?
   A. Store the history of the SIDs that have accessed a resource
   B. Maintain a history of all the SIDs that have been assigned in the domain
   C. Store a cloned or copied object's original SID
   D. Store a list of objects that have been assigned a specific SID

2. What are the most common operations in an inter-forest restructure?
   A. Cloning security principals
   B. Moving security principals
   C. Copying security principals
   D. Modifying security principals

3. What tool would you use to determine if an object has been migrated or replicated between domain controllers?
   A. LDP
   B. MoveTree
   C. ClonePrincipal
   D. NETDOM

4. What tool would you use to clone users in an inter-forest restructure?
   A. NETDOM
   B. ADMT
   C. MoveTree
   D. ClonePrincipal

5. How can you move computer accounts?

    A. Remotely, using MoveTree

    B. Remotely, using the ADMT

    C. Remotely, using NETDOM

    D. Manually configuring each computer to join the target domain

6. What type of objects can you move with MoveTree?

    A. OUs

    B. Resources

    C. Users

    D. Groups

7. Which tool would you use to view and list trust relationships between Windows NT 4.0 and Windows 2000 domains as well as between two Windows 2000 domains?

    A. MoveTree

    B. NETDOM

    C. Ldp

    D. ClonePrincipal

8. Which tool is a collection of sample Visual Basic scripts?

    A. NETDOM

    B. ADMT

    C. MoveTree

    D. ClonePrincipal

9. Which tool would you use to determine if any naming conflicts exist?

    A. ClonePrincipal

    B. ADMT

    C. NETDOM

    D. Ldp

10. What type of objects are security principals?

    A. Users

    B. Resources

    C. Groups

    D. Computers

Answers to Lesson 8 Quiz

1. Answer C is correct. The sIDHistory attribute is used to store a cloned or copied object's original SID.

    Answer A is incorrect. The sIDHistory attribute is not used to store the history of the SIDs that have accessed a resource.

    Answer B is incorrect. The sIDHistory attribute does not maintain a history of all the SIDs that have been assigned in the domain.

    Answer D is incorrect. The sIDHistory attribute does not store a list of objects that have been assigned a specific SID. A SID is unique to a single object in a single domain.

2. Answers A and C are correct. The most common operations in an inter-forest restructure are cloning or copying security principals.

    Answer B is incorrect. Security principals are not moved in an inter-forest restructure.

    Answer D is incorrect. Modification of a security principal is not a part of the migration process.

3. Answer A is correct. You would use Ldp to determine if an object has been migrated or replicated between domain controllers.

    Answer B is incorrect. The MoveTree utility is used to move objects between domains in a single forest.

    Answer C is incorrect. The ClonePrincipal utility is a set of scripts that clone users and groups.

    Answer D is incorrect. The NETDOM utility is used to query for and create trust relationships.

4. Answers B and D are correct. To clone users in an inter-forest restructure, you can use either the ClonePrincipal utility or the ADMT

    Answer A is incorrect. The NETDOM utility is used to query for and create trust relationships.

    Answer C is incorrect. The MoveTree utility is used to move objects between domains in a single forest.

5. Answers B, C and D are correct. You can accomplish moving computer accounts remotely, using the ADMT or NETDOM, or you can do it manually configuring each computer to join the target domain.

Answer A is incorrect. You cannot use MoveTree to move a computer account.

6. Answers A, C and D are correct. The Active Directory objects that can be moved using MoveTree include OUs, Users, and Groups

    Answer B is incorrect. You cannot move resources with MoveTree.

7. Answer B is incorrect. You would use NETDOM to view and list trust relationships between Windows NT 4.0 and Windows 2000 domains as well as between two Windows 2000 domains.

    Answer A is incorrect. MoveTree is used to move security principal objects between domains in a single forest.

    Answer C is incorrect. Ldp is used to query the attributes of an object in Active Directory.

    Answer D is incorrect. ClonePrincipal is used to clone users and groups to a new Windows 2000 environment.

8. Answer D is correct. ClonePrincipal is a Microsoft migration tool consisting of a suite of sample Microsoft Visual Basic scripts used to copy users and groups from a Windows NT 4.0 or Windows 2000 domain to a Windows 2000 native-mode domain.

    Answer A is incorrect. NETDOM is a command-line utility used to query or create trust relationships.

    Answer B is incorrect. The ADMT is a MMC interface wizard-based utility that allows you to generate reports and can analyze migration impacts before the migration occurs.

    Answer C is incorrect. MoveTree is a command-line utility that moves Active Directory security principals between domains in a single forest.

9. Answer B is correct. You would use ADMT to generate a pre-defined report that identifies naming conflicts.

    Answer A is incorrect. ClonePrincipal is used to clone users and groups.

    Answer C is incorrect. NETDOM is used to query and create trust relationships.

    Answer D is incorrect. Ldp is used to query the attributes of any object in Active Directory.

10. Answers A, C and D are correct. A security principal can be a user, group or computer.

    Answer B is incorrect. Resources are not security principals.

Lesson 9: Account Migration Issues

When you restructure a domain, you move or copy accounts to your target Windows 2000 domain. This involves careful planning because you can adversely affect several network functions including password continuity, application functionality, service accounts, and user rights. Therefore, it is critical that you understand the impact of a domain restructure on accounts.

After completing this lesson, you should have a better understanding of the following topics:

- Authentication issues

- Service account operation

- Hard-coded account mappings

- User rights assignments

- User profiles

- Exchange and Active Directory interoperability

- Application functionality

Authentication Issues

You need to plan for any issues involved with user authentication when you clone accounts to a new forest. During an inter-forest restructure, you clone accounts from a source domain to a Windows 2000 domain. When you do so, user passwords are not maintained, as illustrated in Figure 9.1.

Figure 9.1 User Passwords Are Not Maintained During a Restructure

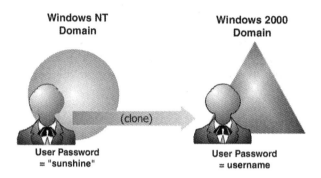

In an inter-forest restructure, the source domain can be either a Windows NT 4.0 domain or a Windows 2000 domain. During the restructure, you will migrate users from the source domain to a Windows 2000 domain. To ensure that you minimize the impact on user authentication during the restructure, you need to understand the affect migration has on user authentication.

 Warning: Authentication issues arise because passwords are not cloned when the user is cloned.

Understanding User Authentication

To clone or copy objects from one domain to another, you must create and maintain trust relationships between the source and target domains, as illustrated in Figure 9.2. If you clone users with the Active Directory Migration Tool (ADMT), by default the new accounts are enabled. Since these new accounts are enabled, it is then possible for a cloned user to log on with credentials from either the source or cloned account. The ability to log on with either account can cause administrator or user confusion. This is especially true if configuration changes are applied to the source account rather than to the cloned account.

Figure 9.2 Trust Relationships Created for the Migration

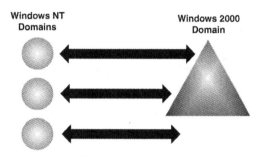

Another potential issue that arises is because passwords are not migrated during an inter-forest domain restructure, and logon attempts will fail. Significant support issues can be generated by failed logon attempts due to the use of incorrect passwords.

Minimizing Authentication Service Issues

You can implement the follow tasks to minimize authentication service issues:

- Determine how to set passwords for cloned accounts

- Determine how to securely distribute passwords for cloned user accounts

- Determine whether accounts must be disabled during the cloning process

- Determine when clients will be allowed to log on using cloned accounts

Setting Passwords on Cloned Accounts

You will need to determine how to set passwords on cloned accounts. At your disposal are several tools for cloning accounts. Each of the following tools handles passwords differently:

- MoveTree maintains the password when a user account is moved

- ADMT sets a random complex password on user accounts

- ADMT sets the password to the username on migrated accounts

- By default, ClonePrincipal sets the password to NULL on cloned accounts

---

 Note: Additional scripting is required to set initial passwords if ClonePrincipal is used.

Securely Distributing Passwords for Cloned User Accounts

If you use ADMT to clone user accounts, then you must decide how to distribute passwords to all the users in a secure manner. You can choose to physically deliver the passwords or you can distribute them using e-mail.

 Tip: If you set the user password to match the user's name or leave the password field blank, then it is recommended that you set the **User must change password at next logon** option.

Disabling Accounts During the Cloning Process

You must determine if you want to disable accounts during the cloning process since ClonePrincipal disables the newly-cloned accounts by default. An administrator must enable them using Active Directory Users and Computers in the Microsoft Management Console (MMC). This concept is illustrated in Figure 9.3.

Figure 9.3 Enabling a User with Active Directory Users and Computers

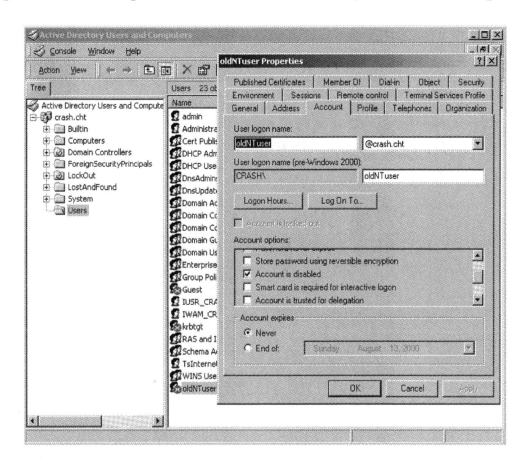

You will have move flexibility in your decisions if you use the ADMT tool because this choice (Figure 9.4) allows you to disable either the source or target account.

Figure 9.4 Disabling Accounts with the ADMT

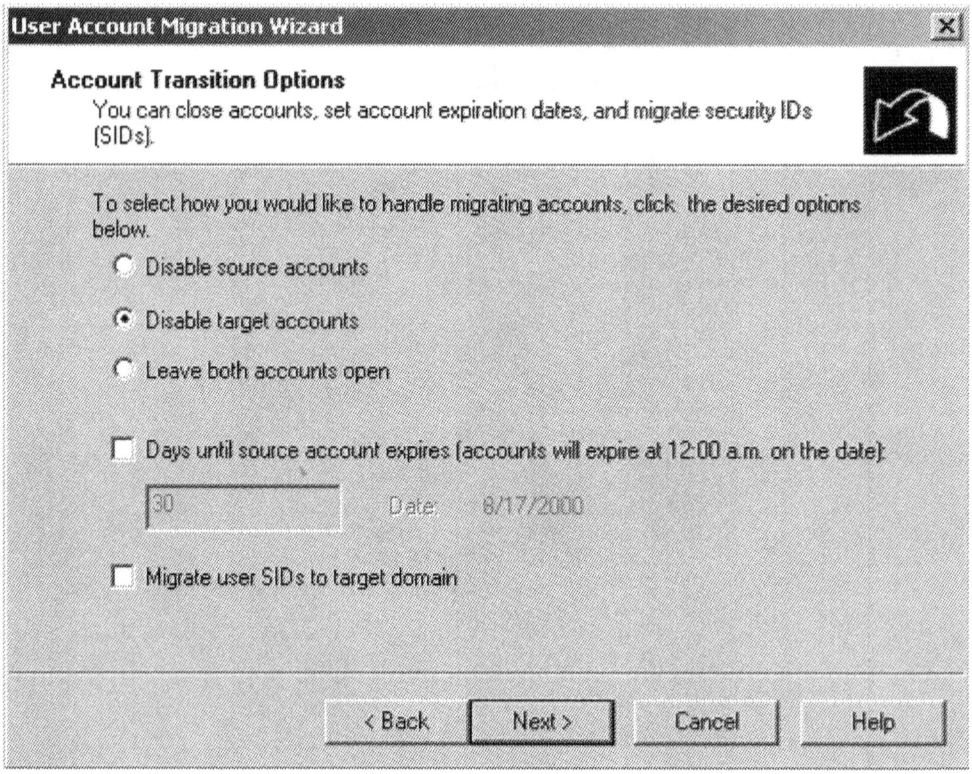

Allowing Clients to Log On Using Cloned Accounts

Cloned accounts must not be made available to a user until you have completely and thoroughly deployed and tested the target environment. The deployment includes the distribution of any new passwords. Further, the new accounts should not be made available until all source accounts have been disabled. You can configure the ADMT to disable cloned accounts.

Service Account Operation

You must ensure that all cloned service accounts maintain all necessary rights. This requires some careful planning.

Microsoft Exchange 5.5 and other network applications and services require access to various network components, such as the SAM database. A special type of user account called a service account, authenticates the application or service in the domain and provides access to these components. Service accounts are often defined within both the SAM database and the application. Because of this, you must take special care to ensure that related applications or services continue to function when you migrate these service accounts.

Planning for Service Account Functionality

To reduce the risk of times when a service or application is not functional, your domain restructure plan should address the following concerns:

- Identifying all service accounts used in the source domain

- Migrating all service accounts to the target domain

- Resetting all passwords on service accounts

- Identifying service accounts that cannot be updated with ADMT

- Creating the necessary trust relationships

Identifying All Service Accounts in the Source Domain

For each server with service accounts, you will need to document all of the service accounts that are in use. Your documentation must include the following:

- Service account name

- Password

- Related services

- Any additional rights assigned to the service account

You can use the Service Accounts Migration wizard in ADMT to identify or enumerate all service accounts in a domain. This is illustrated in Figure 9.5. You will need to manually document all specific password information.

Figure 9.5 Using the Service Accounts Migration Wizard

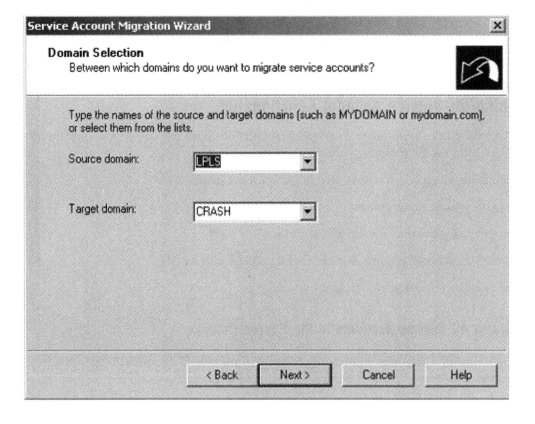

Migrating All Service Accounts to the Target Domain

After you have enumerated all service accounts with the Service Accounts Migration wizard, you can use the User Migration wizard in the ADMT to clone or move accounts. The User Migration wizard is shown in Figure 9.6.

Figure 9.6 The ADMT User Migration Wizard

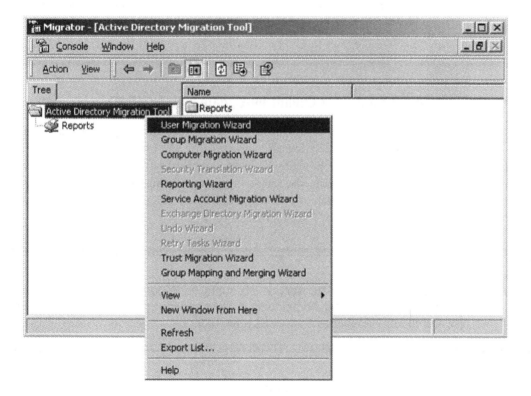

Resetting All Passwords on Service Accounts

When you use the ADMT to clone service accounts, it generates complex random passwords for each service account. You can find these passwords in the PASSWORD.TXT file. All source domain references to the service account must be manually reconfigured with the new password.

 Warning: A failure of a service using the migrated service account may result if not all necessary rights have been defined. Document all special rights assignments to the service prior to the migration to ensure that they can be reconstructed if necessary.

Identifying Service Accounts That Cannot be Updated Using ADMT

The Service Account Migration wizard will note the service accounts requiring manual updating. Some applications will create application-specific services that run under the security context of a specific service account. In this case, the ADMT will be unable to update the service account information. Since the ADMT cannot update the service account information, all service account references must be manually updated to reference the cloned service account. For example, ADMT cannot update service account information for Exchange Server 5.5.

 Tip: You can manually update service accounts in Windows NT 4.0 target by using Services in Control Panel. To manually update service accounts in Windows 2000, use the Computer Management administrative tool.

Creating the Necessary Trust Relationships

After the migration is completed, you must create the necessary trust relationships so that only the cloned service account is used.

You must establish trust relationships from the resource domains that contain the service to the target domain where the cloned account resides. You must also establish trust relationships from resource domains where an application that requires the service is installed to the target domain where the cloned account is located.

You then have to remove the trust relationship established with the original source domain. Since the cloned service account uses the sIDHistory attribute to retain the original SID of the service account from the source domain, the cloned service account should still work. This concept is illustrated in Figure 9.7.

Figure 9.7 The sIDHistory Attribute Retains the Original SID

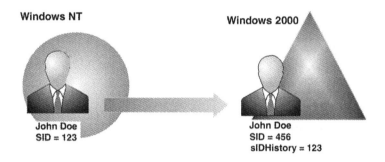

Hard-Coded Account Mappings

A setting that cannot be reconfigured using a migration tool such as ADMT is a hard-coded account mapping. Many applications use hard-coded account mappings, such as Microsoft Exchange Server 5.5. You will need to update these hard-coded account mappings after you complete the domain restructure. Reconfiguration of hard-coded account mappings is accomplished in one of the following ways:

● Registry settings

● Settings within the application

Many applications will have Universal Naming Convention (UNC) mappings in their configurations as well as hard-coded account mappings. For example, Exchange Server 5.5 hard codes the Exchange service account in the Exchange schema.

Configuring Accounts

In all domain-restructuring scenarios, hard-coded account mapping issues can arise. This occurs when the application is migrated between the following domain types:

- Between domains in the same forest

- Between domains in separate forests

- Between Windows NT 4.0 target domains

When you restructure your Windows 2000 forest, you might need to change these mappings to point to the cloned accounts or to new servers that will host the application. If you do not configure the account information correctly, an application may cease to function. To allow the application to continue to function in a manner consistent with the pre-migration environment, you will have to manually reconfigure the hard-coded configuration.

Cloning Hard-Coded Accounts

You need to ensure that all hard-coded account settings issues are resolved during your Windows 2000 migration. To accomplish this, consider the following tasks:

- Determine if any application have hard-coded setting

- Determine the steps required to change hard-coded settings

- Deploy changes to the configuration

- Verify that the application performs as expected after the migration

Determining if Any Applications Have Hard-coded Settings

You can determine hard-coded account settings that require manual reconfiguration with the Service Account Migration wizard in the ADMT as shown in Figure 9.8.

Figure 9.8 Services Accounts Migration Wizard

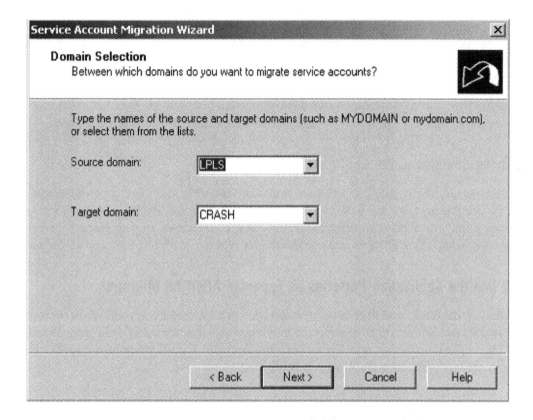

You will also find many hard-coded settings in your test lab, during migration trial testing.

 Note: You must manually configure Exchange Server 5.5 when the service account is migrated.

Determining the Required Steps to Change Hard-coded Settings

To determine how you will change hard-coded settings, you first need to locate and define the needed changes. To find these changes, you may have to search through Knowledge Base articles. You may also need to contact the software manufacturer. The changes you make could require changes to specific registry entries or an application's configuration. If you are unable to determine the changes, you may have to install the application on a new server.

Any solution that you deploy must be tested in your test lab first, and you must document the steps for performing the changes. This documentation should be included in your restructure plan.

Deploying Changes to the Configuration

It is best to minimize the time that an application is off-line when it is migrated to the target environment. Ensure that you develop well-documented procedures in the test lab as you reconfigure hard-coded accounts. You must completely understand the ramifications of any changes to hard-coded account mappings. These changes must be thoroughly tested in both a test lab and a pilot project.

Verify that the Application Performs as Expected After the Migration

Regardless of the results and findings in your test lab and pilot project, you will still need to verify that a migrated application functions as expected in the new environment. After you complete the migration of the application to the target forest, you should employ a small group of the application's users to determine that the application functions as required.

User Rights Assignments

When you perform your domain restructure, you might encounter issues with specific user rights that have been assigned to user accounts in the source domain. User rights must be migrated to the Windows 2000 forest to ensure correct operability of service accounts.

Understanding User Rights Restructuring

All user rights must be migrated to the target forest with the user accounts so that the user's rights function correctly. Sometimes certain operations will fail if the user rights are not migrated. An operation can fail because it is not running in a security context that allows it to perform required functionality.

An example of this interoperability between user rights and service accounts is found in Exchange Server 5.5. Exchange Server requires that the service account be assigned the Act as Part of the Operating System user right, allowing Post Office Protocol 3 (POP3) e-mail users to access their mailboxes.

Migrating User Rights

It is essential that you ensure user rights are correctly migrated to the new Active Directory forest. To do this, you will need to perform the following tasks:

- Determine the accounts with assigned special access rights

- Migrate users with assigned special rights

- Migrate groups with assigned special rights

- Run the Security Translation wizard to update group changes

Determining Accounts with Assigned Special Access Rights

You must determine which accounts have been assigned special access rights. You can accomplish this using one of the following tools:

- User Manager For Domains in Windows NT 4.0 target

- Group Policy console in Windows 2000

You can use the list of groups and users generated by these tools to ensure that all user rights are migrated correctly. You can also use the Service Account Migration wizard, illustrated in Figure 9.9, to determine all accounts that have been assigned as logon accounts for services.

Figure 9.9 Service Account Migration Wizard

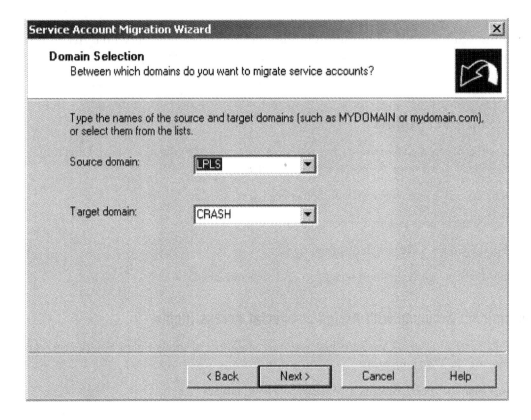

Migrating Users with Assigned Special Rights

To migrate users who have been assigned special user rights, use the ADMT tool. It will flag any accounts that have been identified by the Service Account Migration wizard on a Service Account information page, as illustrated in Figure 9.10.

Figure 9.10 ADMT Service Account Information

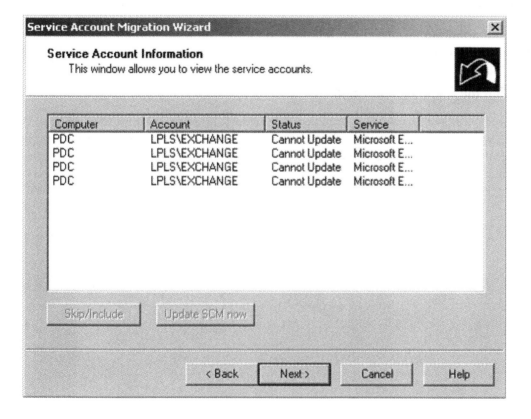

For any items on the Service Account information page that include the "On the machines where they reside" option, be sure to enable "Migrate all service accounts" and update the Service Control

Manager. This action ensures that all service account entries are changed from the original source accounts to the cloned accounts.

Migrating Groups with Assigned Special Rights

To migrate groups with assigned special rights, you must clone any administrator-created local groups to the target domain using one of the following tools:

- ADMT

- ClonePrincipal

A requirement of group migration is that any specific user rights assigned to groups are reconstructed in the target Windows 2000 forest.

Running the Security Translation Wizard

You need to run the Security Translation wizard (Figure 9.11) to update any group changes. You must run the wizard against the source computer if user rights have been assigned directly to groups. This ensures that the user rights assignments all point to the cloned account instead of the original source account.

Figure 9.11 Security Translation Wizard

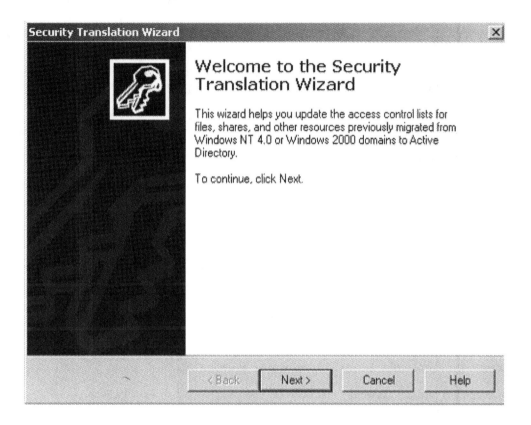

User Profiles

During your inter-forest restructure, you will modify user profiles to allow access by the cloned user accounts. Access to user profiles is based on an account's SID. During the migration, cloning an account generates a new SID for the account, which will not be recognized by the user profile.

It is important that you understand what happens when a user logs on to a Windows NT 4.0 client. Once the user is authenticated, the system determines the correct user profile to load by matching the user's SID to a subkey under the registry key that maintain the user profile list. When the user's account is cloned and a new primary SID is assigned, the user will lose access to his or her logon profile.

 Note: A user's Windows NT 4.0 profile is found as a subkey under the registry key HKEY_LOCAL_COMPUTER \ SOFTWARE \ Microsoft \ Windows \ NT \ CurrentVersion \ ProfileList.

During an intra-forest restructure, profile modification is not an issue when accounts are moved, because the profile can be matched to the target account by using the Globally Unique Identifier (GUID) of the object. The GUID is not changed when the account is moved.

Migrating User Profiles

You must ensure that user profiles are available to users who have been migrated to the new Active Directory forest by performing the following tasks:

- Determine if profile migration is necessary

- Determine whether any manual configuration is required

- Ensure that all roaming user profiles have been activated

- Determine if protected storage has been implemented in the source domain

Determining if Profile Migration is Necessary

You must determine if profile migration is necessary to meet migration goals. You may want to ease user transition to the new environment by maintaining user profiles. However, doing so may cause problems for users who continue to authenticate against both the source and target domains. Problems arise when profile configuration settings are made and saved to the profile in the target domain are not compatible with the operating system of the source domain.

The ADMT migrates profiles and application data to the target domain by altering the registry key. This allows the key to point to the user account's new primary SID. This functionality is not found in either ClonePrincipal or NETDOM.

Determining if Manual Configuration is Required

You must determine if any manual configuration is required for the migrated profile. By default, all application-based data is migrated to the target domain. Several third-party applications that store configuration data in the user profile may require additional configuration. You can automate the additional configuration by using the ADMT tool, which allows you to add additional code.

Ensuring That All Roaming User Profiles Have Been Activated

Prior to the migration, you will need to make sure all roaming user profiles have been activated. Before an account is cloned to the new target domain, roaming user profiles must be used so that all files in the roaming user profile have been created and security settings can be reapplied to match the new SID.

Determining if Protected Storage Has Been Implemented in the Source Domain

If Protected Storage (PStore) has been implemented in the source domain, PStore allows applications to maintain secret user data such as private keys. PStore encryption and decryption private keys are not available to a migrated user and must be migrated to the cloned user account.

Prior to the migration, you can use CryptoAPI (CAPI) to export the contents of PStore under the security context of the user to be migrated. Ensure that you store the exported keys securely during the migration. Use CAPI to re-import the exported keys into the migrated user's PStore under the security context of the migrated user.

 Note: In Windows NT 4.0 target, very few applications use PStore. As you begin to deploy Windows 2000, more applications will use PStore, and you should consider this fact when planning your migration strategy.

The Encrypting File System (EFS) uses PStore to protect its core secrets such as keys and key management information. If you implement EFS before an account is cloned without exporting all keys in the source PStore prior to migration, the cloned user will not have access to the encryption keys. You should not implement EFS until the source account domain is decommissioned.

Exchange Server and Active Directory Interoperability

One of the primary tasks during a domain restructure is to ensure that resource access is maintained both during and after the migration. A common and effective way of doing this is to ensure that the original SID of each Windows NT 4.0 target user account is preserved in the sIDHistory attribute of its cloned account.

All attributes are maintained for a user account in an intra-forest migration. However, not all attributes are cloned during an inter-forest domain restructure. For example, passwords are not migrated during an inter-forest migration. The recommended method of populating the target Active Directory is by using either the ADMT or ClonePrincipal utilities. You may select the Active Directory Connector (ADC) as an alternative method. You can use the ADC to both extend the attribute set of Active Directory and to populate attribute values for user objects that have been migrated using ADMT or ClonePrincipal.

Leveraging Exchange 5.5 Information

If you have deployed Exchange Server 5.5 in your existing source network, you can migrate user attributes from the Exchange directory service to Active Directory by performing the following tasks:

- Migrate all source user accounts to the target Active Directory

- Determine where you can perform writes to user attributes

- Determine how Exchange attributes will be mapped to Active Directory attributes

- Determine who will install the ADC

- Ensure that Exchange Server has the latest Service Pack installed

- Determine where the ADC will be installed

- Configure the ADC connection agreement.

Migrating Source User Accounts to Active Directory

Using migration tools, you can migrate all source user accounts to the target Active Directory. You can use the ADC to populate accounts in Active Directory, however, the new SIDs assigned to the objects that it creates must be manually mapped to the source account SIDs. This can be accomplished by using either the ClonePrincipal script Sidhist.vbs, or by using ADClean from Exchange Server 2000.

If you use the ADC to create new accounts in Active Directory, they will not have their previous primary SID stored in the sIDHistory attribute. It is better to use the ADC to synchronize account attributes between the source and target directories.

Determining Where You Can Perform Writes to User Attributes

Your administrative structure will determine where you can perform writes to user attributes. If changes to the user attributes will only occur in Exchange or in Active Directory Users and Computer, you will want to configure the Connection Agreement as a one-way connection.

Mapping Exchange Server Attributes to Active Directory

If you have not customized any Exchange Server attributes, then you can use the default mapping. However, if you customized Exchange attributes, some modification may be required to map the Exchange attributes to Active Directory attributes.

Determining Who Will Install the ADC

ADC installation extends the Active Directory schema.

Tip: The person who performs the schema portion of the ADC installation must be a member of the Schema Admins group.

Ensuring That Exchange Server Has the Latest Service Pack Installed

You must ensure that the latest Service Pack has been installed on the Exchange Server. You must apply Exchange Server 5.5 SP3 to the Exchange Server to use the ADC. Exchange Server 5.5 SP3 extends the Exchange schema with attributes that are located in Active Directory.

Determining Where the ADC Will Be Installed

You should install the ADC on a Windows 2000 member server to obtain the best performance. The server needs to be on the same physical network segment as a global catalog server and the Exchange 5.5 bridgehead server.

Configuring the ADC Connection Agreement

You can configure a connection agreement in ADC to define how data will be shared or synchronized between Exchange and Active Directory. You can also configure which directory service user attributes can be modified and how those attributes will be mapped between Exchange and Active Directory.

Application Functionality

After you have determined your migration methodology, you need to carefully plan that application functionality is not disrupted during the migration process. Your organization depends upon the functionality of its applications to perform daily job tasks. It is critical to the business that these operations continue to function without interruption, or with as little interruption as possible, during the migration to Windows 2000 Active Directory services.

Understanding Application Functions

To conduct your migration with little or no interruption of application functionality, you need to understand the interoperability of several business applications. For example, your organization might employ database applications that depend upon a Structured Query Language (SQL) database server such as Microsoft SQL Server. You must ensure that the migration process does not adversely impact the performance or accuracy of such interactions.

You must identify and prioritize your business applications, determining their usage, relative value to the organization, number, and types of users, the working environment, and any application dependencies. Determine the use and functionality of an application as well as all application dependencies, and document what you find.

Prior to the migration, you should thoroughly test all business applications to determine their functionality under Windows 2000. You also need to test any applications or services that your applications rely on.

No amount of testing will be completely successful in discovering all issues related to migration. You must verify the results of your tests in a pilot project that models your business environment. Use the pilot project to ensure that the interoperability and functionality of applications and the resources will operate correctly in the target environment.

Vocabulary

Review the following terms in preparation for the certification exam.

Term	Description
ADC	The Active Directory Connector is a synchronization agent in Windows 2000 that provides an automated way of keeping directory information consistent.
ADClean	A utility provided with Exchange Server2000.
ADMT	The Active Directory Migration Tool is a wizard based Microsoft Management Console (MMC) interface that can be used to facilitate inter-forest and intra-forest restructures. It is licensed from Mission Critical Software.
API	An Application Programming Interface is a set of routines that an application can use to request low-level services from a computer's operating system.
connection agreement	A configurable section in the ADC that holds information such as server names to contact for synchronization and the synchronization schedule.
CAPI	CryptoAPI is a Windows 2000 Application-Programming Interface (API) that provides a set of functions that allow applications to encrypt data while providing protection for private keys.

Term	Description
ClonePrincipal	A set of Visual Basic scripts that are used to copy users and groups while populating the sIDHistory attribute. The scripts can be modified to suite the needs of your organization.
EFS	The Encrypting File System is a method of encrypting data files using a randomly generated key.
GUID	The Globally Unique Identifier is a 16-byte value that is generated from the unique identifier on a device, the current data and time, and a sequence number. It is used to identify a particular device or component.
MMC	The Microsoft Management Console is a framework that hosts administrative consoles and provides some commands and tools for authoring consoles.
MoveTree	A command-line tool used in intra-forest restructures to move Active Directory objects between domains in a single forest.
NETDOM	A command-line utility used to manage Windows 2000 domains and trust relationships. It is also used to facilitate inter-forest and intra-forest migration operations.
POP3	Post Office Protocol 3 is a protocol that allows a client computer to communicate with a post office computer and retrieve e-mail.
PStore	Protected Storage provides an application with a protected place to store per-user data that must be kept secret or free from modification.

Term	Description
SAM	Security Accounts Manager is a Windows 2000 service used during the login process that maintains user information.
service account	A special type of user account used to authenticate an application or service in the domain and provide access to network components.
SID	A Security Identifier is a domain-specific identifier that is used by the operating system to distinguish security principals.
SP	A Service Pack is an installation package that upgrades an application or operating system.
Sidhist.vbs	A Visual Basic script provided with ClonePrincipal migration utility.
SQL	The Structured Query Language is a standardized database query language used by large, high-performance database programs such as Microsoft SQL Server.

In Brief

If you want to...	Then do this...
Manually update service accounts in Windows NT 4.0	Use Services in Control Panel.
Manually update service accounts in Windows 2000	Use the Computer Management administrative tool.
Populate accounts in Active Directory	The recommended method of populating Active Directory is by using either the ADMT or ClonePrincipal utilities. You may select the ADC as an alternative method, however, the new SID assigned to the objects that ADC creates must be manually mapped to the source account SID.
Migrate profiles and application data to the target Windows 2000 domain	Use the ADMT to migrate profiles and application data into a Windows 2000 domain.

Lesson 9 Activities

Complete the following activities to better prepare you for the certification exam.

1. Discuss the impact of and reason for failed logon attempts during an inter-forest domain restructure.

2. Describe how you can configure the ADC connection agreement.

3. Discuss how to ensure that resource access is maintained both during and after the migration.

4. Describe how to map Exchange Server attributes to Active Directory.

5. Describe how user account attributes affect an intra-forest migration.

6. Discuss the need for profile modification when accounts are moved during an intra-forest restructure.

7. Describe where to install the ADC to obtain the best performance.

8. Discuss the conditions that allow a user to log on to either a source or cloned account.

9. Describe how to migrate user attributes from the Exchange directory service to Active Directory.
10. Discuss how the EFS used PStore.

Answers to Lesson 9 Activities

1. Significant support issues and demands can be generated by failed logon attempts due to the use of incorrect passwords because passwords are not migrated during an inter-forest domain restructure.

2. You can configure a connection agreement in ADC to define how data will be shared or synchronized between Exchange and Active Directory. You can also configure which directory service user attributes can be modified and how those attributes will be mapped between Exchange and Active Directory.

3. A common and effective way of ensuring that resource access is maintained both during and after the migration is to ensure that the original SID of each Windows NT 4.0 target user account is preserved in the sIDHistory attribute of its cloned account.

4. If you have not customized any Exchange attributes, then you can use the default mapping. However, if any customization of Exchange attributes has been made, some modification may be required to map the Exchange attributes to Active Directory attributes.

5. All attributes are maintained for a user account in an intra-forest migration.

6. During an intra-forest restructure, profile modification is not an issue when accounts are moved because the profile can be matched to the target account by using the Globally Unique Identifier (GUID) of the object. The GUID is not changed when the account is moved.

7. You should install the ADC on a Windows 2000 member server to get the best performance. The server needs to be on the same physical network segment as a global catalog server and the Exchange 5.5 bridgehead server.

8. If you clone users with the Active Directory Migration Tool (ADMT), the new accounts are enabled by default. Because the new accounts are enabled, it is possible for a cloned user to log on with credentials from either the source or cloned account.

9. You migrate user attributes from the Exchange directory service to Active Directory by using the ADC after you migrate all source user accounts to the target Active Directory, determine where you can perform writes to user attributes and decide how Exchange attributes will be mapped to Active Directory attributes. You will need to determine who will install the ADC and where it will be installed. You also need to ensure that Exchange Server has the latest Service Pack installed and configure the ADC connection agreement.

10. The EFS uses PStore to protect its core secrets, for example keys and key management information

Lesson 9 Quiz

These questions test your knowledge of features, vocabulary, procedures, and syntax.

1. Who can perform the schema portion of the ADC installation?

    A. An administrator with privileges in the source and target domains

    B. A domain administrator

    C. A member of the Schema Admins group

    D. A backup operator

2. What are the recommended methods for populating a target Active Directory?

    A. ADC

    B. ADMT

    C. Netdom

    D. ClonePrincipal

3. Which tool would you use to synchronize account attributes between source and target directories?

    A. ClonePrincipal

    B. Netdom

    C. ADMT

    D. ADC

4. Which tool do you use to find service accounts that will require manual updating?

    A. Service Account Migration wizard

    B. ADMT

    C. Netdom

    D. ClonePrincipal

5. Which tool do you use to export the contents of PStore?

    A. ADMT

    B. Netdom

    C. CAPI

    D. ClonePrincipal

6. What types of source domains are migrated during an inter-forest restructure?

    A. Windows 2000 domain in the same forest

    B. Windows NT 4.0 target domain

    C. Windows NT 3.1 domain

    D. Windows 2000 domain in a different forest

7. How can you determine accounts that have been assigned special access rights?

    A. User Manager For Domains in Windows NT 4.0 target

    B. Group Policy console in Windows 2000

    C. NETDOM

    D. ClonePrincipal

8. How can you map a new object SID to a source account SID?

    A. MoveTree

    B. ClonePrincipal script Sidhist.vbs

    C. NETDOM

    D. ADClean from Exchange 2000 server

9. What extends the Exchange schema with attributes that are located in Active Directory?

    A. Active Directory Schema

    B. MoveTree

    C. ClonePrincipal

    D. Exchange Server 5.5 SP3

10. Which tool migrates profiles and application data to the target domain by altering the registry key to refer to the user account's new primary SID?

    A. ADMT

    B. ClonePrincipal

    C. MoveTree

    D. NETDOM

Answers to Lesson 9 Quiz

1. Answer C is correct. The person who performs the schema portion of the ADC installation must be a member of the Schema Admins group.

    Answer A is incorrect. An administrator with privileges in the source and target domains cannot perform the schema portion of the ADC installation unless he or she belongs to the Schema Admins group.

    Answer B is incorrect. A domain administrator cannot perform the schema portion of the ADC installation unless he or she belongs to the Schema Admins group.

    Answer D is incorrect. A backup operator, by default, cannot perform installations.

2. Answers B and D are correct. The recommended method of populating the target Active Directory is by using either the ADMT or ClonePrincipal utilities.

    Answer A is incorrect. You can use the ADC, but it will require additional work.

    Answer D is incorrect. NETDOM is not used to populate Active Directory.

3. Answer D is correct. Use the ADC to synchronize account attributes between the source and target directories

    Answer A is incorrect. ClonePrincipal is used to copy users and groups to a native-mode domain.

    Answer B is incorrect. NETDOM is a command line utility used to manage Windows 2000 domains and trust relationships.

    Answer C is incorrect. The ADMT can be used to facilitate inter-forest and intra-forest restructures.

4. Answer A is correct. Use the Service Account Migration wizard to determine accounts that will require manual updating

    Answer B is incorrect. The ADMT will not find accounts that require manual updating. It is used to facilitate inter-forest and intra-forest restructures.

    Answer C is incorrect. NETDOM is a command line utility used to manage Windows 2000 domains and trust relationships.

    Answer D is incorrect. ClonePrincipal is used to copy users and groups to a native-mode domain.

5. Answer C is incorrect. You use CryptoAPI (CAPI) to export the contents of PStore under the security context of the user to be migrated.

    Answer A is incorrect. The ADMT is used to facilitate inter-forest and intra-forest restructures

    Answer B is incorrect. NETDOM is a command line utility used to manage Windows 2000 domains and trust relationships.

    Answer D is incorrect. ClonePrincipal is used to copy users and groups to a native-mode domain.

6. Answers B and D are correct. In an inter-forest restructure, the source domain can be either a Windows NT 4.0 target domain or a Windows 2000 domain that resides in a different forest than the target Windows 2000 domain.

    Answer A is incorrect. For an inter-forest restructure, the Windows 2000 source domain must be in a different forest.

    Answer C is incorrect. You must upgrade a Window NT 3.1 domain to Windows NT 4.0 target prior to migration.

7. Answers A and B are correct. You use User Manager For Domains in Windows NT 4.0 target and Group Policy console in Windows 2000 to determine which accounts have been assigned special access rights.

    Answer C is incorrect. NETDOM is a command line utility used to manage Windows 2000 domains and trust relationships.

    Answer D is incorrect. ClonePrincipal is used to copy users and groups to a native-mode domain.

8. B and D are correct. You can manually map a new SID assigned to a new object to the source account SID by using either the ClonePrincipal script Sidhist.vbs, or ADClean from Exchange 2000 server.

    Answer A is incorrect. MoveTree is a command-line tool used in intra-forest restructures to move Active Directory objects between domains in a single forest.

    Answer C is incorrect. NETDOM is a command line utility used to manage Windows 2000 domains and trust relationships.

9. Answer D is correct. Exchange Server 5.5 Service Pack 3 extends the Exchange schema with attributes that are located in Active Directory

    Answer A is incorrect. The Active Directory Schema defines objects stored in Active Directory.

Answer B is incorrect. MoveTree is a command-line tool used in intra-forest restructures to move Active Directory objects between domains in a single forest.

Answer C is incorrect. ClonePrincipal is used to copy users and groups to a native-mode domain.

10. Answer A is correct. The ADMT migrates profiles and application data to the target domain by altering the registry key to refer to the user account's new primary SID.

    Answer B is incorrect. This functionality is not found in ClonePrincipal, which is used to copy users and groups to a native-mode domain.

    Answer C is incorrect. MoveTree is a command-line tool used in intra-forest restructures to move Active Directory objects between domains in a single forest.

    Answer D is incorrect. This functionality is not found in NETDOM, which is used to manage Windows 2000 domains and trust relationships.

Lesson 10: Migration Deployment

You have put considerable effort and consideration into developing your Windows 2000 migration strategy. You have selected a migration path, developed an upgrade or restructure strategy, and determined ways to ensure continued productivity during the migration. In addition, you have assessed the risks to your production environment.

Now you must create a project plan for deploying your migration strategy. The documentation that is required to create your deployment plan, as well as selecting an installation strategy are key considerations. You must plan for testing and conducting a pilot program that will ensure a smooth transition to Windows 2000.

After completing this lesson, you should have a better understanding of the following topics:

- Migration deployment plan

- Migration planning documents

- Installation strategies

- Migration deployment components

- Migration plan testing

- Migration pilot

- Windows 2000 transition

- Migration scenarios

Migration Deployment Plan

You will need to carefully plan how you will deploy your Windows 2000 migration strategy to ensure a successful migration. A migration can be a large and complex task that can appear overwhelming. Creating a thoroughly planned migration strategy and project plan will help to break your project down into manageable tasks.

Without a deployment plan, your project may fail to deliver its key business value. Your migration goals and vision may conflict with those of the Information Technology (IT) group or executive management. Without a deployment plan, your project will appear to lack integrity and will certainly appear to be missing the careful consideration and thought that you have already expended in developing your migration strategies.

Identifying Deployment Goals

During the deployment phase, the technical dependencies of Windows 2000 features become more important. The deployment teams in your organization will need to collaborate and share insight into the various capabilities, functionality, and interdependencies of these features.

Further, you will need to test and refine your design specification to ensure that it meets the needs of your organization. For example, you may have different IT and business requirements that have resulted in several namespace design variations for your Microsoft Active Directory. Each of these designs needs to be evaluated against your business and IT requirements and criteria to ensure that they are appropriate for your organization.

Through careful analysis and testing, you will be able to select the appropriate design and implement the correct namespace. You must remember that the results of your testing and decisions are going to be specific to your organization.

Creating a Deployment Plan

Your project deployment plan will include various aspects of your business and your technical network infrastructure. When creating your migration deployment plan, you must accomplish the following:

- Define your migration scope
- Define your migration vision
- Establish personnel requirements
- Organize the migration team
- Create the appropriate documentation

Defining Migration Scope and Vision

It is important to define and document the scope of your migration project as well as your vision of the future of your network. You should document both the scope and your vision for your migration efforts.

Migration Scope

The bounds for the migration project are defined by its scope. The scope document clarifies and differentiates between what the migration must accomplish and what is desirable but non-essential. In your scope document you can prioritize the components of a Windows 2000 network that you must put in place first to meet the most pressing business needs.

For each phase of the project, you should begin with a scope statement that defines what the project phase seeks to accomplish. For example, for the pilot project, your scope statement may perhaps read like the following:

"The scope of the pilot project is to investigate and test the features of Windows 2000 and the interoperability of existing application programs. You might want to develop a scope statement for each phase of the project. A scope statement for the pilot project is shown in Figure 10.1."

Figure 10.1 Pilot Project Scope Statement

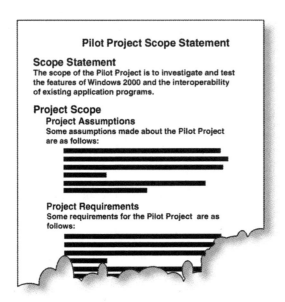

Migration Vision Statement

A vision statement is an unbounded view of the future. Your migration vision establishes both your long-term and short-term goals for your future network. A vision statement can motivate and inspire the migration teams for the long-term success of the migration effort. It can also help to establish short-range goals and objectives. Inclusion of both long-term and short-term goals leads to dedication and a high-quality effort of your migration teams. Your vision statement might read like the following:

"The vision of the Windows 2000 migration project is to deploy a cost-effective, high-value architecture with improved reliability, reduced total cost of ownership, that provides for end-to-end management of all systems in the enterprise."

Each department within the organization has its own business vision. You can ensure that the migration project aligns with the long-terms goals of the organization by collecting and documenting information about the visions and goals of the various departments and keeping these goals in mind while you create your migration vision document. A vision statement is illustrated in Figure 10.2.

Figure 10.2 Vision Statement

Your vision and scope documents will provide the necessary data to enable you to make trade-off decisions during the migration about which features can be sacrificed if the schedule becomes impossibly tight or if resources become scarce. Your documents may also be used to define the following:

Tasks related to the project implementation but excluded from the migration project

- A schedule of when certain functionality will be required

- Any assumptions made that are associated with the project

- Business constrains that may affect the project

- The effort required in completing the planning

Defining Personnel and Migration Team Members

Organizing your migration team is the next step in planning your deployment. You will need to assign specific roles to team members. If the size of your organization permits, you might want to consider forming sub-teams to assist in the migration planning and deployment.

You will have to identify specific tasks and determine the resource requirements for each. Once you have identified all the required responsibilities and determined the necessary resources to accomplish these tasks, you can decide which groups within the organization will need to be involved in the migration. You can then also determine if there is a need for additional resources from outside the organization.

Your teams should be planned so that they reflect your internal structure, your business needs, and the Windows 2000 features and services that you want to deploy.

Team Roles

The six general roles of a complete planning team are illustrated in Figure 10.3. Each team member should participate in designing the migration strategy and its deployment.

Figure 10.3 Team Roles

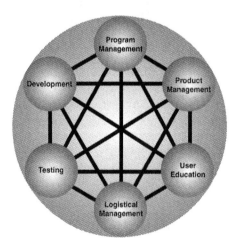

At a minimum, you will need to fill the following roles:

- Product management
- Program management
- Development
- Testing
- Logistics Management
- User education

Product Management

There should be only one product manager. The person who fills the role of product manager is responsible for driving the project vision and maintaining the scope of the deployment. This person also manages customer or executive expectations and develops, maintains, and executes the business interests. The product manager is responsible for meeting business goals and attaining the corporate vision.

Program Management

Program managers are responsible for facilitating team communications and negotiations. Program managers are the people who approve changes to the functional specification and make the decisions that reduce network functionality to ensure project timeliness. The program management team typically fulfills the following tasks:

- Allocate resources
- Schedules projects
- Create status reports

Development

A development manager, who is an experienced implementation architect and is able to understand the key issues of all technical areas of the project, usually leads the development team. The team plays an important role in the migration design and in the selection of the features that will be deployed. They help to define the deployment schedule by estimating the time and resources that will be necessary to implement each feature. The team members will configure or customize the use of the selected features. Development team members provide the scripts and programs to facilitate deployment.

Testing

The primary mission of the test team is to ensure that all issues are known and addressed before releasing the design. To ensure a successful migration, the test team members will perform the following tasks:

- Prepare a test plan
- Prepare the test specifications
- Prepare the test cases
- Conduct the tests

Logistics Management

The mission of the logistics management team is to ensure that the new environment is manageable, supportable and deployable. Logistics management team members are responsible for ensuring that the operational needs are served by the migration and that the migration can be successful, given the physical environment. The logistics management team must work closely with the development team to ensure that all of the necessary data is packaged to facilitate installation and subsequent administration.

User Education

User education is necessary to minimize the impact of the migration to the new operating system on the users of the systems. This will also reduce the support costs associated with transitioning users to a new environment. The job of the user education team is to make the new environment easier to understand and use. This team designs and conducts the user and the team training systems. The user education teams' primary mission is to ensure that the end user's needs are protected throughout the migration.

Migration Planning Documents

Over the course of your migration planning and deployment, you will need to produce a number of documents. It is essential to create documents that define your vision and encourage support for the migration plan. You will also need to craft documents that guide the deployment process and summarize it so others can understand the scope of the migration.

Creating Project Planning Documents

In the planning of the implementation of your migration strategy, you will need to create a number of deployment and administrative documents.

Deployment Documents

As part of your project plan, you should create a number of deployment documents such as those shown in Figure 10.4, and those shown in the following list:

- Summary of the current network environment
- Migration strategy
- Gap analysis
- Capacity plan
- Risk plan
- Problem escalation plan
- Testing and deployment strategies
- Pilot plan

Figure 10.4 Deployment Documents

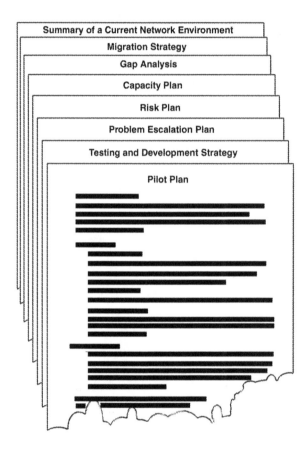

Summary of the current network environment—When you summarize the current networking environment, you should include a high-level description, which includes the following:

- Physical network infrastructure

- Logical network infrastructure

- Network hardware

- Network policies

- Number and types of users

- Geographic locations

Migration strategy—When you develop your migration strategy, you should detail how the transition to Windows 2000 will occur. The following should be included in your migration strategy documentation:

- Migration plan for domains and domain controllers

- Where, when and how the migration will take place

- Who will be involved

Gap analysis—When you create a gap analysis you address the differences between the existing environment and the desired target environment. This document should then address the steps needed to arrive at the desired environment. The gap analysis document provides a bridge between the summary of the current network environment and the migration strategy.

Capacity plan—When you develop your capacity plan, you ensure that there is sufficient hardware and network capacity for the Windows 2000 environment you plan to deploy. The capacity plan should identify the following:

- Expectations

- Potential risks

- Contingencies

For example a capacity plan can be used to identify the possible effects of the additional replication traffic created by Active Directory or it could access the impact of a remote installation.

Risk plan—When you construct your risk plan you identify the risks in your plan and then develop contingency plans for dealing with those risks. You should continually reevaluate your deployment plan during the deployment process. You should also make a formal evaluation after each phase of the project is completed.

Problem escalation plan—The problem escalation plan is created to specify an escalation path that your organization can use to resolve and escalate issues. You should match the different types of problems and situations that could arise to the people who are best capable of addressing them.

Testing and deployment strategies—You must document how you plan to test and deploy Windows 2000.

Pilot plan—When you create your pilot plan you identify the roles and objectives for the servers that will participate in the first rollout. This plan documents the features you will implement and the security principal groups that will take part in each pilot phase. You will also need to document when and which security principal groups.

Administrative Documents

You use administrative documents to identify your goals and to define your objectives. As shown in Figure 10.5, you will need to include the following in your administrative documents:

- Scope and vision
- Phases and milestones
- Budget
- Staffing
- Communications strategy

Figure 10.5 Administrative Documents

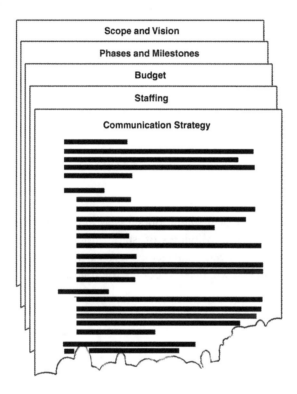

Scope and vision—Your scope and vision ensure that your plan clearly states the project objectives. This document defines the scope of the project and provides the methods that can be used to measure progress and success. The scope and vision document is used to define the business problem or opportunity that led to the decision to migrate. It also defines the audience for the solution as well as the solution.

Phases and milestones—Your phases and milestones document breaks down the deployment project into smaller manageable phases. This will give your staff time to get oriented and will help you to verify the assumptions that you made in the planning stage. You will need to establish and monitor milestones to ensure the project keeps on schedule.

Budget—Your budget document is used to identify and track the expected and unexpected costs of the project. It also documents the cost constraints for the project and identifies backup sources of funding to cover unexpected expenses. Items that should be tracked in your budget include the following:

- Development

- Hardware

- Facilities

- Training

- Personnel

- Testing

- Deployment

Staffing—You need to plan your post-migration site staffing requirements. You should also document and define the roles and responsibilities of staff during the migration, as you roll out new administrative features. This will prevent management gaps as the migration progresses. For each task or feature that you implement, you will need to outline the following:

- Reporting structure

- Responsibilities

- Frequency of meetings

- Communication strategies

- Owners of the overall task

- Owners of the feature

Communications Strategy—You will need to communicate your plans to your organization to raise management and user awareness of the deployment project. By formalizing your communications strategy, and then implementing it, you ensure that you reduce the resistance to change that a migration normally introduces and you increase acceptance among the user community.

Creating a Purposeful Specification

To create a purposeful functional specification you need to establish an agreement between the migration team and the organization's key project stakeholders. Expectations and deliverables are clearly stated in the functional specification and they are documented for future reference.

To create a purposeful specification, you should begin by creating a draft-functional specification that provides a definition of the migration. Define a team to create the specification. As the team works out the details during the design of the migration strategy, it should document and describe all of the functionality at a high level in the functional specification. A completed initial functional specification is used to begin laying out project plans for the deployment of the migration strategy and acts as a blueprint for the following:

- Development

- Testing

- User education

- Logistics management

 Note: The functional specification is not a complete description of your design.

The functional specification needs to be complete enough to be tested against. It should secure agreement on desired functionality among the stakeholders. Your functional specification should be considered a living or fluid document that is revisited and revised regularly during the deployment process. It will need to be updated to reflect any changes in goals, risk, direction, or design.

Installation Strategies

You will need to select an installation strategy. The chosen strategy will vary depending upon the needs and policies of the local IT organization, as well as the supporting infrastructure. You will need to be adaptable during the migration. For example, during the migration, you may determine that you need additional domain controllers to support the new Active Directory forest.

Choosing an Installation Strategy

The strategy you choose will depend upon your local IT policies and the supporting infrastructure. It will also depend upon the action you take at a particular moment in time. The strategy you employ for a new installation of Windows 2000 will be entirely different than that of an upgrade. As much as possible, you will want to automate the installations to ensure consistency and reliability.

Automating New Installations

You can use the following methods to automate the installation of Windows 2000 Server:

- Unattended
- Syspart
- Sysprep
- Bootable CD

Unattended

To carry out an unattended installation, you can use the Setup Manager wizard to create an answer file that is used by Setup to perform unattended installations or upgrades of Windows 2000. An unattended setup consists of the following tasks:

- Create an answer file
- Determine and implement a process to configure computer-specific information
- Determine and implement a process to automate the selected distribution method

Distribution methods can include using network distribution point or hard disk duplication. The Setup Manager wizard is shown in Figure 10.6.

Figure 10.6 Setup Manager Wizard

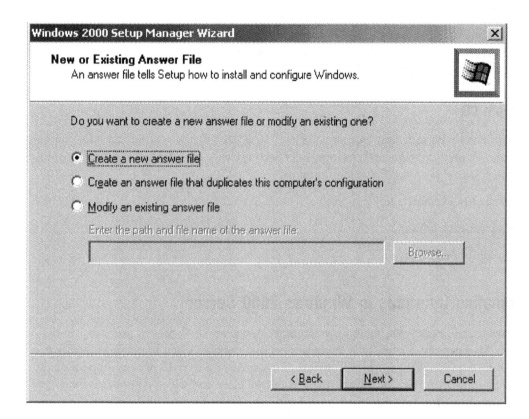

Syspart

Syspart is used for clean installations on computers that have dissimilar hardware. In this case, you will want to create a master set of files containing the necessary configuration information and driver support using Syspart. You then image the files.

Sysprep

For clean installations on computers that have identical hardware, use Sysprep. Identical hardware includes the Hardware Abstraction Layer (HAL) and mass storage device controllers. The Sysprep utility prepares the hard disk on the master computer so that you can use a disk imaging utility to transfer an image of the hard disk to other computers.

Bootable CD

If a computer's Basic Input/Output System (BIOS) allows it to start from CD, you can use the bootable CD method to install Windows 2000 Server. Using a bootable CD is useful for installing on computers with one of the following restraints:

- Located at a remote site

- Slow network links

- No local IT department

Automating Upgrades to Windows 2000 Server

To manage the upgrade of multiple systems to Windows 2000 Server, you can use the Microsoft Systems Management Server. This utility is especially valuable when upgrading systems that are geographically dispersed. The Microsoft Systems Management Server allows you to perform upgrades in a centralized fashion and control when upgrades take place and which computers are upgraded.

If you use Microsoft Systems Management Server to upgrade the server operating system to Windows 2000, you can use scripting to automate domain controller promotion. This provides a hands-off method to create domain controllers for the new Windows 2000 network.

Migration Deployment Components

In addition to careful planning and documentation, you should employ two essential components during migration deployment. These components are a test lab and a pilot project. However, before you can fully appreciate these components, you need to understand the components of your deployment plan.

Understanding the Components of a Deployment Plan

Your deployment plan will consist of several documents, which will include a functional specification as well as vision, scope, administrative and deployment documents. Each of these documents is related to the others by virtue of intent.

The functional specification lays the ground rules. It establishes an agreement between the migration team and the important players in the organization.

The vision document provides an unbounded view of the future. It defines the ideal network environment.

The scope document bounds the migration project. It defines what must be accomplished and what can be considered non-essential

Administrative documents help to identify goals and define objectives. They define the budget, staffing requirements, project phases, and project milestones.

Deployment documents identify the actual migration from the current network environment to the planned environment. They detail how to accomplish the desired goals and provide plans for risk mitigation, problem escalation and testing and deployment strategies.

You will need to cross-reference these documents to ensure that they do not conflict with one another and that each reflects the same organizational goals. These documents should be used in conjunction with one another to help ensure a successful migration project.

Migration Plan Testing

You must test your Windows 2000 migration strategy in a test lab before you perform the actual migration. Use testing as a risk management technique to proactively identify and resolve any issues that might hamper the deployment project.

You will need to examine issues that belong in any of the following categories:

- Technical

- Political

- Administrative

The primary goal of testing is to identify and eliminate the possibility of a negative impact on the production system or its services. You should create a test plan that describes the scope of the project, the project objectives, and all testing methodologies.

Creating a Test Environment for Migration

The test environment that you construct will depend upon whether you are performing a domain upgrade or a restructure. For a domain upgrade, the test environment must duplicate as closely as possible the existing physical and logical production environment of your network. You will need to recreate the current Windows NT 4.0 domain model. In the test environment, you will also need to configure and implement the hardware, software, network services, and any devices currently used in the production environment. The two environments must match each other as closely as you can get them, if not an exact mirror of one another.

If your migration strategy requires a domain restructure, you may ultimately use the test environment as the production environment. In this situation, the goal is to model the hardware and services that your organization will require in the future production environment. For this migration scenario, the test environment should reflect at minimum, a subset of the Active Directory design. The Active Directory design defines the domain hierarchy; sites, services, and Windows 2000 features that must be available in the future network. You will not need to deploy all the domain controllers or domains; however, you will need adequate forest components to perform restructure test cases.

In either migration case, a domain upgrade or restructure, you must create the test environment on a dedicated subnet that is isolated from production servers and users. This is done to prevent unnecessary network traffic and to protect the existing network from problems such as naming conflicts.

 Note: Your test environment should use dynamic Domain Name System (DNS) and Windows Internet Name System (WINS) in an isolated infrastructure.

Testing the Migration Plan

To test your migration plan, you will need to define all likely permutations of your environment. You then analyze these variations to prioritize them, to create specific test cases that will evaluate the proposed change, and to identify any problems the changes may create. Not all problems will be obvious, so your test cases must be well defined.

Defining Test Cases

Whey you create a test case, you specify a detailed procedure to fully test a feature or an aspect of a feature. The test case specifies exactly how a particular test is to be performed. Test cases can be used for any of the following:

- Determine interoperability
- Determine compatibility
- Provide baselines for capacity or performance

When you create a test case, you should include the following:

- The goal of the test
- Any hardware, software or configuration requirements of the test
- The steps to perform the test
- The expected results or success criteria for the test

Your test team develops test cases that will describe the scenarios and issues that you need to address during the pilot. Some examples of migration scenarios are as follows:

- Installing servers and promoting domain controllers
- Controlling inter-site replication traffic

The primary purpose of a test case is the identification of issues and risks that will need to be resolved prior to a full-scale migration. You will not be able to test every possible permutation, so you should focus on limits. Test the items that may present limitations to your implementation. For example, one of the following items:

- The slowest client computer
- The busiest server
- The least reliable network link

You should focus on areas that have the greatest risk or have the greatest probability of occurring. Your suite of test cases must be kept manageable.

 Tip: Wherever possible, automate test cases to save time and overhead. You can use scripts to perform test cases and generate result reports. Scripts can also be used to clean up after a test to ensure a clean environment for any subsequent testing.

Migration Pilot

You need to understand the purpose and components of a pilot project. A pilot project is used as a trial run of the migration processes that you have thoroughly tested in the test lab environment. During the pilot project, users have the opportunity to give you feedback about how features work. You can then use this feedback to resolve problems and to help determine the level of support required after the migration is fully deployed. The pilot project can act as a gating factor in you migration, as the results can help you decide whether to proceed with a full deployment or to slow the project down to give you time to resolve problems that could jeopardize the implementation.

Creating a Migration Pilot

Consider the following factors when planning a pilot project:

- Demonstrate that the migration strategy works as expected

- Demonstrate that the migration strategy meets business requirements

- Give the migration team a chance to practice and refine the deployment process

If the pilot project team discovers issues during the pilot, you have the opportunity to refine the migration strategy and any other deployment documents. The pilot project gives you the ability to ensure a smooth full-scale deployment.

The pilot project should be conducted as a series of small, manageable project phases. The test plan for each phase should include the following:

- Clearly defined objectives

- A description of the work

- A list of requirements

- A list of the criteria

- What you must successfully test before moving to the next phase

- A series of deliverables

Your test plan for each phase must clearly document the outcome of each stage of the testing and you must track these outcomes over time. You must be sure that the team thoroughly documents test results, either on paper or by using electronic forms. It is difficult to recreate a test without documentation that states what has been done and in what order.

Windows 2000 Transition

The ultimate goal of planning your deployment of Windows 2000 is a smooth conversion from the pilot project to the production environment, while minimizing any interruption to the network, its users, and the core business functions of the organization that are supported by the network.

Transitioning to Windows 2000

To ensure a smooth transition to Windows 2000, consider the following tasks:

- Phase your migration efforts

- Create a backup or recovery plan

- Provide appropriate training

- Keeps teams informed

- Schedule major migration activities around business operations

Phasing Your Migration Efforts

When you phase your migration efforts, you break the project down into smaller, more manageable pieces. This allows you to test smaller segments of the migration.

Creating a Backup or Recovery Plan

If you encounter any problems during the migration, a reliable and tested backup plan will enable you to quickly and easily recover. You must have a tested system disaster recovery plan because a computer or site disaster can overcome even the best data protection strategies. You must be prepared.

Providing Appropriate Training

Your support and administrative teams need to be fully trained and prepared for the migration. You should ensure that users are informed of the migration and have received appropriate user training before the new technologies are deployed.

Keeping Teams Informed

You must make sure that all migration teams are aware of the migration plan as a whole. All teams need to be aware of the scope of their responsibility and involvement and how they fit into the whole deployment. They should be informed of any changes to the plan or schedule.

Schedule Major Migration Activities Around Business Operations

With thoughtful scheduling of major Windows 2000 migration activities, you can minimize the impact on your users and the network. For example, if a group needs to complete a major project, or meet a deadline, you should wait before you deploy Windows 2000 to that group. You should upgrade domain controllers during off-peak hours when the fewest number of users will require network access.

Migration Scenarios

No two organizations are exactly the same. Every organization will need to create a unique project plan that is based upon its own business needs and project management procedures. The migration scenario for a particular organization might be to upgrade, then restructure later; or it might be to restructure from the start. While it is not possible to address all the possible migration scenario variations, the following is an example of a pilot plan for a restructure scenario. If you plan to restructure, your pilot plan may include more or fewer steps, depending upon the migration path and complexity of your migration project.

Restructuring Scenario

The following methods provide time to evaluate the impact of Widows 2000 on a production environment before converting the test environment into a production environment. In the restructure migration scenario, you most likely would want to include the following tasks:

- Isolated lab testing

- Limited integration testing

- Extended integration testing

- Limited pilot testing

- Extended pilot testing

Isolated Lab Testing

The primary goal of testing in an isolated lab is to develop and test a Windows 2000 Server configuration that can be connected to the production network during later testing phases. You must thoroughly test this configuration. You need to ensure it creates no adverse impact on the production network.

During this test phase, you will install Windows 2000 servers and create domains on an isolated lab network that simulates the production environments. You will need to simulate both Local Area Network (LAN) and Wide Area Network (WAN) functionality. This phase of testing has the complete documentation of server installation and configurations appropriate for the desired Active Directory design as its deliverable.

Limited Integration Testing

During this phase of testing, you will move the test Windows 2000 servers used in the last phase from an isolated lab into a single segment of the production LAN. You will need to configure servers, service domains, and domain controllers using the recommendations that were made during the isolated testing phase. The goal of this phase of testing is to rule out any coexistence problems with Windows 2000 and the existing production systems while both systems are operating on the same network segment. The primary deliverable of this test phase is an updated and revised version of the documented server installation and configuration recommendations created during the previous phase.

 Note: Do not introduce any new features during this phase. You should not make any configuration changes unless they are required to address a co-existence issue.

Extended Integration Testing

Extended integration testing shifts the focus from a single network location to multiple locations situated across the WAN, if it exists. The objectives of extended integration testing include the following:

- To install Active Directory in a few remote locations to analyze replication traffic

- To test client authentication and resource access in the new environment

- To continue to perform interoperability testing

Another objective is to finalize integration of the Active Directory namespace with the existing Domain Name System (DNS) namespace. You need to ensure that DNS queries for Windows 2000 services are referred to Windows 2000 DNS servers.

Consider documenting the following deliverables during the testing phase:

- DNS configuration

- Completion of the server installation and configuration

- Client configurations

Limited Pilot Testing

There are two objectives to this phase of testing. The first is to extend the deployment of the Windows 2000 pilot to additional locations. The second objective is to migrate a limited population of users to the new environment. In order to achieve these objectives you must install additional servers and domain controllers throughout the organization so that you can accomplish the following tasks:

- Provide Global Catalog and logon services

- Create trust relationships between the production and test environments to enable resource access

- Test the applications required by the pilot users to complete their daily responsibilities

- Test and deploy remote access services to pilot users

This phase of testing has the following deliverables:

- Documentation of application compatibility testing

- A user migration checklist

- Documentation of the trusts created during the testing

- Identification of the requirements for the next phase of testing

Extended Pilot Testing

During extended pilot testing, you will perform the following tasks:

- Expand the pilot project to a larger population of users

- Identify procedures for migrating existing servers to the new environment

- Finalize the comprehensive migration project plan

- Solving application compatibility issues identified in earlier testing

- Deploy additional servers

- Migrate additional users

- Complete application and compatibility testing

- Define processes for completing the migration to Windows 2000

The deliverables for the extended pilot-testing phase include documentation of the following tasks:

- Results of application testing

- Processes used to complete the migration of users and servers

- A final and fully tested migration project plan

 Note: The documentation developed during pilot testing will provide all the necessary information needed to develop a plan that transitions the pilot environment to the production environment.

Vocabulary

Review the following terms in preparation for the certification exam.

Term	Description
BIOS	The Basic Input/Output System is a set of essential software routines that test hardware on startup, start the operating system, and support the transfer of data among hardware devices.
DNS	The Domain Name System is a hierarchical naming system used for locating domain names on the Internet and on private TCP/IP networks.
HAL	The Hardware Abstraction Layer is a layer of software that hides or abstracts hardware differences from higher layers in the operating system.
IT	The Information Technology group is an organization that is concerned with the security and dissemination of information within the organization.
TCP/IP	Transmission Control Protocol/Internet Protocol is a set of software networking protocols that are widely used on the Internet to provide communications across interconnected networks with diverse computer hardware architectures and operating systems.
WINS	Windows Internet Name Service is a software service that dynamically maps IP addressed to computer names.

In Brief

If you want to...	Then do this...
Perform clean installations of Windows 2000 on computers that have identical hardware.	Use Sysprep to create a master set of files with the necessary configuration information and driver support.
Perform clean installations on computers that have dissimilar hardware.	Use Syspart to prepare a hard disk for imaging.
Ensure a smooth transition to Windows 2000.	Test in a test lab followed by a pilot project to minimize the negative impact of migration changes.

Lesson 10 Activities

Complete the following activities to better prepare you for the certification exam.

1. Discuss the purpose of a migration scope document.

2. Describe a migration vision statement.

3. Discuss the use of administrative documents.

4. Discuss the objective of extended integrated testing in relation to DNS.

5. Describe the primary goal of testing in an isolated lab.

6. Discuss the roles that need to be filled in your migration team.

7. Describe the importance of a backup plan.

8. Discuss how you can minimize the impact of a migration on users.

9. Describe the ultimate goal of planning your transition to Windows 2000.

10. Discuss the value of finding issues during a pilot project.

Answers to Lesson 10 Activities

1. The bounds for the migration project are defined by its scope. The scope document clarifies and differentiates between what the migration must accomplish and what is desirable but non-essential.

2. A vision statement is an unbounded view of the future. Your migration vision statement establishes both long-term and short-term goals of your future network.

3. You use administrative documents to identify your goals and to define your objectives.

4. One of the objectives of extended integration testing is to finalize integration of the Active Directory namespace with the existing Domain Name System (DNS) namespace.

5. The primary goal of testing in an isolated lab is to develop and test a Windows 2000 Server configuration that can be connected to the production network during later testing phases.

6. At a minimum, your team will need people to fill the roles of product management, program management, development, testing, logistics management and user education.

7. If you encounter any problems during the migration, a reliable and tested backup plan will enable you to quickly and easily recover.

8. You can minimize the impact on your users and the network with thoughtful scheduling of major Windows 2000 migration activities.

9. The ultimate goal of planning your deployment of Windows 2000 is a smooth conversion from the pilot project to the production environment while minimizing any interruption to the network, its users, and the core business functions of the organization that are supported by the network.

10. If the pilot project team discovers issues during the pilot, you have the opportunity to refine the migration strategy and any other deployment documents. The pilot project gives you the ability to ensure a smooth full-scale deployment.

Lesson 10 Quiz

These questions test your knowledge of features, vocabulary, procedures, and syntax.

1. When would you use a bootable CD to install Windows 2000 Server?
    A. When the computer is located at a remote site
    B. When there is a slow network link
    C. When you wish to switch to native mode
    D. When there is no local IT department

2. What is the situation where you would you use Sysprep?
    A. To prepare a system to a Windows 2000 upgrade
    B. To prepare a Windows 2000 server for native mode operation
    C. To install Windows 2000 on computers with identical hardware
    D. To install Windows 2000 on computers with dissimilar hardware

3. What tool is used to create answer files for unattended installations?
    A. Microsoft Systems Management Server
    B. Sysprep
    C. Setup Manager wizard
    D. A text editor

4. Which of the following are administrative documents?
    A. Phases and Milestones
    B. Staffing
    C. Scope and vision
    D. Capacity plan

5. Which of the following is not a deployment document?

    A. Testing and deployment strategies

    B. Pilot plan

    C. Gap analysis

    D. Communications strategy

6. Who is responsible for driving the project vision and maintaining the scope of the deployment?

    A. The program manager

    B. The logistics manager

    C. The development manager

    D. The product manager

7. What type of document(s) helps to identify goals and define objectives?

    A. Administrative documents

    B. Deployment documents

    C. Functional specification

    D. Pilot project plans

8. What is a vision statement used for?

    A. Define short-term goals

    B. Define the bounds for the project

    C. Prioritize components to meet business needs

    D. Define long-term goals

9. What is a living or fluid document?

    A. A document that is updated to reflect changes

    B. A document that is shared between team members

    C. A document that is continually revisited and revised

    D. A document that is now owned by anyone

10. What tool is used to automate upgrades to Windows 2000?

    A. Syspart

    B. Microsoft Systems Management Server

    C. Sysprep

    D. Setup Manager wizard

Answers to Lesson 10 Quiz

1. Answers A, B, and D are correct. You would use a bootable CD to install Windows 2000 Server on computers that are located at a remote site, have slow network links or where there is no local IT department.

    Answer C is incorrect. You cannot switch to native mode using a bootable CD.

2. Answer C is correct. You use Sysprep to install Windows 2000 on computers with identical hardware.

    Answer A is incorrect. Sysprep is not used to prepare a computer for a Windows 2000 upgrade.

    Answer B is incorrect. Sysprep is not used to convert to native mode

    Answer D is incorrect. Use Syspart to install Windows 2000 on computers with dissimilar hardware.

3. Answer C is correct. You use the Setup Manager to create answer files for unattended installations.

    Answer A is incorrect. You use Microsoft Systems Management Server to upgrade multiple systems to Windows 2000 Server.

    Answer B is incorrect. You use Sysprep to install Windows 2000 on computers with identical hardware.

    Answer D is incorrect. You cannot use a text editor to create setup answer files.

4. Answers A, B, and C are correct. Administrative documents include phases and milestones, staffing, and scope and vision.

    Answer D is incorrect. A capacity plan is a deployment document.

5. Answer D is correct. The communications strategy document is an administrative document.

    Answers A, B, and C are incorrect. The capacity plan, pilot plan and testing and deployment strategies documents are all deployment documents.

6. Answer D is correct. The product manager is responsible for driving the project vision and maintaining the scope of the deployment.

    Answer A is incorrect. A program manager is responsible for facilitating team communications and negotiations.

    Answer B is incorrect. The logistics manager's job is to ensure the new environment is manageable, supportable, and deployable.

Answer C is incorrect. The development manager contributes his or her expertise in setting the deployment schedule.

7. Answer A is correct. Administrative plans help identify goals and define objectives.

    Answer B is incorrect. Deployment documents are part of your project plan and show how you will attain your goals and objectives.

    Answer C is incorrect. A functional specification is used to establish agreements between the migration team and business departments.

    Answer D is incorrect. The pilot plan specifies how you will carry out your pilot project to enable you to meet your goals and objectives with a minimum interruption to user access

8. Answers A and D are correct. The vision statement is used to define short-term and long-term goals.

    Answer B is incorrect. The bounds of the migration project are specified in the scope document.

    Answer C is incorrect. The scope document specifies the priority of component installation to meet business needs.

9. Answers A and C are correct. A living or fluid document is a document that is continually revisited and revised to reflect changes.

    Answer B is incorrect. Many documents can be shared. A living or fluid document can be shared but the act of sharing does not make it living or fluid.

    Answer D is incorrect. A document that is not owned by a person is not necessarily a fluid or living document. Ownership does not define type.

10. Answer B is correct. To manage the upgrade of multiple systems to Windows 2000 Server, you can use the Microsoft Systems Management Server.

    Answer A is incorrect. You use Syspart to install Windows 2000 on computers with dissimilar hardware.

    Answer C is incorrect. You use Sysprep to install Windows 2000 on computers with identical hardware.

    Answer D is incorrect. You use the Setup Manager to create answer files for unattended clean installations.

Glossary

Term	Description
ADC	The Active Directory Connector is a synchronization agent that ensures that the two directories, Active Directory and Exchange Server 5.5 directory service, remain consistent.
ADMT	The Active Directory Migration Tool is a wizard based Microsoft Management Console (MMC) interface that can be used to facilitate inter-forest and intra-forest restructures. It is licensed from Mission Critical Software.
API	An Application Programming Interface is a set of routines that provide an application with the ability to request and perform services provided and performed by a computer's operating system.
ATM	Asynchronous Transfer Mode is a high-speed, connection-oriented, fixed-sized packet protocol with data transfer speeds ranging from 25 to 622 Mbps.
BDC	A Backup Domain Controller is a computer running Microsoft Windows NT 4.0 Server that receives a copy of the domain's directory database in a Microsoft Windows NT 4.0 Server domain.
BIND	Berkeley Internet Name Domain is a name resolution service that runs under UNIX.
BIOS	The Basic Input/Output System is a set of essential software routines that test hardware on startup, start the operating system, and support the transfer of data among hardware devices.

Term	Description
child domain	For DNS and Active Directory, a child domain is located in the namespace tree directly beneath another domain name (the parent domain).
ClonePrincipal	A set of Visual Basic scripts that are used to copy users and groups while populating the sIDHistory attribute. The scripts can be modified to suite the needs of your organization.
complete trust domain model	This is a domain model with few benefits. It is used to support organizations that require completely decentralized administration. This model is difficult to manage because it forms an interconnected web of trust relationships.
cross-link trust	Another name for a Shortcut Trust, it is a two-way trust that is explicitly created between two domains in different domain trees within a forest and optimizes the inter-domain authentication process. A shortcut trust can be created only between Windows 2000 domains in the same forest.
DACL	A Discretionary Access Control List is a part of an object's security descriptor that is used to grant or deny access to the object by specific users or groups. It defines the access rights of users and groups to the object and can only be modified by the owner of the object.
DC	A Domain Controller is the server that authenticates domain logons and maintains the security policy and the master database for a domain.
DDNS	Dynamic Domain Name System is a service that allows clients with a dynamically assigned address to register directly with a server running the DNS service. It also allows such clients to update the DNS table dynamically.
DFS	The Distributed File System is a Windows 2000 service that consists of software that resides on network servers and clients. It transparently links shared folders located on different file servers into a single namespace. The benefit is improved load sharing and data availability.

Term	Description
DHCP	The Dynamic Host Configuration Protocol is a networking protocol that provides dynamic configuration of IP addresses for client computers. It ensures that address conflicts do not occur and provides centralized management of address allocation.
Distinguished Name	Every object in Active Directory has a distinguished name that is used to uniquely identify the object. It contains the name of the domain in which the object resides as well as the complete path through the container hierarchy to the object.
DLL	Dynamic Link Library is a file containing a set of functions to which applications can be dynamically linked at run time.
DNS	The Domain Name System is a hierarchical naming system that maps domain names to IP addresses as well as the reverse. The DNS provides a mechanism by which a computer can query remote systems based upon a name rather than an IP address.
domain	An administrative and security boundary. Active Directory data is replicated between domain controllers within a domain.
domain controller	A Windows 2000 server that is used to manage user access to the network.
DS	Directory Services client software allows Windows 95 and Windows 98 client computers to take advantage of Windows 2000 Active Directory features.
forest	A group of one or more trees that trust each other. All trees in a forest share a common schema, configuration, and global catalog. When a forest contains multiple trees, the trees do not form a contiguous namespace. All trees in a forest trust each other through transitive bi-directional trust relationships.

Term	Description
FRS	The File Replication Service is used by distributed file systems to synchronize content and by Active Directory Sites and Services to replicate topological and Global Catalog information between domain controllers.
GC	The Global Catalog is a highly optimized Active Directory service that stores directory information from all source domains in a single location. Users submit queries to the GC to obtain information about objects in the network regardless of their physical or logical location.
HAL	The Hardware Abstraction Layer is a layer of software that hides or abstracts hardware differences from higher layers in the operating system.
HCL	The Microsoft Hardware Compatibility List is a catalog of hardware that has been certified by Microsoft as compatible with Microsoft Windows 2000.
IETF	The Internet Engineering Task Force is a large, open community of network designers, operators, researchers, vendors, and others concerned with the evolution of the architecture of the Internet.
inter-forest restructure	During an inter-forest restructure, you copy security principals from a Windows NT 4.0 domain to a Windows 2000 domain or from a Windows 2000 domain in one forest to a Windows 2000 domain in another forest
IP	The Internet Protocol is a routable protocol belonging to the TCP/IP suite. IP is responsible for packet addressing and routing as well as deconstructing and later reconstructing of IP packets.

Term	Description
IPX/SPX	A combination of two network protocols native to the Novell Netware product. The Internetwork Packet Exchange works on the network layer to provide packet addressing and routing controls within and between networks. The Sequenced Packet Exchange protocol works on the transport layer to ensure that all packets are received error-free and in their correct order.
IT	The Information Technology group is an organization that is concerned with the security and dissemination of information within the organization.
JScript	Java Script is a cross-platform programming language from Sun Microsystems that can be used to create animations and interactive features.
KDC	A Key Distribution Center is a network service that is used to supply session tickets and temporary session keys used in the Kerberos authentication protocol. Under Windows 2000, the KDC uses Active Directory to manage sensitive account information for user accounts.
L2TP	Layer 2 Tunneling Protocol encapsulates Point-to-Point frames to be sent over IP, X.25, Frame Relay, or ATM networks.
LAN	A Local Area Network is made up of computers and other devices connected by a communications link that allows one device to interact with any other in a limited area.
LANE	Local Area Network Emulation is a service consisting of a set of protocols that provide a mechanism by which existing Ethernet and Token Ring LAN services are emulated on an ATM network.

Term	Description
LDAP	The Lightweight Directory Access Protocol is a directory service protocol that runs directly over TCP/IP. LDAP is the primary access protocol for Active Directory.
LDP	A Windows Explorer like administrative tool that allows user to perform LDAP operations.
Mbps	A communications speed measurement indicating millions of bits transferred per second.
mixed environment	A mixed environment is a Windows 2000 domain that contains pre-Windows 2000 clients or servers. The domain can be in either mixed or native mode.
mixed mode	Mixed mode is the default domain mode setting for Windows 2000 domain controllers. It allows Microsoft Windows NT 4.0 and Windows 2000 domain controllers to coexist in a network.
MMC	The Microsoft Management Console is a framework that hosts administrative consoles and provides some commands and tools for authoring consoles.
MoveTree	A command line tool used to facilitate intra-forest migration operations. It provides a mechanism by which security principals can be moved between domains in the same Active Directory forest.
multiplemaster domain model	A domain model in which there are multiplemaster user domains and an administrative hierarchy.
NetBEUI	The NetBIOS Enhanced User Interface is a Microsoft network protocol usually used in small Local Area Networks (LANs). It is the Microsoft implementation of the NetBIOS standard.

Term	Description
NetBIOS	The Network Basic Input/Output System is an Application Programming Interface (API) used by computers on a LAN. It provides a set of functions that provide access to low-level network services.
NETDOM	A command-line utility that manages Windows 2000 domains and trust relationships. It also facilitates inter-forest and intra-forest migration operations.
NIC	A Network Interface Card is an adapter card that provides the mechanism by which a computer can communicate with a network.
NOS	A Network Operating System is an operating system that is network-aware. Examples of a NOS are Windows 95, Windows for Workgroups v3.11, Microsoft Windows NT 4.0 and Microsoft Windows 2000.
NTFS	New Technology File System is a file system that is designed for Windows 2000 and supports many features, such as file system security, Unicode, recoverability, and long file names.
NTLM	Microsoft Windows NT LAN Manager is a security protocol used for pass-through network authentication, remote file access, and authenticated Remote Procedure Call (RPC) connections to earlier versions of Windows.
one-way trust	A trust relationship where only one of the two domains trusts the other domain. All one-way trusts are non-transitive.
OU	An Organizational Unit is an Active Directory container object that provides a mechanism by which users, groups, computers, printers, and other organizational units are placed.

Term	Description
parent domain	For DNS and Active Directory, domains located in the namespace tree directly above other domain names (child domains).
PDC	A Primary Domain Controller is a computer running Microsoft Windows NT 4.0 Server that authenticates domain logons and maintains the directory database for a domain in a Windows NT 4.0 Server domain.
PPP	The Point-to-Point Protocol is an industry-standard set of Internet protocols that facilitates dial-up networking.
RADIUS	The Remote Authentication Dial-in User Service provides authentication and accounting services for distributed dial-up networking.
RAID	A Redundant Array of Inexpensive Disks is used to store data securely by distributing it over several disk drives in such a way that the loss of one disk will not cause corruption of the data. In some RAID configurations, a failed disk may be replaced and the new disk will be automatically populated with the data from the failed disk.
RAS	The Remote Access Service is a Microsoft Windows NT 4.0 service that provides remote networking access. It is used by system administrators who must monitor and manage network servers at remote locations as well as by remote users to access the network.
RFC	A Request For Comment is a document published by the Internet Engineering Task Force (IETF) requesting comments on a proposed standard affecting network protocols, programs, and concepts.

Term	Description
RID	The Relative Identifier identifies an account or group and is a part of a Security Identifier (SID). They are unique to the domain in which the entity was created.
RIP	The Routing Information Protocol is used to propagate routing information.
RPC	A Remote Procedure Call is a message-passing facility allowing a distributed application to call services available on network machines. RPC is used during remote administration of computers.
SAM	Security Accounts Manager is a Windows 2000 service used during the login process that maintains user information.
SAP	A Service Advertising Protocol is a protocol that advertises the services of the server upon which it resides.
schema	A description of the object classes and attributes stored in Active Directory. For each object class, the schema defines what attributes an object class must have, what additional attributes it may have, and what object class can be its parent.
SCSI	The Small Computer System Interface specification is a standard for a high-speed parallel interface between a small computer system and various peripheral devices.
security principal	An entity that is assigned a security identifier. Security principals include users, groups, and computers.
shortcut trust	A shortcut trust is a two-way trust that is explicitly created between two domains in different domain trees within a forest and optimizes the inter-domain authentication process. A shortcut trust can be created only between Windows 2000 domains in the same forest. They are transitive.

Term	Description
SID	A Security Identifier is a unique name that is used to identify a user who has logged on to a Windows NT 4.0 or Windows 2000 security system. A SID can be used to represent an individual user, a group of users, or a computer.
sIDHistory	The sIDHistory attribute of a security principal object is used to store the former SID of the restructured security principal
site	Sites are a collection of IP subnets. A site object represents a site in Active Directory. Sites are not tied in any way to the Active Directory domain namespace. The name of a directory object does not reflect the site or sites in which the object is stored. A site may contain Domain Controllers (DCs) from several domains, and DCs from a domain may be present in several sites.
site-aware client	A site-aware client is a computer running Windows 2000 or Windows 95 or 98 with the DS client installed.
SMS	The Microsoft Systems Management Server is a part of the Windows BackOffice suite of products. SMS includes inventory collection, diagnostic, and deployment tools that can automate the task of upgrading software on client computers. SMS can also be used to manage software licenses and to monitor computers and networks.
SRV	A Service resource record is used in a zone to register and locate TCP/IP services. It is used in Windows 2000 to locate domain controllers for Active Directory services.
SYSVOL	The System Volume stores the server's copy of the domain's public files. These files are replicated between all domain controllers in a domain.

Term	Description
TCO	The Total Cost of Ownership includes the total amount of money and time associated with purchasing, configuring, and maintaining hardware and software. This includes updates, maintenance, administration, and technical support.
TCP/IP	Transmission Control Protocol/Internet Protocol is a set of software networking protocols used on the Internet. It provides communication across interconnected networks of computers with diverse hardware architectures and operating systems. TCP/IP includes standards for how computers communicate and conventions for connecting networks and routing traffic.
transitive trust	A trust relationship among domains, where if domain A trusts domain B and domain B trusts domain C, then domain A trusts domain C.
trees	A set of domains connected to each other through transitive bi-directional trusts. Trees share the same configuration, schema and global catalog. The domains in a tree form a hierarchal contiguous namespace.
two-way trust	A trust relationship where both of the domains in the relationship trust each other. In a two-way trust relationship, each domain has established a one-way trust with the other domain. Two-way trusts can be transitive or non-transitive. All two-way trusts between Windows 2000 domains in the same domain tree or forest are transitive.
UPN	A User Principal Name consists of a user account name and a domain name that identify the user's logon name and the domain in which the user's account is located.
UPS	An Uninterruptible Power Supply provides power to a computer system or other device in the advent of a power failure. Many such devices can notify a computer system of such a failure so that the computer can initiate shutdown procedures.

Term	Description
VBA	Visual Basic for Applications is a programming environment that is designed specifically for creating application macros. It is the standard macro language in the Microsoft Office suite of products.
VBScript	The Visual Basic Scripting language is based on the Visual Basic programming language, but it is similar to JScript and much simpler.
VPN	A Virtual Private Network is a logically constructed WAN that uses existing public transmission mediums. A VPN allows an organization to emulate a private WAN connection.
WAN	A Wide Area Network is a network that extends beyond a single location, which utilizes leased lines to connect geographically separate computers or other network devices.
WINS	Windows Internet Name Service is a software service that maps IP addresses to computer names permitting users to access resources by name rather than IP address.

Index